SEE
TOUCH
SMELL
HEAR
TASTE

{ *"One cannot think well, love well, sleep well, if one has not dined well."* }
— VIRGINIA WOOLF

CRAVE

THE FEAST OF THE 5IVE SENSES

LUDO LEFEBVRE

With | *Martin Booe*

10 ReganBooks
Celebrating Ten Bestselling Years
An Imprint of HarperCollinsPublishers

HarperCollins books may be purchased for educational, business, or sales promotional use. For information please write: Special Markets Department, HarperCollins Publishers Inc., 10 East 53rd Street, New York, NY 10022.

FIRST EDITION

Designed by Richard Ljoenes/Kris Tobiassen

Printed on acid-free paper

Library of Congress Cataloging-in-Publication Data

Lefebvre, Ludovic.
    Crave / Ludovic Lefebvre with Martin Booe
        p. cm
    ISBN 0-06-001285-4
    1. Cookery. 2. Gastronomy. I. Booe, Martin. II. Title.

TX714 .L45 2005
641.5—dc21

                                                    2002021375

05 06 07 08 09 IM 10 9 8 7 6 5 4 3 2 1

FOR KRISSY

I was only a rumor, but you believed in me;
Los Angeles was a mirage, but you've made it my home;
This book was a fever dream, but you've made it real.

I love you.

ACKNOWLEDGMENTS

THIS BOOK OWES ITS EXISTENCE TO MANY PEOPLE, SOME WHO WERE DIRECTLY INVOLVED, OTHERS WHO WEREN'T. I'D LIKE TO EXPRESS MY DEEP APPRECIATION TO THEM.

My first thanks go to my family: my dad, Jean-Luc; my mom, Colette; my stepmother, Laurence; and my grandpa and grandma, Gilbert and Marcelle. Their love, support, and encouragement allowed me to follow my dream.

Pierre Gagnaire, Marc Meneau, Alain Passard, Guy Martin, and Jean-Pierre Saulnier are, to a man, truly great chefs who inspired me to create all the recipes in this book, and I am blessed to have had them as mentors. They taught me to love cooking and to cook with love. From them I learned passion and perfectionism.

I am especially grateful to Judith Regan for her belief in me and for the opportunity to write this book; to my editor, Cassie Jones, for her infectious enthusiasm and great patience with all my drama; and to my agent, David Vigliano, for bringing us all together.

Thanks to Martin Booe for translating my French into English and my passion into print, without even speaking French; to Rochelle Palermo, who tested the recipes, for her intrepid devotion to making them work on the page and in the kitchen; to Rachel Weill for making the food look beautiful and for making our rigorous photo shoots such a pleasant experience, and to her assistant, Andrea Santos Gomez; to Mark Husmann for always being there in a pinch; to Frank Otte for helping me scale down my recipe proportions for the home cook; and to Venacio Campa for providing me with the Swatches that always keep me on time.

This book, and a lot of other things, could never have happened without Gerard and Virginie Ferry, the owners of L'Orangerie. They brought me to the United States when I was only twenty-four, took care of me as if I were their son, and gave me the chance of a lifetime.

Many thanks to Christian Jarry of World Cuisine for outfitting me with his superb Priority line of kitchenware; to Derrick Foy for providing the beautiful Bernardau porcelain from Limoges for the photographs; to Stefan Simchowitz for his photographic contributions; to John Gatti, Esq., for much good advice; to Marilyn Grabowski for her unconditional generosity; to Steve Wayda and his team for making me look the best I can look (the jacket is awesome); to Lee Zeidman for always making me believe in myself, in his own special way; to Pam Engler for always being there, anytime, notice or not; to Chris and Samantha Robichaud for your belief, support, and vision that has helped create the future; to Jeannine De La Torre for letting me borrow your sexy mouth; and to Timmi and Heather from Energy Muse for reflecting my spirit in your jewelry.

I am deeply grateful to my kitchen staff—Kevin Meehan, Donna Claxton, Manuel Alfaro, Frank Otte, and Damien Dovio Rinaldi—for their loyalty and patience with me when I was stressed out and showing it.

And finally, a hug for my auntie Leonce Loire for taking me into her kitchen when I was just a child and letting me experience the joy of making a truly terrible mess.

INTRODUCTION

COOKING IS MY JOB, BUT TO ME IT HAS ALWAYS SEEMED MORE LIKE PLAY THAN WORK. I WISH IT COULD BE LIKE THIS FOR EVERYONE, FOR THE HOME COOK AND THE PROFESSIONAL ALIKE, BUT UNFORTUNATELY, IT'S NOT. PEOPLE BUY COOKBOOKS AND THEY FOLLOW RECIPES. THE OUTCOME MAY BE EITHER EXCELLENT OR DISASTROUS, BUT EITHER WAY, SOMETHING IS OFTEN MISSING: THE COOK IS SO FOCUSED ON PRODUCING THE FINAL PRODUCT THAT HE OR SHE MISSES OUT ON THE ACTUAL *EXPERIENCE* OF COOKING. WHEN I SAY THAT MAKING GREAT FOOD SHOULDN'T BE A CHORE, THOUGH, I'M NOT PROPOSING THREE-STEP RECIPES THAT CAN BE ACCOMPLISHED IN THIRTY MINUTES FLAT. THERE'S NO WAY AROUND IT: GOOD COOKING REQUIRES A LOT OF CON- CENTRATION. BUT THEN, SO DOES SURFING, WHICH IS MY SECOND LOVE.

WHEN YOU THINK ABOUT IT, THE TWO HAVE A LOT IN COMMON. THEY AWAKEN YOUR SENSES. THEY MAKE YOU FEEL MORE ALIVE. AND OUR SENSES REALLY *DO* NEED AWAKEN- ING FROM TIME TO TIME. WE USE THEM ALL DAY, EVERY DAY, BUT WE TAKE THEM FOR GRANTED. THEY GROW TIRED AND DULL, AND WE LOOK FOR SOMETHING TO ENERGIZE THEM ALL OVER AGAIN. SURFING! BUNGEE JUMPING! MOUNTAIN CLIMBING!

COOKING.

The recipes collected in this book range from simple to rather intricate. However, my aim is not to create a set of paces with the goal of simply reaching the finish line. Instead, I hope this book will help all who truly love food to open their minds, stretch their creativity, test their limits—just as they would while surfing, bungee jumping, or climbing Mount Everest. Approached with the right frame of mind, cooking (and certainly eating) can be as exhilarating and enlivening as any extreme sport. Or it can be as calming, mind clearing, and spiritually nourishing as meditation or yoga, a safe haven from the hectic pace and numbing cares of our daily lives.

Learn to play with your food, and don't be afraid to experiment because every failure brings you one step closer to success. (Tobacco-infused eggs and scallops dusted in cocoa powder are just a couple of my more spectacular missteps.) Food offers us much more than physical nutrients. It connects us to the earth; breathes life into our spirits; binds us to others socially, communally, and romantically. And we *need* these things. Otherwise, we'd all be content squeezing our meals out of tubes and popping vitamins, which is what thirty years ago the futurists were predicting would take the place of regular meals by now. They were, of course, wrong, as they usually are. After all, anyone who thinks kelp paste and ascorbic acid will bump roasted rack of lamb, potatoes au gratin, and fresh green beans (sautéed with garlic and basil, perhaps) off the human dinner table doesn't understand humans very well.

Still, from the traditional American family dinner to the long, languorous Parisian-style lunch, our culinary rituals have taken a pretty good whack in the shorts over the past few decades, in Europe as well as America. Maybe that is why we have become so crazy. Cooking, and enjoying the fruit of our labor with all of our five senses, is one road I know to peace of mind. "You must cook with love!" Alain Passard, one of my mentors, would tell me repeatedly, and the fact that he was usually screaming at the top of his lungs and smashing everything in sight when he said this only underscored his sincerity. (We French are a demonstrative people, to say the least—especially when it comes to food and love, and here he was talking about *both*.)

What does it really mean to cook with love? It means a commitment to excellence and a passion for perfection. But those things are still a matter of outcomes and goals. On a deeper level, cooking (and, of course, eating) with love means opening all of our senses to each step of the process. That's why I've organized this book into five sections, each corresponding to one of the five senses: sight, touch, smell, hearing, and taste. Naturally, there's a lot of crossover; after all, what's the point in creating the most beautiful dish in the world if it has no flavor? But I truly believe that exercising each of your senses individually as you cook will open your creativity, increase your appreciation of food, and enhance your technical skill in the kitchen. Listen to the meat as it sizzles on the grill—it's singing to you! Inhale the vapors of the chicken in herbs before you eat—you can taste it even before you put it into your mouth. Pay attention to the textures of the cod as you bite into it, wonderfully crispy on the outside and soft and succulent within, and understand how your sense of touch enhances your enjoyment. Learn to see art when you gaze at a stall heaped with summer-ripe tomatoes. Run through all of your senses one by one whenever you come into contact with food, and then you will truly be cooking with love.

Bon appétit!

Ludo Lefebvre

THE EDUCATION OF
A FRENCH *Chef*

PART *I*

WHEN I WAS THIRTEEN, I TOLD MY DAD THAT I WANTED TO BE A CHEF. I MIGHT AS WELL HAVE TOLD HIM I WANTED TO BE AN ELEPHANT TRAINER; COOKING WAS A PROFESSION NOBODY IN MY FAMILY HAD FOLLOWED, AND HE HAD MORE CONVENTIONAL JOBS IN MIND FOR ME. HE ALSO FIGURED THAT BEING A CHEF WAS BETTER THAN BEING A JUVENILE DELINQUENT, WHICH HAD BEEN MY PREVIOUS CAREER CHOICE, AND ONE FOR WHICH I SHOWED A LOT OF PROMISE. I HAD ALREADY BEEN KICKED OUT OF TWO SCHOOLS FOR LOCKING ONE TEACHER IN A STORAGE CLOSET AND THROWING ANOTHER'S HANDBAG OUT A SECOND-STORY WINDOW. I WAS ANGRY, REBELLIOUS, AND ALWAYS GETTING INTO TROUBLE.

THIS NEW CONCEPT OF MY DESTINY SEEMED TO COME MORE OR LESS OUT OF THE BLUE, BUT MAYBE NOT. I PRETTY MUCH CAME OUT OF THE WOMB WITH A GIGANTIC APPETITE. MY MOTHER SAYS THAT, AS A KID, I WAS *ALWAYS* HUNGRY. I SPENT A LOT OF TIME WITH HER IN THE KITCHEN WHEN I WAS A YOUNG BOY. A LITTLE LATER, WHEN I WAS EIGHT OR NINE AND MOM WAS WORKING, I SPENT MANY HOURS EACH WEEK MAKING BREAD AND PASTRIES WITH MY AUNT. IN THOSE DAYS, I LOVED TO GO TO THE GROCERY STORE BY MYSELF AND JUST WANDER THROUGH THE AISLES, GAZING AT ALL THE WONDERFUL INGREDIENTS. WHEN I WAS TEN, I ASKED FOR SOME COOKWARE FOR MY BIRTHDAY. MY PARENTS THOUGHT THIS STRANGE, BUT THEY GAVE ME A BEAUTIFUL COPPER POT NONETHELESS. I NEVER USED IT. IT WAS SO BEAUTIFUL THAT I DIDN'T WANT TO GET IT DIRTY.

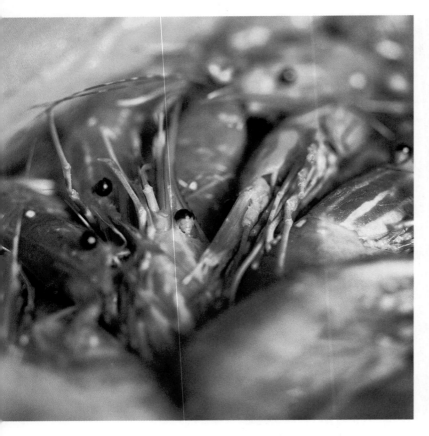

of my ridiculous ambition, and hopefully point me toward a more sensible profession. So for two weeks, I chopped, scraped, washed, and did all of the grunt work of the kitchen. The hours were long. I would return home at the end of the day looking like some gothic warrior, my hair matted in animal fat and my face caked with flour. But I liked the energy in the kitchen, and within a few days, I made up my mind: One day I would be giving the orders. To me, being a chef seemed like being the conductor of an orchestra. All that shouting, barking, and clanging translated into a beautiful, musical feast, and I wanted to be the one waving the baton.

At the end of the two weeks, Jean-Pierre gave me 200 francs. I felt rich and proud. I went straight to the village store and bought my own knife. When I got home, Dad called me into the living room. "So, Ludovic, after all that grunt work, I'd imagine you're ready to think about a *real* job." I told him no, I'd decided to become a chef. It was the first time I ever saw my father speechless. Still, he took me at my word.

My grandfather, it turned out, was an old friend of Marc Meneau, whose restaurant, L'Espérance in St.-Père-sous-Vézelay, had won three Michelin stars. Meneau agreed to give me a one-month tryout, and off I went to the village of St.-Père-sous-Vézelay, forty miles from Auxerre, to work for free. Though located in a village of two hundred in the middle of a forest, L'Espérance was a rare opportunity. It was decided that I'd finish college (the equivalent of high school in America) and go to work for Meneau. This brought about an almost magical change in my attitude. I studied hard and my grades improved dramatically. I stopped causing trouble. I now had something to work toward. Six months later I was accepted to the Castle Culinary School in Dijon. I would spend one week a month there and three weeks working for Meneau. I was fourteen.

So when this idea of becoming a chef suddenly took shape, my father called his friend Jean-Pierre, who had a small restaurant called Maxime in our village of Auxerre, in the region of Burgundy, where the men of the village gathered daily at noon and whiled away the lunch hours drinking copious quantities of wine and neglecting their wives. It was a pleasant place where everyone knew everyone, and its comfortable terrace overlooking the river certainly encouraged leisure—as if Burgundians needed any encouragement in that direction. Anyway, Jean-Pierre agreed to take me on in the kitchen, which dished up simple, classic Burgundian dishes like coq-au-vin, steak béarnaise, and wonderful potato gratins.

My father figured that two weeks of sweating my buns around hot stoves in cramped conditions, washing mountains of pots and pans, chopping bushel baskets of vegetables, and generally being treated like a slave would cure me

Any chef of Meneau's stature would be papered with requests from experienced chefs to learn at his elbow, so I was lucky to get a tryout. Dad gave me enough of an allowance to support me in fine style in a flophouse eight miles outside the village. Mornings I hitchhiked to the restaurant while my fellow residents passed the days drinking and watching porno movies, which was a good way for them to spend their time because they had to save their energy for the fistfights they would have later in the evening. It was a good thing I'd discovered cooking because compared to my neighbors, I would have been a failure as a juvenile delinquent.

I was scared to death of the flophouse denizens (I was even afraid to take breakfast with them in the communal dining room), but I was more scared of Meneau. True, the flophouse guys might slit my throat to steal 5 francs for a cheap bottle of wine, but Meneau had a real way of wielding psychological terror. My grandfather had not told me that my tenure with Meneau was an audition, and that after thirty days I might well get canned. It was better not to know, or I would have been even more nervous.

My first day of work, I showed up wearing jeans and a T-shirt. "Why are you dressed like that?" Meneau snarled. "You look like a bum!" He grumbled some more and found me a chef's jacket that was six sizes too big, which I flopped around in until I got my own. Meneau was a large man with a booming voice, and a hush came over the kitchen whenever he passed through.

The kitchen itself was tiny, and with twenty-five chefs at work, about to burst from overcrowding, so I was exiled to the corner where the garbage cans were. I spent my first shift sitting on top of the garbage cans, cleaning game, learning as I went along. As it happened, I was still exhausted from running a forty-mile race the day before,

and after an hour I passed out cold in the kitchen. I came to and found the kitchen crew encircled around me, looking at me like I was a hopeless case.

I can't explain the kind of magical transformation I went through when I was in the kitchen. Through most of school I was contrary, rebellious, and sullen. But here in the restaurant, ordered around like a private in boot camp, I was a fountain of "yes, chefs!" and "right away, chefs!" "Never stand there with your arms folded like that!" Meneau screamed at me at the top of his lungs (his normal speaking voice). "There's always something to be done!" He only had to tell me once.

I was in awe of Meneau's chefs and their neurotic obsession with perfection, and even at my young age, I realized that to work in a three-star restaurant, foot soldier that I was, was a rare opportunity. At first, I teetered on the verge of disaster. I was always afraid of being shouted at for chopping the carrots too large, or failing to master the myriad of prep work fast enough. Once I was asked to fetch a crate of lobsters from the storage room. It was bad enough that I was terrified of lobsters; their claws weren't bound and I was sure they would snap off my fingers. But when I tried to open the door, the key broke. With no idea what to do, and certain that as punishment Meneau would fling *me* into a lobster pot full of boiling water, I went to Fernand, the old pastry chef, who had become kind of an uncle to me, and begged for advice. Together, we quietly broke into the storage room and got the lobsters.

For four years, I worked six days a week, never taking off a single holiday, including Christmas. I returned at night to the dismal flophouse and listened to my radio in my room while the young criminals watched their pornos in the TV room. In some ways, the work was grueling, but sensing my shared obsession with food, Meneau's chefs gradually took me under their wing and began to teach me.

One night as I was leaving, Meneau took me aside. "Your hands are like gold," he said. "I'm glad to have you in my kitchen." I didn't expect this kind of praise and could barely respond. As time went on, I told him I wanted to go to the United States. "You're too young," he admonished me (not the first time I would be told this). "But I think it's time for you to move on." He arranged a meeting with chef Pierre Gagnaire, another three-star chef, whose Restaurant Pierre Gagnaire was in Saint-Etienne. In France it's normal for chefs eventually to kick their best apprentices out of the nest to gain experience with others. I guess you could say there is a kind of communal commitment to enriching the culinary gene pool. Meneau had not only taught me a lot; he had taken an interest in my future.

When Gagnaire invited my parents and me to lunch to discuss a job, I couldn't believe how pleasant and easygoing he seemed. He ended up offering me $700 a month as commis de cuisine, a step up from apprentice, and I felt like I'd just become a millionaire. I could rent my first real apartment. No more hitchhiking; no more unshaven, porno-afflicted derelicts for roommates. No more screaming.

His tone changed when I showed up for work. "Get a goddamn haircut, you look like a bum!" he railed. (Déjà vu!) My first challenge: to feed and walk Gagnaire's dog, Lucas, a huge black lab whose domain was Gagnaire's office. Secondly, I was put to work in the pastry kitchen. On the first day, I was told (once again) that I had thirty days to prove myself, which was news to me. Here, I'd moved everything to St.-Etienne, a depressing and filthy mining town, with no assurance of continuing employment.

Gagnaire's kitchen was small in comparison even to Meneau's. There were five chefs working in the main kitchen and two in the pastry kitchen. Gagnaire was a very different chef from Meneau, whose brand of *cuisine terroir* was exquisitely refined. He would put his own spin on traditional fare, but he was hardly experimental. Gagnaire was always testing the limits with unusual flavor combinations. Avocado cream with bananas, beet chips served with cheese, oyster and foie gras with cod pancakes—wacky, but wonderful, combinations. Here, I began to learn to color outside the lines of tradition. But I'm glad I started with Meneau; it would have been harder to learn the fundamentals from Gagnaire, who was more like a jazz musician.

Gagnaire drove us hard. He had two Michelin stars and he wanted the third. Difficult as he was, Gagnaire and I had a more personal relationship than I'd had with Meneau. On the weekends, he would lend me to Lucas as a chauffeur, and the dog and I would take off for jaunts in the country. After one year, I told him I should leave to do my year of obligatory military duty. "Nonsense!" he roared. "You need more time with me! Now is a bad time to interrupt your training!"

There are no meteoric ascents in French kitchens. For two years, I continued doing prep work until one day Gagnaire finally put me to work on the seafood line. After six years of kitchen work I got to cook my first fish for an actual customer: cod stuffed with pistachio and red bell pepper. It was exciting finally to have direct contact with heat.

From Gagnaire I learned a lot about plating. He'd play with the sauce like Jackson Pollock played with paint, making crazy designs, hurling it at the plates so that anyone who passed within ten feet of him would be sloshed with it. Even when the kitchen was really busy, he'd often make us replate as often as seven times. From Gagnaire I learned to cook with my eyes.

After two years, I reminded Gagnaire that I really had to get on with my military service. He said he would use his influence, and he arranged for me to cook for the Minister of Defense in Paris. Being a private chef was a new experience, and it wasn't lost time. The pantry was lavishly stocked, I had a lot of freedom, and money was no object. (I now understood why the French pay such high taxes!) I cooked twice for François Mitterand and once for Bill Clinton. There was a certain amount of status, too. Twice, when I told them whom I worked for, the cops let me off for speeding. Those ten months were a nice time for me, and it's saying something that it was after I'd joined the army that I got some vacation for the first time in my working life.

After I'd put in my time, I called Gagnaire and told him I wanted to stay in Paris. He arranged a meeting with Alain Passard, the chef of L'Arpège, a fifty-seat affair and an excellent restaurant. Passard offered me $1,000 a month. In terms of salary, this was a step down from Gagnaire, because Paris was so expensive. I had to pay $600 for a filthy, depressing studio on the fifth floor of a decrepit building. Not quite as bad as the flophouse, but almost.

I thought I'd seen a lot of pressure, but it was nothing compared to L'Arpège. Passard made me chef de partie of fish right off. This made some of the others jealous, which made a difficult situation even harder. I started at 8 A.M. and worked until 2 A.M. Before dining room service opened, Passard would come in and start shadowboxing against the wall, as if he were already about to explode. He called his cooking philosophy "Ecole de Feu"—"The School of Fire"—meaning that he placed proper use of heat above all else in cooking. When the plates came back from the kitchen, he would seize them from the waiters and maniacally pick through the leftovers, examining the bones. If they weren't the specific rose color that denotes perfect cooking, he would start screaming, smashing plates, and hurling pots and pans. "You're no good!" he would howl. "You're a bad chef! This isn't a school!" Like Gagnaire, Passard had two Michelin stars and he wanted three. He was like a Roman general hell-bent on sacrificing as many troops as it took to achieve his conquest. Still, I learned from his obsession. He refused to allow the use of timers, and you were forbidden to touch the fish—it had to be done on instinct.

I lived in constant fear. For a while I had a girlfriend, whom I hardly ever saw. She didn't last long because in the middle of the night I'd wake up screaming about the color of John Dory bones. "Ludo, you're going crazy!" she'd wail.

"But you saw the bones!" I'd holler, still caught up in my dream. "They were pink! I swear they were pink!"

I wasn't the only one having a nervous breakdown. The whole kitchen staff kept themselves going by eating caffeine pills or taking amphetamines. It wasn't unusual to see my co-workers stumbling around talking to themselves. Sometimes they were hallucinating. In one year, I saw sixty cooks come and go. I lost so much weight that my parents barely recognized me when they came to visit.

A gas fire in the kitchen put two cooks in the hospital and burned the hair off my head. We were down to four, but Passard didn't care; the restaurant remained open and we stayed until 3 A.M., getting a head start on prep work. Not too long after this I cut my foot and had to have seven stitches. The doctor said not to walk for ten days. I was at work that night. Later I was in a car accident, and the doctor said not to work for three weeks. I was in the kitchen that afternoon working in a neck brace. I knew that if I didn't show up, I'd lose my position, and I also felt bad for the rest of the staff. It was also about this time my girlfriend said, "Adieu."

But I always felt good cooking. There was a passion that ran in my blood when I cooked, and it still does. I can still hear Passard screaming, "Cook with your ears! Listen to it cook! Use your senses!"

After three years, I weighed 150 pounds and I was exhausted. I called Meneau, who had become a godfather of sorts, and told him I wanted to go to the United States. "No," he said firmly. "You need to work in one more French restaurant."

My next assignment: Le Grand Véfour, headed by Chef Guy Martin, perhaps the most beautiful and historic restaurant in Paris. (Napoleon and Josephine, as well as Victor Hugo, had eaten there.) It was difficult at first; I fought with the sous-chef, but by now I was used to facing off against people older than I but with less experience, so I wasn't scared. Also, Martin, who would go on to win the coveted three Michelin stars, had a cooler head than my previous bosses, so the situation was much more relaxed. I'd learned so much technique that now I felt I really had something to contribute. Martin was young and innovative, and he taught me a lot about the use of spices. I went to Asia with him for several cooking events, and there I learned some new techniques. He was also a good businessman and from him I learned how to run a kitchen.

After three years, I went to lunch again with Meneau. I wasn't even going to bring up going to the United States; I knew he'd tell me to wait longer. But I was wrong. "Now you're ready," he said, and he repeated what he'd told me a few years earlier. "Your hands are like gold." He faxed recommendations to five restaurants, and I was accepted by all of them. One was L'Orangerie, a well-respected French restaurant in Los Angeles. It turned out that the owner, Gerard Ferry, was visiting Paris. I met with him and he offered me a job right away as chef de partie at L'Orangerie. I don't know why I chose Los Angeles; having spent nearly half my life in kitchens, I didn't even know it was the center

of the movie business. But I think I felt more comfortable with a Frenchman; at this point I spoke no English.

I cried the day I left my parents behind in France, but when I arrived there with only two suitcases and my knives, Los Angeles was like a dream. I only worked nights, so I had time off. I started gaining weight back and I learned to surf. Finally, I had a life!

Then something completely unexpected happened. After five months, there was a shakeup in the kitchen and the chef de cuisine left. Mr. Ferry summoned me to his house and asked point-blank if I would take over as head chef. I was astonished. I didn't think I was ready. I asked him if I could take some time to think about it, but he said he needed an answer immediately. I took the plunge and said yes. I was twenty-four.

Up until now I'd been young, angry, and eager to cook. I had learned a lot about how to do things without really understanding *why*. Meneau had taught me the fundamentals of classic cuisine. Passard had taught me both to use my eyes for plating and my ears for cooking. Gagnaire had taught me how to combine flavors, and how to use my sense of taste. Guy Martin had taught me how to cook smart, how to manage and organize a kitchen. I still thought many of the things they had taught me ("Cook with your ears!") were crazy, and in those first months, I was still like a highly trained robot. But as I shouldered this new responsibility and gained control of the kitchen, I began to understand and truly appreciate their wisdom. It was as if they were all there with me and I became infused with their passion for excellence, their maniacal perfectionism, and in some cases, their tempers. I learned to cook with love.

And at some point in those first two years, I grew up. I had become a chef.

the FUNDAMENTALS

Respect for the Market

Seasoning

The School of Fire

Synchronicity

PART *II*

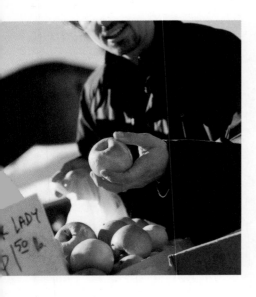

RESPECT FOR THE MARKET

COOKING BEGINS WITH SHOPPING, AND AT THE MARKET OUR SENSES ARE FULLY ENGAGED.

SURE, YOU'VE GOT A BUSY DAY AND YOU WANT TO GET IN AND OUT OF THE MARKET AS FAST AS

POSSIBLE. BUT TRY TO SLOW DOWN AND BECOME AWARE OF THE DIFFERENT SELECTIONS OF PRO-

DUCE THAT EACH CHANGE OF SEASON BRINGS TO THE SHELVES AND MARKET STALLS. IMAGINE

THE FIELDS AND GARDENS FOR THAT TIME OF THE YEAR, THE ANGLE OF THE SUN AS IT RISES

OVER THE LAND, THE MORNING DEW ON THE CROPS, THE SCENT OF THE EARTH AS IT WARMS TO

THE HEAT OF THE DAY. IF POSSIBLE, TRY TO VISIT A LOCAL FARMER. THEN, COOK WITH THE SEA-

SONS. ARTICHOKES, CHARD, AND ASPARAGUS IN SPRING; STRAWBERRIES, PEACHES, AND TOMA-

TOES IN SUMMER; IN AUTUMN, TRUFFLES AND TURNIPS; AND OTHER ROOT VEGETABLES IN WIN-

TER. THIS WILL MAKE YOU FEEL CLOSER TO NATURE, WHICH IS ALWAYS A GOOD THING, AND IT

CAN TRANSFORM YOUR SHOPPING FROM A TEDIOUS, HURRY-THROUGH EXPERIENCE INTO A

LEISURELY MENTAL STROLL THROUGH THE COUNTRYSIDE.

We want fresh, vibrant flavors, but without all of the cream and butter, and the way to achieve this is to get the freshest, most lovingly grown produce.

I can't overemphasize the importance of developing a strong bond to the market. The longer I cook, the more strongly I believe that any cuisine is only as good as the quality of its ingredients. It is, in a way, like making a movie. You can have the greatest actors, the best director, and the most accomplished technical crew, but if the script is lousy, the movie will be too, because the script is its foundation. So it is with produce, the essence of any dish, no matter how simple or elaborate. Before the mid-nineteenth century, French cuisine was perversely obsessed with sauce and little else; if the sauce was rich, flavorful, and creamy, it didn't matter if underneath it you were serving a carriage wheel. That has changed. Now we want to eat healthier. We want fresh, vibrant flavors, but without all of the cream and butter, and the way to achieve this is to get the freshest, most lovingly grown

produce. Fortunately, with the resurgence of farmers' markets in many cities, fine fresh produce has become more accessible than it's been in generations, and there has been a proliferation of small, fanatically devoted organic farmers whose produce now rivals the best of France. Respect for these people is crucial. They love what they do, and your enthusiasm infects them. I highly recommend getting to know them, learning about their growing techniques and the land they work. Let them know when you've been especially pleased with their crops. That way you'll find your way to the best of the best. And you'll make a lot of new friends. Continually try new things, and when you want to create a menu of your own, first visit the market and see what's available.

SEASONING

When you want to cook simply, without sauces or other adornments, these seasoning techniques will work miracles on your produce, whether it's meat, chicken, or fish. As you'll see, I'm strongly partial to using fleur de sel in place of common table salt; its flavor is much more delicate and lacks the bitterness of ordinary salt. A basic mixture of two parts fleur de sel and one part white pepper, which is less assertive than black pepper and has great flavor-enhancing powers, really amplifies the natural flavor of produce when properly applied. White pepper is best when freshly ground.

FOR RED MEAT, including beef, veal, and pork, rub with the salt and pepper, then rub with grapeseed oil. The oil serves two purposes: It will tenderize the meat and promote the conduction of heat, making it cook more evenly.

FOR POULTRY, rub with the salt and pepper mixture the day before. This will give the seasonings time to penetrate the skin. After applying the salt and pepper, brush the skin with heavy cream. This will make the skin wonderfully crisp, protect it from becoming too brown, and seal in the juices. Store the poultry in your refrigerator overnight.

SEASON FISH with the salt and pepper one or two hours before cooking and store in the refrigerator. Brush the fish with a little fish stock or shellfish liquor. This will reinforce the natural, open-sea flavor of the fish and reduce the need for salt.

DON'T SALT VEGETABLES before cooking; it will make them tough. Salt may be added sparingly to the cooking water, but take care not to add too much or the vegetables will taste salty. Add salt to taste *after* cooking.

THE SCHOOL OF FIRE

Let's return to my mentor Alain Passard, who believed that the key to brilliant cooking was all in the way you manage food's contact with heat. "I am a human rotisserie!" he would declare, and he really was. He called his philosophy of cooking "Ecole de Feu"—the School of Fire. It's a good school in which to study. Especially when you're cooking simply, the use of heat—whatever the source—is half the battle. And if you can master just a few basic techniques, you'll be amazed at how much more delicious chicken, fish, and meat will turn out.

As always, though, the first issue is produce. Everyone wants to cook fillets these days, and we've all gotten hooked on the convenience of having our meat deboned. But I want to tell you that whatever kind of meat you're cooking, it's going to be more tender, juicy, and flavorful, and will have a more pleasing texture, if you cook it with the bone or bones intact. (If you ask me, the boneless chicken breast is the worst thing to happen to American cookery since the TV dinner!) Nobody has come up with a definitive scientific explanation for why this is, but any seasoned chef will tell you it's true.

Plus, it's much more exciting to cook a big piece of meat, whether it's a whole fish, a rack of lamb, or a prime rib. In this way, the meat will retain more flavor and juice.

There are a couple of basic ideas behind the School of Fire. The first is pretty obvious: Food must be cooked evenly on each side or sides. But that is easier said than done. Whole fish, for example, are shaped like, well, whole fish—sort of lopsided. So the tail will cook first and dry out unless you take measures to correct this. One trick to avoid overcooking the tail is to prop it up with an inverted spatula while it cooks in the oven or on the stove, reducing its contact with the heat source.

This is what Passard meant when he called himself the human rotisserie; he could always manipulate the meat over and around the heat source in a way that compensated for its uneven density, resulting in complete uniformity of doneness. It's important *not* to flip the fish, steak, or chicken over and over because you interrupt the cooking process on each side, then begin it all over again, which will toughen the meat. Instead, cook one side before turning it to the other. This will allow a consistent amount of heat to penetrate the meat from each side. Also, keep in mind that you'll probably cook the second side less than the first because heat will already have begun building up inside the meat.

The second principle is to remove flesh from the heat before it's as done as you want it to be, then allow it to rest. Although you may embrace the romantic ideal that meat should be served straight out of the oven or off the stove, this isn't so. As we say in France, cook it à *la goutte de sang*—"a little bloody" (in France, we tend to be pretty visceral when we're talking about food). Then cover it with aluminum foil for a few minutes, and return it to the heat just long enough to rewarm. There are two benefits to this. The meat will continue cooking while away from the heat, and the juices, which have migrated to the center, will have a chance to redistribute as it cools, making it all the more succulent and moist. Frankly, I don't like thermometers and have never used them for cooking meat, fish, and poultry. I prefer to rely on my senses, and I think you'll find that, ultimately, you'll have far more control if you do too. I think it makes you work too much like a robot! Here are a few general guidelines for cooking and resting flesh.

BEEF, PORK, VEAL. Allow the meat to stand outside the refrigerator for a couple of hours, covered in plastic. The closer it is to room temperature when you cook it, the better. Cook beef rare and allow it to rest for five minutes. Veal and pork should be cooked more toward medium rare. Let the meat rest for five to ten minutes, then return it to a 400-degree oven for five to seven minutes, depending on the size of the cut—longer for bigger pieces of meat and shorter for smaller ones.

FISH. Cook to medium rare, usually at 375°F in the oven (the degree of heat when cooking fish on the stovetop varies considerably with different recipes). If cooked whole, on the bone, allow to rest for ten to fifteen minutes before returning it to the oven for five to seven minutes, again depending on the size. Fillets, however, should be served immediately.

CHICKEN. Roast to medium rare at 350°F and let rest for five minutes before returning it to the oven for five to seven minutes. A two-and-a-half-pound chicken, for example, should be roasted at 350°F for about forty-five minutes to an hour. (I really don't like to be too scientific about these things; nature has many variables.) Test by pressing on the breast with your fingers; if it is very soft, it's undercooked. When it starts to feel more firm, it's close to being done, so remove it and let it rest for fifteen minutes before rewarming for five to seven minutes at the same temperature. (I've noticed that in the United States people tend to roast birds for more like an hour and a half, which is too long.) Another method of testing it is to run a thin knife down to the bone; leave it there for fifteen seconds, and then touch the knife to your lip. If the knife is warm, the chicken is done. Don't worry if the juice is still pink. The chicken will continue to cook while resting, and it's better to err on the side of rareness, which can be corrected, than to overcook it.

Another excellent method for cooking chicken is *à l'étouffée,* which means that you seal the lid of a pot or Dutch oven with pastry dough before placing it in the oven. This creates a concentration of vapor, which lulls the flesh into a state of exquisite softness and intensifies the flavors. (Check out the recipe for Chicken Etouffée in Dried Verbena and Curry Leaves on page 138.)

VEGETABLES. Vegetables should be cooked at a strong boil. You want to cook them as fast as possible so they don't lose their color, so always bring the water to a boil before you add the vegetables. They're vastly more appetizing when they retain their natural hues. For most green vegetables, such as green beans, broccoli, and Brussels sprouts, I recommend that you first bathe them in ice water for five minutes before cooking, then plunge them into an ice water bath after cooking for another five minutes. This preserves the chlorophyll, which is the source of their color. If you're incorporating them into a salad, cook them to doneness, and they're ready to go. If you're serving them as a side dish, cook them to a sharp crispness and finish by sautéing in two or three tablespoons of olive oil until they're warm again.

With cooking, as with life, timing is everything. Timing is like the law: It must be obeyed. You can learn to anticipate that perfect level of underdoneness, which with time away from heat will transform your food into a perfectly cooked delight. With practice and attention, you will be able to throw away your stopwatch and have your timer in your head. Which is the best timer of all.

SYNCHRONICITY

Cooking should be a pleasure, not a headache. Preparing even a simple three-course meal can quickly become an exercise in stress management if you're not prepared. I've known a fair number of highly accomplished home chefs who've mastered a lot of sophisticated techniques. They can roast meat to perfection, blanch vegetables to the most beautiful al dente, render the perfect crème brûlée. But when they try to bring all of these things together in preparing a meal that may kick off with appetizers, move on to salad and soup, and culminate with entrée and dessert, they fall to pieces. The spice-crusted rack of lamb comes out of the oven fit for a king, but the mashed potatoes are only halfway done, and the guests have long ago finished off their salads. And while the host correctly calculated that the side dish of wilted spinach would take only eight or nine minutes to prepare, he or she overlooked the fact that spinach requires soaking. The result: Canned green beans are substituted for fresh spinach, the lamb has dried out in the oven, and the potatoes are lumpy because they were fixed in haste. Fried to perfection, however—wonderfully crisp on the outside and molten within—is the cook's nervous system.

I don't cook well when I'm angry, upset, or frustrated. Like anything else, we can do a better job when we're happy, and this goes for professionals too. Once not long ago we were visited by an influential national food critic. This makes any kitchen staff nervous, and we were trying too hard. When the sous-chef removed a perfectly baked John Dory fillet from the oven and it slipped out of his hands, it was almost like watching a disaster in slow motion as it plummeted to the floor. We had to start all over.

Fortunately, when it comes to kitchen stress, it's pretty easy to create a mental nonstick surface. Get organized, mentally and physically. I know this may sound obvious, but so many home cooks approach the kitchen randomly (and with disastrous results) that I feel it's worth bringing up. Whether you're the chef of a large high-end restaurant or the host of a dinner party for four, it's important to have a strategy. I've watched many of my nonprofessional friends come to the brink of meltdown because they couldn't find their whisk or vegetable peeler or paring knife at a crucial moment in the cooking process.

Always lay out your tools, cookware, seasonings, and spices *before* you start work. Sharpen your knives, wipe out your pans, and take inventory of your tools so everything will be ready when you need it. It's a simple step, but it will save you rummaging through the cabinets and drawers hunting for a jar of cardamom or a garlic press while your food simmers into oblivion on the stove.

Second, anything you can do in advance, do it. In France we call this *mise en place*, which simply means advance preparation. I believe that solid *mise en place* is half of good restaurant service, and this is no less true for the home chef. It's another simple organizing principle. Vegetables should be peeled, chopped, and rinsed, meat should be cleaned and seasoned, butter should be softened (if necessary), all at the outset. With all of your ingredients ready for the saucepot, skillet, or roasting pan, you will be free to focus fully on cooking.

Finally, always start with the component of your meal that will take the longest to cook. There seems to be some quirk in human nature that makes people want to tackle protein first. Maybe it's left over from our days as hunter-gatherers. When protein flashes across our field of vision in the form of a buffalo or mountain trout, we want to immediately spear it before we return to picking nuts and berries. At any rate, I've seen a lot of people shove, say, sea bass in the oven before they even begin preparing their vegetables. I guess it gives them a sense of accomplishment, however false. But a sea bass may cook in five minutes and carrots in twenty. In this case, the poor fish has died for nothing! He languishes, growing cold and soggy, while the vegetables get under way. This is bad karma. A badly treated fish may communicate telepathically to a school of sharks, instructing them to devour you the next time you jump in the ocean.

Most likely, you'll want to start with your sauce. Then red meat or chicken, depending on how it's to be prepared. Whatever medley of foods you're preparing, first sit down and make a plan. It's actually a fun part of the process, and it helps you avoid frustration and allows you to work in a pleasant state of mind.

SPICES, HERBS, & SPECIALTIES

PART *III*

SPICES

I AM FASCINATED WITH SPICES, FROM BOTH A HISTORICAL AND A CULINARY POINT OF VIEW.
ANCIENT ROMANS DEMANDED PEPPER AS TRIBUTE FROM THEIR SUBJECTS. IN THE MIDDLE AGES,
SPICES WERE USED FOR MONEY, AND MANY ADVENTURERS RISKED LIFE AND LIMB, SAILING INTO
TREACHEROUS WATERS AND SOJOURNING TO MYSTERIOUS REGIONS TO ACQUIRE THEM. IT'S
ALMOST AS IF SPICES HAVE A MAGIC HOLD OVER US. IN COOKING, THEY CAN MAKE ALL THE DIF-
FERENCE, TURNING SOMETHING ORDINARY INTO SOMETHING MAGICAL.

YOU MAY NOT BE ABLE TO FIND MANY OF THE SPICES WE USE HERE AT THE GRO-
CERY STORE, BUT DON'T WORRY. IF YOU'RE LUCKY ENOUGH TO LIVE IN A CITY WITH A SPICE STORE,
BY ALL MEANS TAKE ADVANTAGE OF IT. THE SPICES WILL BE FRESHER, THE SELECTION WIDER, THE
QUALITY BETTER, AND BELIEVE IT OR NOT, THE PRICES ARE LIKELY TO BE LOWER. OTHERWISE, THE
INTERNET IS LADEN WITH NUMEROUS SHOPPING SITES FEATURING SPICES, AND FROM THESE,
ALONG WITH SPICE HOUSES THAT DO MAIL ORDER, YOU CAN GET JUST ABOUT ANYTHING. THIS HOLDS
TRUE FOR A NUMBER OF OTHER INGREDIENTS CALLED FOR IN THIS BOOK THAT AT FIRST GLANCE MAY
SEEM HARD TO FIND. BE SURE TO CHECK THE RESOURCE GUIDE ON PAGE 246. IT'S ABSOLUTELY
ESSENTIAL TO USE THE BEST SPICES YOU CAN FIND; QUALITY MAKES ALL THE DIFFERENCE.

ALTHOUGH MANY PEOPLE LIKE TO TOAST THEIR SPICES THESE DAYS, BELIEVING
IT BRINGS OUT THE FLAVOR, IN MOST CASES I PREFER NOT TO; I THINK THEY'RE BETTER FRESH.
ALL SPICES SHOULD BE FRESHLY GROUND, THOUGH, AS SHORTLY BEFORE USING AS POSSIBLE. A
FINAL THOUGHT: GROUND SPICES LOSE THEIR FLAVOR WHEN COOKED. I GENERALLY PREFER TO
GIVE MY FOOD A DUSTING WITH THEM *AFTER* COOKING. THAT WAY YOU GET THE FULL INTENSITY OF
THEIR FLAVOR.

HERE ARE A FEW OF MY FAVORITE SPICES:

CARAWAY SEED. Related to cumin, the caraway seed is aromatic and slightly fruity, with a strong hint of anise. It adds verve to cauliflower, Brussels sprouts, zucchini, and potatoes. One of my favorite uses for it is with lamb, such as in Rack of Lamb with Broth, Baby Vegetables, and Caraway Seeds on page 204.

CARDAMOM. If you've had the now-popular Chai tea, you've tasted cardamom, a spice that combines hints of camphor, citrus, and bergamot. There are three types of cardamom: green (the most common), black, and white, though white is nearly impossible to find. Following the Indian tradition, I use green cardamom mostly for desserts. Black cardamom has a more smoky, minty character, and it is good with stronger meats like lamb and wild game, and stronger fish such as anchovies. Cardamom pods can be used whole, as with Chanterelles with Vinegar and Green Cardamom on page 132, or the seeds may be removed and ground and the pods discarded, as with Red Wine–Poached Beef with Star Anise, Long Pepper, and Cardamom Infusion on page 140. If grinding cardamom, toast the pods and using a pestle, bruise the shells and discard them, then grind the seeds to a fine powder. I like to dust fish and meat with it after cooking, but be careful because a little goes a long way.

CINNAMON. One of the most popular spices in the world, cinnamon is most typically added to desserts, but it's also wonderful with chicken and legumes. I find that it blends well with salty foods, particularly shellfish (see Glazed Langoustines with Ceylon Cinnamon and Fried Angel Hair Pasta with Clams on page 210). In my opinion, cinnamon from Ceylon is the best in the world. Cinnamon sticks are actually the dried bark of a tropical evergreen tree, and the best are somewhat soft and have tender skin.

FLEUR DE SEL. All salt is not created equal, and my strong preference is for fleur de sel (flower of salt). Fleur de sel is sea salt that has been slowly evaporated in clay beds. After a few weeks, the fine, lacy crystals that rise to the top like cream are skimmed off, and that is the fleur de sel. Its flavor is more nuanced and less aggressive than any other salt, and it's healthier, due to its lower level of sodium chloride. Because it retains the moisture of the sea, its grains have a tendency to stick together. I recommend spreading it out on a baking sheet and drying it in a 300-degree oven for forty minutes, which will cause it to clump into a gravelly mass. After it is dry, break it into pieces and grind it in a food processor until the granules are fine but not powdered. This will improve the flavor and allow it to infuse better. (You can do this with the entire container and store it for later use.)

CORIANDER
FRANCE
CERTIFIED ORGANIC
1 OUNCE 1.00   1/4 LB. 3.00
1/2 LB. 5.00
1 LB. 10.00

GINGER. This may be my favorite spice of all. It's peppery, aromatic, pungent, slightly bitter, and floral, all at the same time. You can use it with almost anything, and in any way: fresh, dried, or even candied. To test its range, try Sweetbreads with Ginger, Licorice, Roasted Pears, and Lemon Confit on page 97, and Cod Crusted with Ginger, Almonds, and Sesame Seeds with Baby Tomatoes and Candied Ginger on page 213. For a completely different application, see Bavaroise of Goat Cheese with Onions, Beets, and Candied Ginger on page 42.

LONG PEPPER. I fell in love with this Indian black pepper ever since my spice supplier introduced me to it a couple of years ago. It has a sharp flavor and a light floral aroma, and is somewhat bitter and slightly sweet. It will give a mildly acid taste to marinades. It is best when coarsely ground. To experience it, try Roast Beef with Long Pepper and Spiced French Fries on page 170.

MACE. The outer membrane of the nutmeg seed, mace is usually sold ground, but I prefer to buy it whole (in which case it's known as "blade" mace) and then grind it into a powder. A bit stronger than nutmeg, it's a piquant but delicate spice, with a hint of hazelnuts. It's good for infusing broths. It also goes well with chicken, pork, and veal, and with potatoes, such as in Potato Cake with Onions on page 85.

SAFFRON. One of the most difficult spices to describe, saffron is truly unique; there's really nothing else you can compare it to. Use it sparingly; its taste is more of a whisper than an announcement, yet it can overpower anything that comes into contact with it. It adds panache to seafood dishes, and it is wonderful with lentils and rice. For a less typical application, try the Lemon Sorbet with Saffron on page 230.

STAR ANISE. Native to China, star anise is the seed found in the pods of the Badian tree, a small evergreen related to the magnolia. It has the same essential oil as anise and fennel, but it's quite powerful, so be careful when using it. Star anise is best when coarsely ground; then it becomes a textural component in addition to providing flavor, as in King Crab with Avocado Mousse and Water of Tomato and Star Anise on page 44.

VANILLA. Vanilla is one of the most primary spices, yet it is incredibly difficult to describe. Many flavor sensations and aromas are compared to vanilla, but to what can you compare vanilla? If you've only used vanilla extract in the past, you're in for a surprise when you use the whole bean. The difference is huge. In my opinion, the best beans come from Madagascar and Tahiti. Vanilla is more versatile than most people imagine. If you thought vanilla was only for use in desserts, check out Salad of Tomato Confit with Basil and Mint and Vanilla and Raspberry Balsamic Vinaigrette on page 91, and Gently Cooked Ahi Infused with Vanilla on page 102. Vanilla beans are quite expensive, so I recommend keeping the vanilla pod after you've scraped out and used the seeds, drying it for one hour in a 300-degree oven, and grinding it into a powder for later use.

HERBS

FRESH HERBS ARE AN ESSENTIAL COMPONENT OF MY COOKING. THEY ALLOW US TO COOK SIMPLY, WITH CLEAN, UNCLUTTERED FLAVORS, WHILE PROVIDING ANY NUMBER OF SURPRISES FOR THE PALATE. FOR THE MOST PART, I DON'T LIKE TO COOK HERBS; THEY'RE MUCH MORE EFFECTIVE WHEN ADDED RAW AT THE LAST MINUTE SO THEY RETAIN THEIR COLOR AND PUNGENCY. FARMERS' MARKETS HAVE GREATLY EXPANDED THE SELECTION OF HERBS AVAILABLE TO THE HOME COOK. HERE ARE A FEW OF MY FAVORITES:

CHIVES. Chives add zest to cheese, such as fromage blanc; spice up salads; and add sparkle to eggs, as you'll discover with Eggs Caviar on page 162. Though members of the onion family, chives are much more subtle. I use them to season sauces and sprinkle on meat and fish. Chives are especially delicate, so always add them at the last minute.

LEMON VERBENA. An amazingly versatile herb, with a strong, citrusy perfume and delicately bitter aftertaste, lemon verbena gives chicken an aromatic tanginess and provides a sharp high note for desserts.

LEMONGRASS. A staple of Thai and other Asian cuisines, lemongrass imbues any kind of seafood with an irresistible bang of citrus, combined with a hint of ginger, as in Caramelized Black Sea Bass with Lemongrass-Infused Consommé, Clams, and Basil on page 57.

SORREL. Popular in France for centuries, sorrel is a slightly sour, leafy green, visually resembling spinach. It mades a wonderful salad and goes well with fish, as in Whole Dorade with Salt Crust, Yellow Wine Sauce, and Sorrel Salad on page 174.

TARRAGON. If you've only used dried tarragon in the past, the herb in its fresh form will surprise you with its delicate, savory flavor. Its properties are shown off to fine effect in Whole Lobster Cooked in Salt and Tarragon on page 166. The scent and flavor of tarragon always transport me to the south of France.

THYME. Another widely used herb in its dried form, thyme is even better fresh, and less likely to overpower a dish. It marries well with almost anything, from veal, chicken, and pork to tomatoes. The recipe for Young Garlic Soup with Thyme, Scallops, and Gold Leaf, on page 165, is a good demonstration of its amiable nature.

SPECIALTIES

YOU MAY NOT BE FAMILIAR WITH A NUMBER OF THE INGREDIENTS CALLED FOR IN THESE

RECIPES, BUT I HOPE THAT EXPERIMENTING WITH THEM WILL BE PART OF THE FUN. IN MOST

CASES, I'VE PROVIDED EASY-TO-OBTAIN SUBSTITUTIONS THAT WILL WORK JUST FINE. STILL, IN

THE SPIRIT OF ADVENTURE, I HOPE YOU'LL TEST THE LIMITS BY EMPLOYING SOME OF THESE

UNUSUAL BUT TRULY DYNAMIC INGREDIENTS.

ACACIA HONEY. This is my favorite honey of all. It's delicately floral and not overly sweet. All honey is not created equal; with cheaper versions, all you taste is sugar. With acacia honey, you experience a whole different dimension of flavor.

ALMOND MILK AND ALMOND FLOUR. These lend a subtle but exotic note to desserts, such as Almond Rice Pudding with Citrus Jelly on page 229, and Fried Candied Milk with Green Cardamom on page 146.

ARGAN OIL. This oil is made from the fruit of the argan tree, which grows in Morocco. Its subtle flavor is nutty, with floral undertones, and it's excellent for finishing soups (such as Chilled Asparagus Soup with Argan Oil on page 194) and spicing up salad dressings. It also adds an exotic touch when drizzled on fish and lamb after cooking.

BANYULS VINEGAR. A fortified wine made in the south of France, Banyuls is similar to a tawny port, but less sweet and with more spice. The vinegar made from it is exquisite for its soft, round character. It's excellent for marinades and salad dressings.

RASPBERRY BALSAMIC VINEGAR. With its fruity, palate-cleansing character, this is a dazzling foundation for any vinaigrette. It goes especially well with tomatoes and greens. Check out Salad of Tomato Confit with Basil and Mint and Vanilla and Raspberry Balsamic Vinaigrette on page 91.

VERJUS. The juice of large, unripened grapes, verjus is a wonderful stand-in for vinegar. It had until recently been all but forgotten, but it is now making a well-deserved comeback. Verjus is tart and slightly astringent, and adds a note of fruity acid to salads and marinades.

VIN JAUNE. A product of eastern France's Jura region, vin jaune—"yellow wine"—is made from grapes fermented on top of hay, which gives it a pungent, earthy essence. It's vaguely similar to a dry sherry, but it makes an excellent sauce, as you'll see with Whole Dorade with Salt Crust, Yellow Wine Sauce, and Sorrel Salad on page 174.

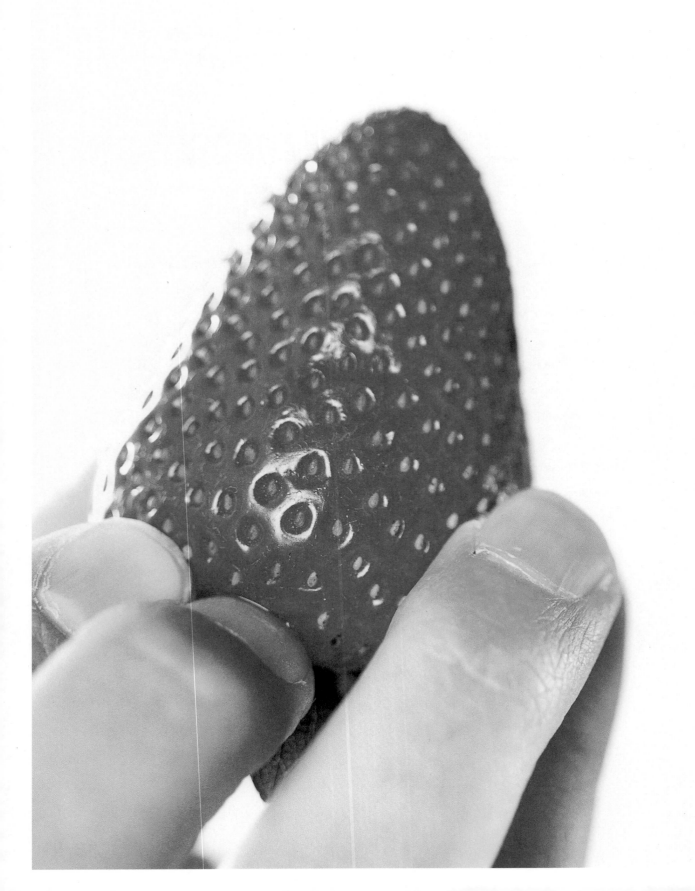

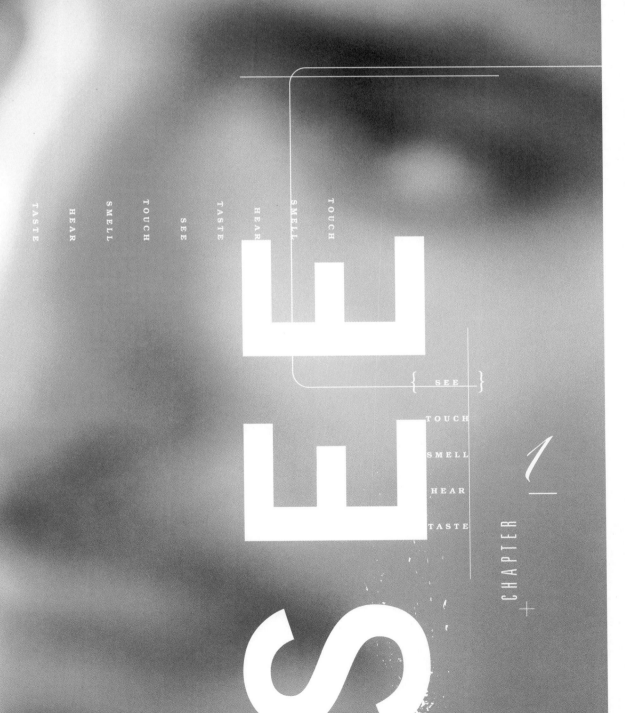

TASTE

HEAR

SMELL

TOUCH

SEE

TASTE

HEAR

SMELL

TOUCH

SEE

E

E

{ SEE }

TOUCH

SMELL

HEAR

TASTE

S

CHAPTER 1

BEFORE THE FIRST FORKFUL OF FOOD ENTERS OUR MOUTHS,
WE HAVE ALREADY BEGUN EATING.

WE HAVE BEGUN EATING WITH OUR EYES. —AS WE ALMOST ALWAYS DO. ALTHOUGH SOMETIMES

OUR NOSES MAY LEAD THE WAY WHEN A DISH IS PARTICULARLY AROMATIC, IT'S USUALLY OUR

EYES THAT MAKE THE FIRST CONTACT WITH FOOD. OUR GAZE FALLS ON A PLATE HOLDING A PER-

FECTLY ROASTED CHICKEN, ITS GOSSAMERLIKE SKIN TAUT AND RICHLY BURNISHED WITH SPICES.

SURROUNDING IT IS A MEDLEY OF STEAMED BABY VEGETABLES, THEIR COLORS VIBRANT AND

TRUE. THE EYE THEN CATCHES THE WISP OF STEAM UNFURLING FROM A FRESHLY BAKED LOAF

OF BREAD. STARING AT THIS SCENARIO AS IF IT WERE A WORK OF ART, YOU BECOME AMAZED AT

THE NATURAL BEAUTY OF FOOD, ITS CONTOURS, ITS FORM, THE WAY LIGHT PLAYS OFF ITS TEX-

TURES. SIGHT HAS AWAKENED YOUR APPETITE BEFORE YOU'VE EVEN TAKEN ONE TASTE OF THE

GORGEOUS DISH IN FRONT OF YOU. OF COURSE, A LOT OF WHAT I'M TALKING ABOUT AMOUNTS TO

PRESENTATION—THE WAY WE DRESS FOOD UP BEFORE SENDING IT TO THE TABLE FOR ITS DATE

WITH DESTINY. THERE ARE CERTAINLY ALL SORTS OF BEAUTY TIPS YOU CAN MAKE USE OF, ALONG

WITH INFINITE POSSIBILITIES FOR CREATIVE GARNISHING, THAT WILL MAKE ANY PLATE RAVISH-

ING TO THE EYE AS WELL AS THE TONGUE. BUT FOR THE MOMENT, I'D LIKE TO GO A LITTLE

DEEPER THAN THAT.

As I've said, cooking begins with shopping, and our appreciation for the food we cook deepens all the more when we stop to let our eyes drink in the splendor of nature's bounty, to behold produce naked in its raw, unfinished state. It's no wonder that so many artists, from the ancient Greeks to the Flemish masters to impressionists like Paul Cézanne, found such rapture in painting still lifes of a simple bowl of fruit or wild game hanging to cure. At the farmers' market, I can easily fall into an absolute trance just staring at a palette of tomatoes, a bin of carrots, a heaping box of spinach. Nowhere in nature will you find such intensity of color as in fresh produce, and it is our eyes that lead us to the best.

The colors tell us much about the quality of our purchase. In fact, our eyes tell us things about the food we're going to eat that we don't even consciously realize. The deep burnished red of the apples whispers to us of their ripeness and readiness, the glossy purple sheen of the eggplant speaks for its goodness, the sunset hues of the tangerines assure us of their sweetness. A fish that's glistening and translucent, its body lambent and shimmering in the light, its eyes sparkling, is bound to be good. We behold the perfect marbling of a beefsteak, ruby-colored and glinting like a precious stone. Our pleasure at the sight of these things is more than simply aesthetic; food visually telegraphs its power (or lack of it) to nourish, and the sight of food frames our expectations of its flavor. It really is worth taking the time to look at food with new eyes.

Our eyes tell us much about the process of cooking as well. A loup de mer starts out translucent, then grows white as it reaches doneness. When a veal chop turns black in the skillet, we know we've ruined it. Vegetables deepen in color as they steam, and we know they're done. There are also situations in which perfect cooking is reflected in visual appeal, and vice versa. Think, for example, of a beef tenderloin cooked to a perfect medium-rare. You slice the meat, revealing a tantalizing color spectrum: It is encased in a ring of rich brown, the color of tree bark glistening in the rain. The brown graduates first toward pink, then into a bright rosy hue, winding up with a ruby core, with many nuances within. At first sight, you know it's going to be delicious. But do you plop the tenderloin onto a board and carve it for your guests one slice at a time? No! Carve the entire piece of meat and arrange the slices, laying one against another, in a circle. Don't hide the beauty of the meat from your guests.

As lovely as food is in its naked state, you can't really overemphasize the importance of presentation.

As lovely as food is in its naked state, you can't really overemphasize the importance of presentation. I like to think of every meal as a wedding; the food and the person consuming it are to become one. You're giving your daughter away at the altar, and you want to see her dressed in a way that shows off her natural beauty to its best advantage. Your presentation may be elaborate or simple; it may be crinoline or it may be calico. In my years of work in restaurants, I've come to the conclusion that if diners are seduced visually by the plate put before them, there's at least a fifty-fifty chance that they'll like the dish—no matter how it tastes.

It's amazing when you look back on the evolution of food presentation. Can you remember the days when a single sprig of parsley resting atop a T-bone steak was the peak of elegance? Along with the gastronomic revolution in this country that began in the 1970s and continues to this day, came a new—and sometimes crazy—emphasis on style. Chefs weren't plating food, they were building monuments, and the trend came to be known as "architectural food." These were garish constructions indeed, and they were at their height in the mid-nineties when I first came to Los Angeles. Towers! Everything, it seemed, had to be a tower that required a hammer, a full set of Allen wrenches, and a consultation with an engineering firm before you dared dismantle it. At first, I was intimidated by all this because I didn't know how to do it. (I still don't.) So I ignored it, hoping the trend would go away.

Fortunately, for the most part, it has. We're back to elegance and simplicity, although there is still plenty of room to be creative. And while I don't like to think of the plate as a foundation for a building project, I do like to think of it as a canvas. And I am fussy about it. I may rearrange the presentation seven or eight times before I send a plate out to the dining room. It's better not to go overboard, though. You don't want to clutter the plate visually. When there's too much going on, it confuses the eyes.

As for the plate itself, I prefer a subtle pattern, if not a simple white plate. There are many beautiful and elaborate designs available, and you can spend a lot of money on them. But in the end I want people to look at the food, not the plate!

There are many inventive ways to bring flair to your food presentation and you shouldn't be afraid to experiment. Personally, I like to play around with geometrical patterns. (My grandfather was an architect, and I seem to have inherited some of his sense of design.) Four fish fillets, for example, can be arranged into a square with your vegetables mounded up in the middle, a configuration that makes the vegetables all the more appealing, thanks to their posi-

tion of prominence. (Speaking of vegetables, proper cooking preserves the intensity of their colors, and we'll talk in this section about how to save them from fading.)

It's also important to set a nice table. A beautiful tablecloth, candles, and an artful centerpiece—something that reflects your own personality—go a long way in enhancing the pleasure of eating. The right ambience creates the feelings of security and relaxation so essential to the full enjoyment of dining.

In the High Middle Ages, superstition dictated that most food should be colored gold. Foods were tinted with saffron and sandalwood, and numerous elixirs containing potable gold were created to enhance health and ward off evil. The belief was that, by ingesting the color gold, you absorbed its fundamental nobility. I wouldn't go as far as to say that an artful presentation of food will bring wealth and fame to the diner, or protect him from malevolent forces. But a beautiful plate, now as then, can make all the difference.

CREAM OF BROCCOLI SOUP

Here's a simple (and tasty) exercise in preserving the color of vegetables. Broccoli is too often overcooked or wrongly cooked, causing it to fade into an unappetizing khaki color. Follow this method and you'll learn how to preserve that beautiful vibrant green.

4 APPETIZER SERVINGS

8 cups broccoli florets (from about
 2 pounds of broccoli)

2 cups Chicken Stock (page 239)

1 cup plus 4 teaspoons heavy
 whipping cream

3 tablespoons unsalted butter
 Fleur de sel and freshly ground white
 pepper

Cook the broccoli in a large pot of boiling water until it is tender but still bright green, about 5 minutes. Drain. Transfer the broccoli to a large bowl of ice water to cool and preserve the color. Drain well. Set 4 very small individual broccoli florets aside.

Combine the chicken stock and 1 cup of the cream in a heavy medium saucepan. Bring to a boil. Remove from the heat. Working in batches, puree the well-drained broccoli, the broth mixture, and butter in a blender until smooth, seasoning the soup to taste with fleur de sel and pepper while blending, about 3 minutes per batch. Thin the soup with water to the desired consistency, if necessary.

DO AHEAD: *The soup and individual broccoli florets can be prepared up to 8 hours ahead. Cool the soup, then cover and refrigerate. Rewarm the soup over medium-low heat before serving. Enclose the 4 individual broccoli florets in a resealable plastic bag and refrigerate.*

Ladle the soup into 4 shallow soup bowls. Drizzle 1 teaspoon cream over each serving. Garnish with the reserved broccoli florets and serve.

OYSTERS ON THE HALF SHELL WITH RED BEET JELLY AND SHALLOT CREAM

Nestled in their shells on a pillow of frothy white shallot cream and garnished with deep-red beet jelly, then arranged on a mound of rock salt, these oysters are not only regal to behold, but delightful to taste.

6 APPETIZER SERVINGS

Red Beet Jelly

1¹⁄₂ cups strained fresh beet juice (from about 2¹⁄₂ pounds of large red beets)

³⁄₄ teaspoon sugar

¹⁄₂ teaspoon unflavored gelatin

Fleur de sel and freshly ground pepper

Shallot Cream

¹⁄₂ cup heavy whipping cream

2 tablespoons strained fresh lemon juice

1 tablespoon minced shallot

1 tablespoon oyster liquor, reserved from oysters

Oysters

Rock salt

24 fresh Fanny Bay oysters, freshly shucked, on the half shell, liquor reserved

1 small red beet, peeled and cut into chiffonade

1 bunch watercress, stems discarded

FOR THE RED BEET JELLY

Combine the beet juice and sugar in a heavy small saucepan. Sprinkle the gelatin over and let soften for 5 minutes. Whisk the gelatin mixture over low heat until the gelatin and sugar dissolve, skimming the accumulated foam off the top, about 1 minute. Strain the beet mixture through a fine-mesh strainer and into a small container. Season to taste with fleur de sel and freshly ground pepper. Cover and refrigerate until the mixture resembles a loose jelly but is not firm, at least 4 hours or overnight. If the jelly is too firm, add a few drops of water or leftover beet juice and whisk to loosen.

FOR THE SHALLOT CREAM

Beat the cream in a large bowl until soft peaks form. Whisk in the lemon juice, shallot, and reserved oyster liquor. Lightly season the shallot cream to taste with fleur de sel and freshly ground pepper.

DO AHEAD: *Cover all the components separately and refrigerate until ready to serve or up to 2 hours. Keep the beet jelly refrigerated.*

TO ASSEMBLE AND SERVE THE OYSTERS

Line 6 large plates with the rock salt. Carefully remove the oysters from their shells. Set the oysters aside in a small bowl. Arrange 4 oyster shells atop the rock salt on each plate. Spoon 1½ teaspoons of the shallot cream into each oyster shell. Top the cream with the oysters. Spoon 1½ teaspoons of the beet jelly atop each oyster. Sprinkle the oysters with fleur de sel and pepper. Garnish with the beet chiffonade and watercress. Serve immediately.

CARPACCIO OF BROCCOLI WITH SAFFRON OIL

Sometimes I think I'm a frustrated painter. I may never make it into the Museum of Modern Art, but I do like to think of the plate as a canvas. Here, the combination of broccoli, tomatoes, and golden saffron oil garnished with crisp fried tomato skin and basil leaves creates a wonderful presentation.

4 APPETIZER SERVINGS

Saffron Dressing

- ¼ cup strained fresh lime juice
- ⅛ teaspoon crumbled saffron threads
- 6 tablespoons extra virgin olive oil
- ¼ teaspoon hot pepper sauce (such as Tabasco)
- Fleur de sel

Broccoli Carpaccio

- 1¼ pounds broccoli, stalks discarded
- 1 firm hothouse tomato
- 8 fresh whole basil leaves
- ¼ cup extra virgin olive oil
- 2 tablespoons shaved Parmesan cheese
- 4 thinly sliced fresh basil leaves
- ½ teaspoon fleur de sel

FOR THE SAFFRON DRESSING

Stir the lime juice and saffron threads in a medium bowl. Cover and set aside for the saffron to infuse the juice, swirling occasionally, about 10 minutes. Whisk in the olive oil and the hot pepper sauce. Season the mixture to taste with fleur de sel.

FOR THE BROCCOLI CARPACCIO

Meanwhile, trim the broccoli stems to ½ inch. Soak the broccoli florets in a large bowl of ice water until crisp, about 10 minutes. Steam the florets just until crisp-tender, about 2 minutes. Drain. Transfer the florets to the ice water to cool. Drain the florets and pat dry with paper towels. Cut the florets in half lengthwise. Cover and refrigerate.

Submerge the tomato in a medium saucepan of boiling water for 10 seconds. Using a slotted spoon, transfer the tomato to the bowl of ice water to cool. Using a small sharp paring knife, carefully peel off the tomato skin into pieces; reserve the skin. Remove the seeds from the tomato and discard. Dice the tomato.

DO AHEAD: *At this point, the saffron dressing, broccoli florets, diced tomato, and tomato skin can be prepared up to 8 hours ahead. Cover each of them separately and refrigerate. Bring the saffron dressing to room temperature and rewhisk before using.*

Pat the tomato skin and whole basil leaves with paper towels to dry well. Heat the olive oil in a small sauté pan over medium-high heat. Using a large pan lid to shield the oil splatters, carefully add the reserved tomato skin pieces and whole basil leaves. Sauté until the tomato skin is crisp and the basil no longer pops, about 20 seconds. Using a slotted spoon, transfer the tomato skin and basil leaves to paper towels to drain.

TO FINISH AND SERVE

Beginning at the outer rim of each of 4 plates, arrange the broccoli florets cut side down and in concentric circles, covering the plate completely. Drizzle the saffron dressing over the broccoli. Sprinkle with the Parmesan, then the diced tomato and sliced basil. Garnish with the sautéed basil leaves and tomato skin. Sprinkle with the fleur de sel and serve.

BAVAROISE OF GOAT CHEESE WITH ONIONS, BEETS, AND CANDIED GINGER

Bavaroise, the French version of Bavarian cream, has lots of variations. With a consistency somewhere between a custard and a mousse, it's usually served for dessert, but this medley of savory flavors, anchored by beets and lent a sparkle by candied ginger, makes for a mouth-watering appetizer. It's also ravishing to the eye, with its garnish of beets in alternating colors and a bit of green provided by the mâche.

4 APPETIZER SERVINGS

Bavaroise

- 2 tablespoons water
- 1 teaspoon unflavored gelatin
- 1 tablespoon extra virgin olive oil
- 1 cup chopped white onion
- ½ cup heavy whipping cream
- ¼ teaspoon Fleur de sel
- ¼ teaspoon freshly ground white pepper
- 5 ounces soft fresh goat cheese (such as Montrachet)
- 1 large egg white

Beet Salad

- 2 golden beets
- 2 red beets
- 3 tablespoons fresh beet juice (from 1 beet)
- 1½ tablespoons extra virgin olive oil
- 2 tablespoons finely chopped crystallized ginger
  Fleur de sel and freshly ground pepper
- 1 cup mâche

FOR THE BAVAROISE

Arrange four 4-inch ring molds with ¾-inch-high sides on a cookie sheet; place in the freezer.

Pour the water into a small bowl. Sprinkle the gelatin into the water and let soften for 5 minutes. Meanwhile, heat the oil in a heavy medium sauté pan over medium-low heat. Add the onion and sauté until very tender but not brown, about 10 minutes. Add ¼ cup of the cream, the fleur de sel, pepper, and gelatin mixture. Stir until the gelatin dissolves.

Whip the goat cheese in a food processor until smooth. Add the onion mixture and process until the mixture is smooth. Transfer the cheese mixture to a large bowl and place the bowl over another large bowl of ice water. Let stand until the mixture begins to thicken, stirring occasionally, about 5 minutes. Using an electric mixer, beat the egg white in a medium bowl until semifirm peaks form. Fold the egg white into the cheese mixture. Beat the remaining ¼ cup cream in the same medium bowl until firm peaks form. Fold the whipped cream into the cheese mixture. Divide the cheese mixture equally among the 4 chilled ring molds. Cover and refrigerate until the cheese mixture is set, at least 1 hour.

FOR THE BEET SALAD

Cook the golden beets in a medium saucepan of boiling salted water until tender, about 20 minutes. Using a slotted spoon, transfer the beets to a work surface. Peel the beets, then cut them into ⅛-inch-thick disks. Set the golden beet slices aside. Repeat with the red beets, keeping them separate from the golden beets in order to prevent discoloration.

Whisk the beet juice and oil in a medium bowl to blend. Whisk in 1 tablespoon of ginger. Season the vinaigrette to taste with fleur de sel and pepper.

DO AHEAD: *At this point, the bavaroise, beets, and vinaigrette can be prepared up to 8 hours ahead. Keep the bavaroise refrigerated. Cover the beets separately and refrigerate. Cover and refrigerate the vinaigrette; return to room temperature and rewhisk before using.*

TO ASSEMBLE AND SERVE

Using a metal spatula, place one bavaroise in the center of each of 4 plates. Run a small sharp knife around the ring to loosen. Carefully remove the ring molds. Arrange the sliced beets atop the bavaroises in concentric circles and alternating colors. Surround with the remaining ginger. Drizzle the vinaigrette over the beets and around the bavaroises. Top the bavaroises with the mâche and serve immediately.

KING CRAB WITH AVOCADO MOUSSE AND WATER OF TOMATO AND STAR ANISE

This is truly a sensual dish, with so many different textures at play in your mouth and so many colors to dazzle the eye. The first time I served it, I knew I had a hit.

6 APPETIZER SERVINGS

Tomato and Star Anise Water

3   large ripe tomatoes
      (about 10 ounces total)

½   cup good-quality dry white wine

2 ¾ teaspoons coarsely ground star anise

½   teaspoon unflavored gelatin

2   ounces fresh crabmeat, preferably
      king crab
      Fleur de sel and freshly ground white
      pepper

1   tomato, seeded and diced

3   tablespoons sliced fresh chives

6   teaspoons extra virgin olive oil

Avocado Mousse

1   ripe avocado, peeled and pitted

3   tablespoons strained fresh lemon juice

1   teaspoon fleur de sel

¼   teaspoon freshly ground white pepper

2   tablespoons heavy whipping cream

FOR THE TOMATO AND STAR ANISE WATER

Line a sieve with cheesecloth. Puree the tomatoes, wine, and 2 teaspoons star anise in a food processor until very smooth. Strain the tomato mixture through the cheesecloth and into a small saucepan, making about 1¼ cups tomato water. Sprinkle the gelatin over the tomato water. Let stand until the gelatin softens, about 5 minutes. Bring the tomato water just to a simmer over medium-low heat, whisking until the gelatin is dissolved, about 1 minute. Transfer the tomato water to a small bowl. Cover and refrigerate without disturbing just until the tomato sediment settles at the bottom of the bowl (the water will have a golden color), about 40 minutes. Spoon off the tomato water; discard the tomato sediment. Return the tomato water to the small bowl. Cover and refrigerate until the tomato water resembles a loose jelly but is not firm, at least 8 hours or overnight.

FOR THE AVOCADO MOUSSE

Puree the avocado, lemon juice, fleur de sel, and pepper in a food processor until very smooth. Beat the cream in a large bowl until firm peaks form. Fold the avocado puree into the whipped cream. Press plastic wrap directly onto the surface of the mousse; refrigerate until cold.

TO ASSEMBLE AND SERVE

Spoon 2 tablespoons of the avocado mousse in the center of each of 6 wide shallow soup plates. Arrange the crabmeat around the mousse. Spoon the tomato water over each serving of crabmeat, covering the crabmeat completely. Generously dust with fleur de sel, freshly ground white pepper, and remaining star anise. Sprinkle with the diced tomato and chives. Drizzle the oil over the crabmeat and serve immediately.

RED SNAPPER CARPACCIO

Sometimes, less is more, and that's the case with this simple dish. Find top-quality red snapper and let its natural flavor do the talking. Also, there's fun to be had in the presentation, and when your guests see the beautiful array of colors, they'll think you've served them edible confetti. This dish should be prepared shortly before serving; otherwise the lime juice will chemically cook the fish and you'll end up with ceviche. Note: Fresh thyme is almost always available, but thyme flowers are a nice addition; you may find them at farmers' markets in the spring.

6 APPETIZER SERVINGS

Dressing

- 6 tablespoons extra virgin olive oil
- 3 tablespoons strained fresh lime juice
- 1/2 teaspoon hot pepper sauce (such as Tabasco)
  Fleur de sel and freshly ground pepper

Toast

- 12 1/2-inch-thick slices French bread (each slice about 3 x 2 inches)
- 2 tablespoons extra virgin olive oil

Carpaccio

- 1 pound boneless, skinless red snapper fillets, cut crosswise into paper-thin slices
- 3 baby red beets, blanched, peeled, and finely diced
- 3 baby golden beets, blanched, peeled, and finely diced
- 8 very small individual broccoli florets, blanched
- 2 teaspoons fresh thyme leaves, preferably with blossoms attached

FOR THE DRESSING

Whisk the oil, lime juice, and pepper sauce in a small bowl to blend. Season the dressing to taste with fleur de sel and pepper.

DO AHEAD: *The dressing can be prepared up to 8 hours ahead. Cover and refrigerate. Return to room temperature and rewhisk before using.*

FOR THE TOAST

Preheat the oven to 400ºF. Brush the bread slices with the oil; arrange the bread on a baking sheet. Sprinkle with fleur de sel and pepper. Bake until the bread is toasted and beginning to color, about 8 minutes.

FOR THE CARPACCIO

Meanwhile, place one 4-inch ring mold with ¾-inch-high sides in the center of each of 6 plates. Layer the sliced fish inside the molds, brushing each layer of the fish with the dressing. Top with the beets and broccoli. Carefully remove the ring molds. Garnish the carpaccio with the thyme and serve with the toast.

EGGS SUNNY SIDE UP ON TOAST WITH PORCINI MUSHROOM COULIS AND TRUFFLE SAUCE

Here's my answer to the traditional American breakfast favorite one-eyed Jacks. In this case, though, the egg yolks are peeking out from a socket of brown porcini coulis with an outer ring of truffle sauce. This is definitely an eye-opener.

6 APPETIZER SERVINGS

Porcini Mushroom Coulis

- 1 teaspoon extra virgin olive oil
- 1 cup coarsely chopped fresh porcini mushrooms
- ¾ cup Chicken Stock (page 239)
- ¼ cup whole milk
- 1 shallot, coarsely chopped
- 1 garlic clove, coarsely chopped
- Fleur de sel and freshly ground pepper

Truffle Sauce

- ¾ cup Chicken Stock
- ¼ cup chopped fresh black truffles (about 1 ounce)
- 2 tablespoons unsalted butter

Toast and Eggs

- 6 slices white bread
- 2 tablespoons plus 2 teaspoons extra virgin olive oil
- 6 large eggs

FOR THE PORCINI MUSHROOM COULIS

Heat the oil in a heavy medium sauté pan over medium-high heat. Add the porcini mushrooms and sauté until golden brown, about 5 minutes. Add the chicken stock, milk, shallot, and garlic. Gently simmer, uncovered, over low heat until the mushrooms are very tender and the liquid is reduced by half, about 20 minutes. Transfer the mixture to a food processor and puree until smooth. Season the coulis to taste with fleur de sel and pepper. Set aside and keep warm.

FOR THE TRUFFLE SAUCE

Combine the chicken stock and truffles in a heavy small saucepan. Simmer gently over medium-low heat until the truffles are tender and the stock is reduced by half, about 15 minutes. Transfer the mixture to a mini–food processor. Add the butter and blend until smooth, adding water to thin, if necessary. Strain the sauce through a fine-mesh strainer. Return the sauce to the saucepan. Season the sauce to taste with fleur de sel and pepper. Set aside and keep warm.

FOR THE TOAST AND EGGS

Preheat the oven to 350°F. Using a 3-inch biscuit cutter, cut out the centers of the bread slices; discard the trimmings. Brush 2 tablespoons of the oil over the bread rounds. Sprinkle with fleur de sel and pepper. Arrange the bread rounds on a baking sheet. Bake until the bread is crisp and golden brown, about 5 minutes per side. Set aside and keep warm.

DO AHEAD: *The porcini coulis, truffle sauce, and toast can be prepared up to 8 hours ahead. Cover the coulis and sauce separately and refrigerate. Rewarm before serving. Keep the toast at room temperature. Rewarm in the oven before serving.*

Heat 1 teaspoon oil in each of 2 heavy large nonstick sauté pans over medium-low heat. Crack 3 eggs near the edges of each sauté pan to prevent them from touching. Cook until the egg whites are almost cooked through but the yolks are still loose in the center, about 8 minutes. Carefully slide the eggs onto a work surface. Using the 3-inch biscuit cutter, cut out the yolks. Don't worry if some of the white remains around the yolks. Discard the excess egg white trimmings.

TO ASSEMBLE AND SERVE

Place the toasts in the center of 6 wide shallow bowls. Place the egg yolks atop the toasts. For each serving, spoon 2 tablespoons of the porcini coulis around the toast, and drizzle 2 teaspoons of the truffle sauce around the outer perimeter of the porcini coulis. Sprinkle with the fleur de sel and serve immediately.

MOUSSAKA OF LAMB WITH CUMIN AND ROASTED TOMATO COULIS

You could say that moussaka is the Greek equivalent of lasagna, with eggplant standing in for pasta, and it's usually piled high on top with browned béchamel sauce. Here we're doing it a little bit differently. A charlotte mold is lined with deep-cut strips of eggplant, which cloak the spiced ground lamb in a purple robe when inverted onto a plate after baking. Your guests will have to do a reality check when they realize it's not a dessert cake.

6 MAIN-COURSE SERVINGS

Moussaka

- 2 tomatoes, peeled, seeded, and chopped
- 3 large eggs, beaten to blend
- ¼ cup chopped fresh mint leaves
- ¼ cup finely chopped onion
- 2 tablespoons chopped fresh flat-leaf parsley
- 1 tablespoon Curry Powder (page 241)
- 1 tablespoon tomato paste
- 1 tablespoon fleur de sel
- 2 teaspoons freshly ground cumin
- ½ teaspoon freshly ground black pepper
- 2 pounds freshly ground lamb
- 6 tablespoons (about) extra virgin olive oil
- 4 large eggplants (about 1 pound each)

Roasted Tomato Coulis

- 6 hothouse tomatoes, quartered
- 6 tablespoons extra virgin olive oil
- 1½ cups Lamb Stock (page 237)
- 2 tablespoons tomato paste
- Fleur de sel and freshly ground pepper

FOR THE MOUSSAKA

Stir the first 10 ingredients in a large bowl to blend. Add the lamb and 2 tablespoons of the oil. Mix just until blended. Cover and refrigerate. Using a large sharp knife, quarter the eggplants lengthwise. Trim the flesh, leaving just ¼ inch of the flesh and skin. Reserve the trimmed eggplant flesh for another use. Heat 2 tablespoons oil in a heavy large sauté pan over medium-high heat. Add 4 eggplant strips and cook for 2 minutes on each side. Transfer the eggplant strips to a paper towel–lined plate to drain. Repeat with the remaining eggplant strips, adding more oil as needed. Refrigerate until cold.

DO AHEAD: *The lamb mixture and eggplant strips can be made up to 8 hours ahead. Keep refrigerated.*

Preheat the oven to 375°F. Oil a 3-quart charlotte mold (8 x 4½ inches). Arrange the eggplant strips, skin side down and overlapping slightly, in the pan to line the bottom and sides completely, and allow some eggplant to overhang the rim of the mold. Spoon the lamb mixture into the mold (it will fill just over half the mold). Fold the overhanging eggplant strips over the meat. Cover the top with any remaining eggplant strips. Cover with aluminum foil. Place the mold in a heavy roasting pan. Add enough hot water to the roasting pan to come halfway up the sides of the mold. Bake until an instant-read meat thermometer inserted into the center of the lamb mixture registers 145°F, about 1 hour. Turn the oven off. Open the oven door. Let the moussaka rest for 20 minutes in the oven.

NOTE: *The coulis can be roasted in the oven along with the moussaka, which takes slightly longer to cook.*

Toss the tomatoes with the oil on a heavy large rimmed baking sheet. Sprinkle with fleur de sel and pepper. Bake the tomatoes in the 375ºF oven until tender and amber brown on the bottom, about 30 minutes. Remove the baking sheet from the oven. Add the lamb stock to the tomato mixture, stirring to scrape up the browned bits on the bottom. Whisk in the tomato paste. Return the baking sheet to the oven and bake until the tomatoes are very tender and the liquid is reduced by half, about 15 minutes longer. Transfer the tomato mixture to a blender and puree until smooth. Strain the tomato coulis through a fine-mesh strainer and into a small saucepan. Season the coulis to taste with fleur de sel and pepper. Rewarm over medium-low heat before serving.

TO ASSEMBLE AND SERVE

Remove the foil from atop the mold. Using oven mitts, carefully invert the mold onto a large rimmed platter. Remove the mold from the moussaka. Drizzle the roasted tomato coulis around the moussaka and serve immediately.

BRAISED VEAL SHANK WITH HONEY, ARTICHOKES, SWISS CHARD, AND GARLIC-PARSLEY BUTTER

When people see this, they say, "Wow!" The shank is first browned on the stove, then basted with honey before baking, which creates an almost iridescent glaze. The result is a beautiful honeyed shank the color of bright amber. The sweetness is counterbalanced by the slightly bitter artichokes and Swiss chard that accompany it.

4 MAIN-COURSE SERVINGS

Veal Shank

One 4- to 5-pound whole veal shank
Fleur de sel and freshly ground pepper
2 tablespoons extra virgin olive oil
1 cup honey, preferably acacia
4 cups Veal Stock (page 238)

Vegetables

12 cups water
6 tablespoons strained fresh lemon juice
2 tablespoons all-purpose flour
16 baby artichokes (about 2½ pounds total)
1 bunch green Swiss chard
¼ cup plus 2 tablespoons unsalted butter, room temperature
2 tablespoons chopped fresh flat-leaf parsley
2 garlic cloves, minced
1 cup Veal Stock (page 238)

FOR THE VEAL SHANK

Preheat the oven to 425°F. Sprinkle the veal shank with fleur de sel and freshly ground pepper. Heat the oil in a heavy roasting pan just large enough to hold the veal shank over medium heat. Add the veal and cook until brown all over, about 18 minutes. Pour the honey over the veal. Add the veal stock to the pan and stir to loosen any browned bits from the bottom of the pan. Bring the pan juices to a boil. Transfer the pan to the oven. Braise, uncovered, until the meat is fork-tender and a rich amber brown all over, basting occasionally with the pan juices, about 2½ hours.

MEANWHILE, PREPARE THE VEGETABLES

Stir the water, 4 tablespoons of the lemon juice, and the flour in a heavy large pot to blend. Bend back the dark green outer leaves of the artichokes (about the outer 3 or 4 layers of leaves) and snap them off at the base of the artichoke until only the pale green and yellow leaves remain. Cut off the top 1¼ inches from each artichoke. Add the artichokes to the lemon water. Bring to a boil over high heat. Reduce the heat to medium and simmer until a skewer can be inserted without resistance into the base of the artichoke, about 4 minutes. Drain the cooking liquid. Cut the artichokes lengthwise in half. Arrange in a single layer on a baking sheet to cool. Set aside.

Cut the chard stems into 1-inch diagonal slices. Cut the chard leaves crosswise into ½-inch-thick strips; set aside. Cook the stem pieces in a small saucepan of boiling water until crisp-tender, about 20 seconds. Drain. Transfer the stem pieces to a bowl of ice water to cool. Drain again. Set aside.

Whisk the ¼ cup of butter, parsley, and garlic in a small bowl to blend. Gradually whisk in the remaining 2 tablespoons lemon juice. Season the garlic-parsley butter to taste with fleur de sel and pepper.

TO FINISH AND SERVE

Bring the 1 cup veal stock to a simmer in a heavy wide saucepan over medium-high heat. Add the artichokes, chard stem pieces, and chard strips. Cook, uncovered, until the chard strips are tender but still bright green and the artichokes are heated through, stirring occasionally, about 6 minutes. Using tongs, transfer the vegetables to a large platter; tent with aluminum foil to keep warm. Boil the cooking liquid over high heat until reduced, about 4 minutes. Whisk in the garlic-parsley butter. Spoon the sauce over the vegetables.

Place the veal shank in the center of the platter. Whisk the remaining 2 tablespoons butter into the veal pan juices. Drizzle the pan juices over the veal and serve immediately.

VEGETABLE-CRUSTED TURBOT FILLETS WITH MINTED COUSCOUS AND OLIVE PUREE WITH LEMON CONFIT

The snow-white turbot is encrusted with eggplant, zucchini, and tomatoes, the couscous is bejeweled with raisins and bell peppers of different colors, and it's all encircled by a ring of purplish olive puree. With its gorgeous, muted hues, this dish could have been painted by Monet.

4 MAIN-COURSE SERVINGS

Olive Puree

- ¹⁄₂ cup pitted kalamata olives
- 5 tablespoons extra virgin olive oil
- ¹⁄₄ cup Lemon Confit (page 244)
  Fleur de sel and freshly ground pepper

Vegetables

- 2 tablespoons extra virgin olive oil
- ¹⁄₂ cup very finely diced (about ¹⁄₈ inch) eggplant, unskinned
- ¹⁄₂ cup very finely diced (about ¹⁄₈ inch) zucchini
- ¹⁄₂ cup very finely diced (about ¹⁄₈ inch) seeded tomato

Fish

- 4 5- to 7-ounce turbot fillets
  Minted Couscous (page 59)
- 1 tablespoon chiffonade of fresh basil

FOR THE OLIVE PUREE

Blend the olives, oil, and lemon confit in a blender until smooth. Strain the olive puree through a fine-mesh strainer and into a medium bowl. Season to taste with fleur de sel and freshly ground pepper. Set aside.

FOR THE VEGETABLES

Heat 1 tablespoon of the oil in a heavy large sauté pan over high heat. Add the eggplant, zucchini, and tomato. Sauté until crisp-tender, about 1 minute. Season to taste with fleur de sel and pepper.

DO AHEAD: *The olive puree and sautéed vegetables can be prepared up to 8 hours ahead. Cover the olive puree and keep it at room temperature. Cover and refrigerate the vegetables.*

TO FINISH AND SERVE

Preheat the oven to 475°F. Drizzle the remaining 1 tablespoon oil over a heavy large rimmed baking sheet. Arrange the fish fillets in a single layer over the baking sheet. Sprinkle the fillets with fleur de sel and pepper. Cover one side of each fillet with the sautéed vegetables to form a thin layer. Bake until the fish is just opaque in the center, about 5 minutes. Remove from the oven and let rest for 5 minutes.

Place the fish on 4 large plates. Using a ring mold, mound the minted couscous alongside the fish. Drizzle the olive puree on the plates. Sprinkle the basil over the sauce and serve.

CARAMELIZED BLACK SEA BASS WITH LEMONGRASS-INFUSED CONSOMMÉ, CLAMS, AND BASIL

There's something peaceful about the presentation of this dish. The beautifully caramelized fish swims in a light-colored consommé, and is encircled by open clams, who seem to be engaged in an underwater corporate conference.

4 MAIN-COURSE SERVINGS

Consommé

- 3 fresh lemongrass stalks, smashed
- ¼ cup chopped carrot
- ¼ cup chopped onion
- ¼ cup chopped leek
- 2 cups Lobster Stock (page 240)
- 2 large egg whites
- 1 1-inch piece of peeled fresh ginger

Sea Bass

- 4 7-ounce black sea bass fillets
  Fleur de sel and freshly ground pepper
- 4 teaspoons sugar
- 2 tablespoons extra virgin olive oil

FOR THE CONSOMMÉ

Combine 1 stalk of the lemongrass, the carrot, onion, and leek together in a food processor and blend until the vegetables are finely minced, stopping the machine and scraping down the sides of the bowl occasionally. Heat the lobster stock in a heavy medium saucepan over medium heat until it begins to boil. Remove from the heat. Whisk in the vegetable mixture. Whisk in the egg whites. Stir the stock over medium-low heat for 5 minutes. Reduce the heat to low and simmer gently without stirring until the vegetable mixture gathers at the top of the stock and forms one large floating piece (known as the "raft"), about 20 minutes. Cool for 5 minutes. Strain the stock through a fine-mesh strainer lined with cheesecloth and into a small saucepan. Gather the corners of the cheesecloth and gently squeeze to extract the excess liquid. Discard the cheesecloth and solids. Add the remaining 2 stalks of lemongrass and the ginger to the consommé. Bring to a simmer over medium heat. Remove from the heat. Cover and steep for 30 minutes to infuse the consommé. Strain the consommé again through a fine-mesh strainer, return to the small saucepan, and discard the solid pieces.

DO AHEAD: *The consommé can be made up to 8 hours ahead. Cool. Cover and refrigerate.*

FOR THE SEA BASS

Preheat the oven to 375°F. Sprinkle the fish with fleur de sel and pepper. Sprinkle one side of each fish fillet with 1 teaspoon of the sugar. Heat 1 tablespoon of the oil in a large nonstick sauté pan over medium-high heat. Place 2 fillets, sugared side down, in the pan and cook until the bottoms are caramelized and crisp, about 4 minutes. Transfer the fillets, seared side up, to a heavy large baking sheet. Wipe out the pan. Repeat with the remaining 1 tablespoon oil and 2 fillets. Place the baking sheet in the oven and bake until the fish is just opaque in the center, about 12 minutes longer.

(continued)

Clams

24 live Manila clams (about 1¼ pounds total), scrubbed

¾ cup water

¾ cup extra virgin olive oil

⅓ cup strained fresh lemon juice

2 tablespoons chiffonade of fresh basil

2 teaspoons very finely sliced fresh lemongrass

MEANWHILE, PREPARE THE CLAMS

Place the clams in a medium saucepan. Add the water and oil to cover the clams completely. Add the lemon juice and basil. Cook over medium-high heat until the liquid comes to a boil and the clams open, about 3 minutes. Strain. Discard any clams that do not open. Discard the cooking liquid. Sprinkle the clams with fleur de sel and pepper.

TO ASSEMBLE AND SERVE

Bring the consommé to a simmer. Place 1 fillet, caramelized side up, in the center of each of 4 wide shallow soup plates (or pasta bowls). Arrange the clams around the fillets, dividing equally. Sprinkle the sliced lemongrass over the clams. Ladle the consommé over the clams and serve.

MINTED COUSCOUS

This aromatic couscous also goes well with Rack of Lamb with Broth, Baby Vegetables, and Caraway Seeds (page 204).

4 SIDE-DISH SERVINGS

½ cup plain couscous

1 tablespoon argan oil or
   extra virgin olive oil

2 tablespoons dark raisins

2 tablespoons golden raisins

1 tablespoon finely diced red bell pepper

1 tablespoon finely diced yellow
   bell pepper

1 tablespoon finely diced green bell pepper

⅓ cup water

¼ cup strained fresh lemon juice

1 tablespoon chiffonade of fresh mint
   leaves
   Fleur de sel and freshly ground pepper

Toss the couscous with the oil in a large bowl to coat. Add all of the raisins and peppers. Bring the water to a boil in a heavy small saucepan. Pour the hot water over the couscous mixture. Stir to combine. Drizzle the lemon juice over and add the mint. Season to taste with fleur de sel and pepper. Stir to combine. Cover the couscous with a clean, damp kitchen towel. Set aside until the liquid is absorbed and the couscous is tender, about 12 minutes. Fluff the couscous mixture with a fork. Season to taste with fleur de sel and pepper.

FILLET OF SOLE WITH SEA URCHIN, TOASTED BREAD CRUMBS, AND RED ONION COMPOTE

This is one of my favorite presentations. The sole fillets are arranged in a square with the red onion compote in the middle, surrounded by a ring of sauce made bright orange by the addition of sea urchin roe.

4 MAIN-COURSE SERVINGS

Sauce

- 1 cup Fish Stock (page 240)
- 1/3 cup heavy whipping cream
- 1/2 cup sea urchin roe
- 1/4 cup strained fresh lemon juice
- Fleur de sel and freshly ground pepper

Fish

- 5 tablespoons Clarified Butter (page 243)
- All-purpose flour (for dredging)
- 4 1 1/2-pound whole Dover soles (heads, fins, and skins removed)
- Red Onion Compote (recipe follows)
- 2 tablespoons bread crumbs, toasted

FOR THE SAUCE

Boil the fish stock and cream in a heavy small saucepan over medium-high heat until reduced to 3/4 cup, about 12 minutes. Whisk in the sea urchin roe. Cook over low heat until heated through, about 5 minutes. Transfer the mixture to a blender and puree until smooth. Strain the sauce through a fine-mesh strainer and into the small saucepan. Bring the sauce to a simmer. Whisk in the lemon juice. Season the sauce to taste with fleur de sel and pepper. Cover to keep warm.

FOR THE FISH

Preheat the oven to 375°F. Coat a heavy large rimmed baking sheet with 1 tablespoon of the clarified butter. Place the flour on a small cookie sheet. Sprinkle the soles with fleur de sel and pepper. Heat 2 tablespoons clarified butter in a heavy large sauté pan over medium-high heat. Dredge 2 soles in the flour to coat; shake off the excess flour. Immediately transfer the soles to the sauté pan and cook until golden brown, about 2 minutes per side. Transfer the sautéed soles to the prepared baking sheet. Repeat with the remaining 2 tablespoons clarified butter and 2 soles. Transfer the baking sheet to the oven and bake until the soles are just opaque in the center, about 5 minutes. Remove the baking sheet from the oven. Let the soles rest for 5 minutes.

TO ASSEMBLE AND SERVE

Run a sharp fillet knife alongside the backbone and down the attached bones to loosen the fillets from the fish; each sole will have 4 fillets. Arrange 4 fillets in the center of each of 4 large plates, overlapping the ends and forming a box shape. Spoon the red onion compote in the center of the box. Drizzle the sauce around the perimeter of the fillets. Sprinkle the sauce with the bread crumbs. Serve immediately.

RED ONION COMPOTE

2 red onions (8 ounces each)

1½ cups good-quality dry red wine

1½ cups water

⅓ cup balsamic vinegar

1 tablespoon unsalted butter

¼ cup honey, preferably acacia

Fleur de sel and freshly ground pepper

Using a mandoline, cut the onions into ⅟₁₆-inch-thin slices. Combine the onions, wine, water, vinegar, and butter in a heavy large saucepan. Bring to a simmer over medium-high heat. Reduce the heat to medium and simmer gently until most of the cooking liquid has evaporated and the onions are tender, stirring occasionally, about 1 hour. Add the honey and simmer gently until the cooking liquid is thick and syrupy, about 15 minutes longer. Season the compote to taste with fleur de sel and pepper.

DO AHEAD: *The compote can be prepared up to 1 day ahead. Cool. Cover and refrigerate. Rewarm over medium-low heat before using.*

SKATE WINGS WITH SALSA OF CUCUMBER, TOMATO, AND SEAWEED

The skate is a peculiar-looking fish, shaped rather like a kite. The pectoral fin is the edible part, and its flesh is firm, sweet, and white, reminiscent of a scallop. After you adorn it with the colorful salsa, you'll think it's still swimming in the ocean. Banyuls is a fortified wine made in the south of France, much like tawny port but less sweet and with more spice. It also makes an excellent vinegar, which is used in this recipe.

4 MAIN-COURSE SERVINGS

½ cup extra virgin olive oil

2 fresh green jalapeño chiles, coarsely chopped

4 ripe but firm tomatoes, peeled, seeded, and finely diced

1 English hothouse cucumber, peeled, seeded, and finely diced

½ cup fresh crabmeat, preferably peeky toe

¼ cup coarsely chopped fresh seaweed

¼ cup strained fresh lemon juice

3 tablespoons finely sliced fresh chives

2 tablespoons Banyuls vinegar or good sherry vinegar

1 tablespoon chopped fresh dill
Fleur de sel and freshly ground pepper

4 7-ounce skate wing fillets

2 tablespoons finely chopped green bell pepper

Combine ¼ cup of the oil and the jalapeño chiles in a heavy medium saucepan. Bring to a simmer over medium heat. Remove from the heat. Steep to infuse the oil with the chiles, about 30 minutes. Strain to remove the chiles. Return the jalapeño oil to the saucepan.

Add the tomatoes, cucumber, crabmeat, seaweed, lemon juice, chives, vinegar, and dill to the jalapeño oil. Season the salsa to taste with fleur de sel and pepper. Stir over low heat just until heated through, about 3 minutes.

Meanwhile, sprinkle the skate fillets with fleur de sel and pepper. Heat 2 tablespoons of the oil in each of 2 heavy large sauté pans over high heat. Add 2 skate fillets to each sauté pan and cook until golden brown, about 4 minutes. Using a large metal spatula, turn the skate fillets over and cook until they are golden brown and just opaque in the center, about 3 minutes longer.

Spoon the salsa over 4 large plates. Top with the skate fillets, sprinkle on the chopped green bell pepper, and serve immediately.

ROASTED MONKFISH WITH PINK GRAPEFRUIT, BASIL, LEEKS, AND POTATO

As I've said, we begin eating with our eyes, and this version of monkfish certainly provides a visual feast (of course, it tastes good too). The sauce is bright pink, the leeks green, and the potatoes yellow.

4 MAIN-COURSE SERVINGS

Potatoes and Leeks

2 cups Clarified Butter (page 243)

2 very large russet potatoes (about 1¼ pounds each)

2 whole leeks (white and pale green parts only)

Fish and Sauce

1 tablespoon extra virgin olive oil

4 6-ounce monkfish fillets

Fleur de sel and freshly ground pepper

1 teaspoon sugar

2 cups strained fresh pink grapefruit juice

⅓ cup strained fresh lemon juice

½ cup finely chopped shallots (from about 3)

10 fresh basil leaves, cut into chiffonade (about ⅓ cup)

3 tablespoons unsalted butter

1 cup Chicken Stock (page 239)

½ cup Citrus Marmalade (page 245)

10 outer leaves of 3 Brussels sprouts, cut into chiffonade (about ½ cup)

¼ cup finely diced peeled raw turnip

2 tablespoons finely chopped toasted husked hazelnuts

FOR THE POTATOES AND LEEKS

Heat the clarified butter to 180ºF in a wide pot over medium heat (do not allow the butter to simmer). Using a large sharp knife, trim the potato into a 5 x 2-inch rectangle. Using a mandoline, cut the potato rectangle lengthwise into ⅛-inch-thick by 2-inch-wide strips to resemble pappardelle pasta. Rinse the potato strips under cold running water until the water runs clear. Pat the potato strips dry with paper towels. Add the potatoes to the warm butter and cook just until tender, but not brown or crisp, about 30 minutes. Using tongs, transfer the potato slices to a baking sheet and arrange in an even layer to cool.

Meanwhile, cook the leeks in a large saucepan of boiling salted water until they are crisp-tender, about 3 minutes. Drain. Transfer the leeks to a large bowl of ice water. Drain again. Cut the leeks lengthwise in half, discarding the tough outer leaves that fall away naturally.

DO AHEAD: *The potato strips and leeks can be prepared up to 8 hours ahead. Cover separately and refrigerate.*

FOR THE FISH AND SAUCE

Preheat the oven to 450°F. Heat the oil in a large nonstick ovenproof sauté pan over high heat. Sprinkle the monkfish with fleur de sel and pepper. Sprinkle one side of the monkfish fillets with the sugar. Add the monkfish to the sauté pan, sugared side down, and cook just until pale golden but not cooked through, turning to brown each side, about 8 minutes total. Transfer the monkfish to a plate; set aside. Add the grapefruit juice and lemon juice to the pan, scraping up any browned bits. Add the shallots, basil, and 2 tablespoons of the butter. Bring to a boil. Return the monkfish to the pan. Transfer the pan to the oven and bake until the fish is just cooked through, about 12 minutes.

Using oven mitts, remove the sauté pan from the oven. Transfer the fish to a plate; tent loosely with aluminum foil to keep warm. Boil the cooking liquid in the sauté pan over high heat until it is reduced to ½ cup and almost syrupy, about 12 minutes. Whisk in the remaining 1 tablespoon butter to form a smooth sauce. Season the sauce to taste with fleur de sel and pepper.

TO ASSEMBLE AND SERVE

Just before serving, combine the potato strips, leeks, and chicken stock in a large sauté pan. Bring the stock to a simmer over medium heat and simmer gently until the vegetables are heated through and just tender, stirring gently, about 8 minutes. Season to taste with fleur de sel and pepper.

Using tongs, mound the potato strips and leeks (not the cooking liquid) in the center of 4 large plates, dividing equally. Place the fish atop the potatoes and leeks. Spoon a dollop of the citrus marmalade alongside. Drizzle the sauce around the fish. Sprinkle the Brussels sprout chiffonade, turnip, and hazelnuts around the perimeter of the plates. Serve immediately.

YELLOW PEACH TART WITH LEMON VERBENA

This is quite a simple tart, but I love the burnished amber color of the peaches; be sure to get the best you can. The lemon verbena is like a low-impact citrus bomb cutting against the sweetness of the tart. It makes all the difference.

MAKES ONE 10-INCH TART

Sugar Crust

- 1 cup all-purpose flour
- ½ cup powdered sugar
- ⅛ teaspoon fleur de sel
- 4 tablespoons chilled unsalted butter, cut into 1-inch pieces
- 1 large egg, stirred to blend

Peach Filling

- 4 fresh ripe but firm unpeeled yellow peaches (about 1½ pounds), halved and pitted
- 2 tablespoons powdered sugar
- 2 tablespoons unsalted butter, cut into small pieces
- 2 tablespoons minced fresh lemon verbena leaves

  Vanilla Ice Cream (page 245)

FOR THE SUGAR CRUST

Blend the flour, powdered sugar, and fleur de sel in a food processor. Add the butter. Using on/off turns, blend until the mixture resembles a coarse meal. Drizzle 2 tablespoons of the beaten egg over the dough; discard the remaining egg. Using on/off turns, blend just until the dough begins to form. Gather the dough into a ball; flatten into a disk. Wrap the dough in plastic; refrigerate at least 30 minutes and up to 1 day.

Preheat the oven to 350°F. Roll out the dough on a lightly floured surface to a 12-inch round. Transfer to a 10-inch cake pan. Gently press the dough in the pan to cover the bottom completely and to come about halfway up the sides of the pan. Refrigerate the crust until it is cold, about 10 minutes. Line the crust with aluminum foil and fill with pie weights. Bake the crust until the sides are set, about 15 minutes. Carefully remove the weights and foil. Bake the crust just until the tops of the edges are pale golden, about 10 minutes longer. Cool the crust in the pan on a rack. Carefully remove the crust from the pan and place it on a heavy baking sheet.

DO AHEAD: *The crust can be prepared up to 8 hours ahead. Store airtight at room temperature.*

FOR THE PEACH FILLING

Increase the oven temperature to 375°F. Place the peach halves, cut side down, on a work surface. Using a large, very sharp knife, cut the peaches lengthwise into ¼-inch-thin slices. Arrange the peach slices attractively in concentric circles in the prepared crust. Sift the powdered sugar over the peaches. Dot with the butter. Bake until the peaches are tender and the crust is brown and crisp, about 30 minutes.

Using a large metal spatula, transfer the tart to a serving platter. Sprinkle the lemon verbena over the top. Cut the warm tart into wedges and serve with the Vanilla Ice Cream.

FRESH TANGERINE MARMALADE
WITH ORANGE JELLY AND CREAM SORBET

Is there any natural color more beautiful than tangerine orange? This gorgeous dessert hits three flavor notes: mostly sweet and sour, but with just a hint of bitter to balance them out.

4 SERVINGS

Tangerine Marmalade

3 clementines or other seedless tangerines (about 1 pound), peeled (peels reserved) and segments separated
¼ cup sugar
2 tablespoons strained freshly squeezed ruby red grapefruit juice
1 tablespoon strained freshly squeezed orange juice
¼ teaspoon unflavored gelatin

Orange Jelly

⅔ cup freshly squeezed orange juice
¼ teaspoon unflavored gelatin

Cream Sorbet

½ cup water
½ cup sugar
1 cup heavy whipping cream
2 tablespoons light corn syrup

FOR THE TANGERINE MARMALADE

Place the tangerine peels in a heavy small saucepan. Fill the pan with enough water to cover the peels. Bring the water to a boil over high heat. Drain the water; rinse the peels. Repeat this process three times to remove excessive bitterness. Combine the peels, sugar, and 2 cups water to cover the peels. Simmer, uncovered, over medium heat until the liquid evaporates and the peels are very tender and coated with syrup, about 40 minutes. Meanwhile, combine the grapefruit juice and orange juice in a small bowl. Sprinkle the gelatin over the top. Let stand until softened, about 5 minutes.

Transfer the warm tangerine mixture to a food processor. Add the gelatin mixture. Using on/off pulses, blend until the tangerine peels are finely chopped but the mixture is not pureed or smooth. Transfer the warm marmalade to a small bowl; stir in ½ cup of the tangerine segments. Cover and refrigerate until the marmalade is set, at least 4 hours.

FOR THE ORANGE JELLY

Pour the orange juice into a small saucepan. Sprinkle the gelatin over the juice; let stand until the gelatin softens, about 5 minutes. Bring the juice just to a simmer in a heavy small saucepan over medium-high heat. Remove from the heat and whisk until the gelatin dissolves, about 1 minute. Transfer the orange jelly to a small container. Cover and refrigerate until the mixture resembles a loose jelly but is not firm, at least 8 hours or overnight. Stir to loosen before using.

FOR THE CREAM SORBET

Bring the water and sugar to a boil in a heavy small saucepan, stirring to dissolve the sugar. Remove from the heat. Stir in the cream and corn syrup. Cover and refrigerate until the cream mixture is cold, at least 2 hours.

Transfer the cream mixture to an ice cream maker. Process according to the manufacturer's instructions. Transfer the sorbet to a container. Cover and freeze for up to 8 hours.

TO FINISH AND SERVE

Spread ¼ cup of the marmalade over the center of each of 4 bowls. Arrange 5 tangerine segments in each bowl atop the marmalade. Spoon 1 tablespoon orange jelly over the segments in each bowl. Spoon an oval-shaped scoop of the cream sorbet atop and serve immediately.

ÎLE FLOTTANTE WITH PRALINE AND MOCHA SAUCE

In English, the name means "floating island," and it's a traditional French dessert. This version is so light you'll think it's about to float away, but the heavier mocha sauce holds it down to earth. Use French pink pralines if you can find them. They look like boulders shimmering in the sunset. Regular pralines are fine; they look like boulders in midafternoon, which is still a pretty sight!

6 SERVINGS

Mocha Sauce

- ¾ cup whole milk
- 1 tablespoon chopped fresh lemon balm or lemongrass
- 1 vanilla bean, split lengthwise
- 4 large egg yolks
- 3 tablespoons sugar
- 1½ ounces good-quality bittersweet (not unsweetened) chocolate, chopped
- 3 tablespoons freshly brewed espresso
- 2 tablespoons heavy whipping cream

Îles Flottantes

- 10 large egg whites
  Pinch of fleur de sel
- 1 cup sugar
- ¼ cup coarsely ground pink pralines

FOR THE MOCHA SAUCE

Place the milk and lemon balm or lemongrass in a heavy small saucepan. Scrape the seeds from the vanilla bean into the milk mixture; add the bean. Bring to a simmer over medium heat. Whisk the egg yolks and sugar in a large bowl until light, about 5 minutes. Gradually whisk in the milk mixture. Return the mixture to the saucepan. Stir over low heat until the sauce thickens (do not allow the mixture to boil), about 5 minutes. Add the chocolate. Whisk until the chocolate melts and the mixture is smooth. Whisk in the espresso and cream. Strain the sauce into a small bowl. Cover and refrigerate until cold.

FOR THE ÎLES FLOTTANTES

Preheat the oven to 300°F. Lightly oil 6 individual 9-ounce soufflé dishes. Place the dishes in a roasting pan. Using an electric mixer on medium speed, beat the egg whites and fleur de sel in a large bowl until foamy. Gradually beat in the sugar. Continue beating just until firm peaks form, about 5 minutes longer. Divide the egg white mixture equally among the prepared dishes; smooth the tops. Transfer the roasting pan to the oven. Carefully add enough hot water to the roasting pan to come halfway up the sides of the dishes. Bake until the îles flottantes rise and are pale golden on top, about 30 minutes. Transfer the îles flottantes to the refrigerator and chill until cold. Cover and keep refrigerated.

DO AHEAD: *The mocha sauce and îles flottantes can be prepared up to 8 hours ahead. Keep refrigerated.*

TO ASSEMBLE AND SERVE

Ladle enough mocha sauce into 6 shallow soup plates or pasta bowls to cover the bottom. Level the tops of the îles flottantes. Run a small sharp knife around the edges of the îles flottantes to loosen. Carefully invert each île flottante into the center of the bowl. Sprinkle the ground pralines over the îles flottantes. Serve cold.

RED BERRIES WITH YOGURT SORBET, GRAINS OF PARADISE, AND HIBISCUS JELLY

Nothing complicated about this one, but with four kinds of fruit topped with a glittering layer of hibiscus jelly and topped with yogurt sorbet, it's a feast for the eyes as well as the taste buds. I recommend that you freeze the sorbet for no longer than eight hours; it's better when served soft. Grains of paradise, also known as maniguette, are African in origin and are actually a member of the ginger family. A pepper substitute in Europe for centuries, they resemble a mild white pepper, but are more aromatic with a hint of camphor that cuts against the sweetness of the dish. Hibiscus flowers can be found in spice shops and Latin markets, where they're usually marketed as Jamaica flowers.

6 SERVINGS

Hibiscus Jelly

1 cup water
¹/₂ cup sugar
³/₄ cup dried hibiscus flowers
¹/₂ teaspoon unflavored gelatin

Berries

1 cup fresh strawberries, hulled
1 cup fresh raspberries
¹/₂ cup fresh blackberries
¹/₂ cup fresh blueberries

³/₄ teaspoon ground grains of paradise
Yogurt Sorbet (recipe follows)

FOR THE HIBISCUS JELLY

Stir ¾ cup of the water and the sugar in a heavy small saucepan over high heat until the sugar dissolves. Bring the syrup to a boil. Remove the syrup from the heat. Stir the hibiscus flowers into the syrup. Cover and steep 15 minutes. Strain the syrup into a small bowl; discard the flowers. Meanwhile, pour the remaining ¼ cup water into another small bowl. Sprinkle the gelatin over and let soften for 5 minutes. Whisk the softened gelatin into the warm flower syrup until dissolved. Cover and refrigerate until the mixture is gelatinous and resembles a loose jelly but is not firm, at least 8 hours or overnight. Stir the jelly to loosen before using.

FOR THE BERRIES

Combine all the berries in a large bowl. Using the back of a fork, coarsely mash the berries.

TO ASSEMBLE AND SERVE

Spoon the berries and accumulated berry juices into 6 wide shallow dessert bowls, dividing equally. Spoon the hibiscus jelly over the berries. Sprinkle with the grains of paradise. Top each with an oval-shaped scoop of the yogurt sorbet. Serve immediately.

YOGURT SORBET

The sorbet is best when made no more than eight hours before serving. If you must freeze it longer, let it melt back to a liquid in a bain-marie and return it to the ice cream maker until soft-solid.

MAKES ABOUT 1 PINT

²/₃ cup sugar

2 tablespoons whole milk

1 tablespoon powdered milk

2 cups plain yogurt

¹/₃ cup light corn syrup

Whisk the sugar, whole milk, and powdered milk in a heavy small saucepan to blend. Cook over medium-low heat until the mixture simmers, whisking constantly, about 3 minutes. Whisk the warm milk mixture, yogurt, and corn syrup in a large bowl to blend. Cover and refrigerate until cold, about 3 hours.

Transfer the yogurt mixture to an ice cream maker. Process according to the manufacturer's instructions. Transfer the sorbet to a container. Cover and freeze for up to 8 hours; the sorbet is at its best when still soft, so avoid overfreezing.

RUM BABAS WITH SPICED SYRUP AND MANGO

This is truly a happy dish; just looking at it makes me smile. A baba is a dense yeast cake heavily doused in a liquid such as kirsch or rum, which moisturizes it. Here, we're making individual servings. The spiced rum syrup imbues the cakes with a lovely, translucent glaze speckled with lemon zest, further brightened by mango slices arranged like rays of the sun.

8 SERVINGS

Rum Babas

Nonstick cooking spray
2 tablespoons warm whole milk (105° to 110ºF)
2 teaspoons active dry yeast
¾ cup all-purpose flour
2 teaspoons sugar
¼ teaspoon fleur de sel
1 large egg
¼ cup unsalted butter, room temperature

Cream

½ cup Pastry Cream (recipe follows)
¼ cup heavy whipping cream

Spiced Syrup

2 cups water
1¼ cups sugar
1 vanilla bean, split lengthwise
⅓ cup dark rum
2 tablespoons cracked pink peppercorns
1 tablespoon finely grated orange peel
1 tablespoon finely grated lemon peel
2 whole cloves

Mangoes

2 tablespoons unsalted butter, room temperature
2 tablespoons sugar
2 mangoes, peeled, pitted, and cut lengthwise into ¼-inch-thin slices
2 tablespoons freshly ground pink peppercorns

FOR THE RUM BABAS

Position the oven rack in the center of the oven and preheat the oven to 375ºF. Arrange eight 1½-ounce savarin molds on a heavy baking sheet. Spray the molds with nonstick cooking spray. Stir the warm milk and the yeast in a small bowl to blend. Let stand until the yeast dissolves, about 5 minutes. Using an electric mixer with the paddle attachment, or a wooden spoon, stir the flour, sugar, and fleur de sel in a large bowl to blend. Add the yeast mixture and egg. Stir to blend well. Gradually beat in the butter (the dough will be sticky). Transfer the dough to a pastry bag. Pipe the dough into the prepared savarin molds, dividing equally. Cover and place in a warm draft-free area until the dough doubles in volume, about 30 minutes. Transfer the baking sheet to the oven and bake until the babas are golden brown and a skewer inserted near the center of a baba comes out clean, about 15 minutes. Invert the babas onto a cooling rack. Remove the molds and cool the babas completely.

FOR THE SPICED SYRUP

Combine the water and the sugar in a large wide saucepan. Scrape the seeds from the vanilla bean into the sugar water; add the bean. Bring to a boil. Remove from the heat. Add the rum, peppercorns, orange peel, lemon peel, and cloves. Bring the syrup to a boil over high heat. Turn off the heat and steep for 15 minutes. Strain the syrup into a medium bowl; discard the solids. Working in batches, submerge the babas in the hot syrup just until soaked through, about 1 minute per side. Using a slotted spoon, transfer the babas to a cooling rack set over a baking sheet to drain. Cool completely. Reserve the remaining syrup in the saucepan.

FOR THE CREAM

Beat the pastry cream and the whipping cream together in a large bowl until thick. Set the cream mixture aside.

DO AHEAD: *The babas, syrup, and cream can be prepared up to 4 hours ahead. Cover separately and refrigerate. Rewarm the syrup before serving.*

(continued)

FOR THE MANGOES

Working in four batches, melt ½ tablespoon of the butter in a heavy large sauté pan over high heat. Add ½ tablespoon of the sugar; stir to blend. Add one fourth of the mango slices and cook until the sugar mixture is golden brown and the mango slices are caramelized, about 2 minutes per side. Transfer the mango slices to a plate. Repeat with the rest of the butter, sugar, and mangoes.

TO ASSEMBLE AND SERVE

Place 1 baba in the center of each of 8 plates. Spoon 2 tablespoons of the cream mixture into the center of each baba. Arrange the caramelized mango slices around the babas, dividing equally. Drizzle 1 tablespoon of the remaining warm syrup over the mangoes. Sprinkle with the ground peppercorns and serve immediately.

PASTRY CREAM

MAKES ABOUT 1 CUP

1 cup whole milk

½ vanilla bean, split lengthwise

¼ cup sugar

3 large egg yolks

2 tablespoons cornstarch

1 tablespoon unsalted butter

Place the milk in a heavy small saucepan. Scrape the seeds from the vanilla bean into the milk; add the bean. Bring the milk to a boil. Meanwhile, using an electric mixer, beat the sugar and egg yolks in a large bowl until light and fluffy, about 5 minutes. Mix in the cornstarch. Gradually mix in the hot milk mixture. Return the mixture to the saucepan. Stir with a whisk over medium-low heat until the pastry cream thickens and bubbles begin to break on the surface of the cream, about 3 minutes. Remove from the heat. Whisk in the butter. Transfer the pastry cream to a small bowl. Press plastic wrap directly onto the surface of the pastry cream. Refrigerate until cold, at least 3 hours and up to 2 days. Remove the vanilla bean.

DO AHEAD: *The pastry cream can be prepared up to 2 days ahead. Keep refrigerated*

SEE

{ TOUCH }

SMELL

HEAR

TASTE

+ CHAPTER 2

TOUCH

TOUCH SMELL HEAR TASTE SEE TOUCH SMELL HEAR TASTE SEE TOUCH SMELL HEAR

BITE INTO A CHICKEN LEG AND YOUR TEETH CRUSH
THROUGH THE FINE, CRISP LAYER OF SKIN BEFORE DELVING INTO
THE PILLOWLIKE SOFTNESS OF THE MEAT.

CUT INTO A TOMATO BEIGNET AND GATHER A MOUTHFUL ONTO YOUR FORK; YOU KNOW BY

INSTINCT THAT YOU WON'T FULLY ENJOY THE DISH UNLESS YOU SCOOP UP BITS OF BOTH THE

BRITTLE CRUST AND THE WARM MUSH OF THE TOMATO—AND EAT THEM TOGETHER. A RISOTTO

MAY BE SOFT ALL THE WAY THROUGH, AND WHILE THE FLAVOR ALONE MAY MAKE IT ENJOYABLE,

THERE'S SOMETHING EXQUISITELY SOOTHING ABOUT DIVING INTO ITS SILKY CONSISTENCY.

WHEN IT COMES TO FOOD, TOUCH MAY WELL BE THE MOST UNDERAPPRECIAT-

ED SENSE OF ALL, BUT NOT THAT MANY OF US ARE FULLY CONSCIOUS OF ITS ROLE. WHEN WE

EAT, WE DON'T JUST TASTE THE FOOD; WE TOUCH IT. I'M NOT TALKING ABOUT EATING WITH YOUR

HANDS OR PLAYING WITH YOUR FOOD THE WAY A TWO-YEAR-OLD DOES (THOUGH I WILL!). RIGHT

NOW, I'M TALKING ABOUT CHEWING. SURE, CHEWING IS THE FIRST STEP IN THE DIGESTIVE

PROCESS. BUT THERE'S A LOT MORE TO IT THAN SIMPLY GRINDING UP FOOD WITH YOUR TEETH.

THROUGH CHEWING, WE HAVE OUR MOST INTIMATE PHYSICAL CONTACT WITH FOOD; IN FACT, THE

ANCIENTS BELIEVED TOUCH WAS THE CLOSEST OF THE SENSES TO TASTE. AND WHENEVER WE

SLOW DOWN ENOUGH TO REALLY FOCUS ON OUR SENSE OF TOUCH, IT WILL REWARD US WITH A

TREMENDOUS AMOUNT OF PLEASURE. WHEN A DISH PROVIDES AN INTERESTING ARRAY OF TEX-

TURES, WE EMBARK ON A WHOLE NEW SENSUAL JOURNEY.

Chew your food thoroughly! Chew each bite at least twenty times! As children, many of us were taught to chew our food as if it were a competitive sport. This indoctrination has left many adults at a disadvantage when it comes to savoring food. I really hate to see someone sit down to a beautifully prepared meal and bolt it down, as if they'd been shivering in a flooded foxhole and these were the first army rations they'd seen in days. They've forgotten how to luxuriate in every bite, letting the food slip around the tongue, encouraging it to flirt with the taste buds, allowing it to caress the roof of the mouth. Such a range of textures to explore.

Layering textures for contrast—soft against crunchy, liquid against solid, crisp against yielding, rough against smooth—does wonders for any dish. Think of a napoleon, for example: What makes eating one so enjoyable is how that wonderfully crisp first layer of pastry gives way to the very different, cloudlike sensation of soft cream. With both of these sensations in your mouth at the same time, there's a sort of yin and yang principle at work. Because they're so different, you feel each one more intensely. Even spices, which we're more likely to associate with the sense of taste, appeal to our sense of touch. Finely powdered and rubbed on meat, cumin creates a delicate crispness. Coarsely ground star anise, added to a soupy tomato aspic, takes on the quality of a jewel in a velvet-lined box, delivering a rowdy *crunch* that is so pleasing to the palate.

Think about the times you've tried to eat after a trip to the dentist, with your tongue numbed by Novocain. Your sense of taste is more or less intact, but your sense of touch has been completely short-circuited. In this situation, eating is reduced to a simple matter of nutrition. It's a mere bodily function, with no real power to lift your spirits or provide enjoyment. You could resurrect August Escoffier, perhaps the greatest French chef of the nineteenth century, to prepare you the finest meal imaginable, but you might as well have a bologna sandwich because food will have no aesthetic value until the inside of your mouth comes back to life.

Another aspect to our sense of touch is the ability it gives us to feel variations in temperature. Playing hot and cold against each other in a single dish is yet another exciting sensual dimension, and I love to experiment with it. I think this is one of the reasons I like Grilled Foie Gras with Roasted Pears and Spice Syrup with Sauternes Jelly, on page 90, so much—having both the hot foie gras and the cold jelly in your mouth at the same time is a truly wonderful sensation.

It is also our sense of touch that allows us to delight in certain chemical properties of food that don't quite fall into the realm of taste: the sharp kick of hot pepper, the acidic tang of a lemon, the subtle but giddy tingling and burning sensations of onions or garlic.

You can also tell a lot about how to cook things by touching them. The degree of firmness offers many clues to cooking time. For example, let's say you're going to make a tomato confit. Press your fingers on the tomatoes. If they are ripe and soft to the touch, they will probably need only twenty minutes in the oven to reduce to a confit. If they are on the green side and firm to the touch, they may take forty minutes. (You could call this "the rule of the thumb.") As a matter of principle, ripe fruits will cook faster and require less heat. Vegetables are another story. They should always be crisp and firm. There is no magic technique for rendering a flaccid spear of asparagus or a squishy head of cauliflower worth eating.

Seafood especially reveals much about itself when touch is applied. The halibut, for example, is a very firm fish with a low fat content. It is extremely delicate, cooks rapidly, and therefore must be treated with great care. The flesh of a sea bass is by contrast very soft and contains much fat. Sea bass will therefore endure a much longer time on the stove and in the oven, so it's very difficult to ruin. But no matter how fat or lean a piece of meat or fish is, it should always have a certain springiness. If your finger leaves an impression, it is most likely no good. You can also test the doneness of meat by applying pressure. The more rare the meat, the more yielding it should be to pressure.

Let's go back to the two-year-old toddler sitting in his high chair. He scoops up hot mashed potatoes and rubs them between his hands. Then it occurs to him the stuff might make a pretty nice facial mask. He notices that the green beans seem designed specifically to be tucked behind (or inside) his ears. I, too, love to touch food, and I like to eat with my fingers. There's something satisfying about feeling your fingertips brush against the rough crust of a crispy piece of bread, or the softness of a ripe peach in your hand.

Now, I'm not suggesting that everybody regress to the age of two, or that washing your hair with carrot soup is going to do much other than get you scratched off a lot of party lists. But there's a lot of joy in that incredibly free, tactile relationship that young children have with food, and I think it's possible to recapture some of that magic in the kitchen without having your family haul you in for a psychiatric evaluation. Call me kinky, but I love the sensation of rubbing salt all over a chicken or a piece of meat; I guess you could say I actually caress it. In the kitchen, I'll plunge my fingers into a steaming pot of soup to test the temperature. I'll even press them inside the skillet to tell if it's hot enough. Which is not as masochistic as it sounds— when you're a chef, your fingers build up an amazing amount of scar tissue!

FRIED STUFFED TOMATO BEIGNETS

One of the greatest pleasures of eating is to experience contrasting dimensions of texture. It's always disappointing to be served a soft beignet, but I guarantee this recipe will result in a wonderfully brittle vessel of crust to hold the warm, voluptuously mushy tomato filling. Be sure to listen for the beautiful crackling sound as you cut into the beignet with your knife.

4 APPETIZER SERVINGS

Pureed Tomato Filling

  2 pounds ripe hothouse tomatoes (about 6)
  2 tablespoons extra virgin olive oil
  1 Vidalia onion, chopped (about 1½ cups)
  1 garlic clove, chopped
1½ tablespoons grated orange peel

Beignets

  4 whole firm tomatoes with stems
     (about 1¾ pounds total)
     Canola oil (for deep-frying)
  1 cup all-purpose flour
⅔ cup cornstarch
1½ teaspoons baking powder
  1 teaspoon fleur de sel
  1 cup ice-cold good-quality lager
¼ cup dried bread crumbs,
     fresh or packaged
½ cup mixed baby greens (for garnish)

FOR THE PUREED TOMATO FILLING

Submerge the tomatoes in a large saucepan of boiling water for 10 seconds. Using a slotted spoon, transfer the tomatoes to a large bowl of ice water to cool slightly. Using a small sharp paring knife, peel off the tomato skins. Quarter the tomatoes.

Heat the olive oil in a heavy large saucepan over medium heat. Add the onion and garlic and sauté until tender, about 3 minutes. Add the tomatoes and orange peel. Cook until the liquid from the tomatoes evaporates completely and the mixture is thick, stirring often, about 30 minutes. Puree the tomato mixture in a food processor until smooth (makes about 2 cups). Cook over medium heat until the puree is very thick like tomato paste and reduced by half, stirring often, about 15 minutes. Season to taste with fleur de sel and pepper. Cover the puree to keep it warm.

FOR THE BEIGNETS

Submerge the tomatoes in a large saucepan of boiling water for 10 seconds. Using a slotted spoon, transfer the tomatoes to a large bowl of ice water to cool slightly. Using a small sharp paring knife, peel off the tomato skins, keeping the stems intact. Using a knife, remove a quarter-size piece from the bottom of each tomato; reserve the small pieces to plug the tomatoes and enclose the filling later. Using a small melon baller, carefully scoop out the pulp and seeds through the hole cut in the bottom of the tomatoes. Set the hollowed tomatoes and tomato pieces aside. Discard the pulp and seeds.

DO AHEAD: *The hollowed tomatoes and tomato puree can be prepared up to 8 hours ahead. Cool. Cover separately and refrigerate. Rewarm the tomato puree before continuing.*

Add enough oil to a deep fryer or a large Dutch oven to come 3 inches up the sides of the pot. Heat the canola oil over medium heat until a deep-fry thermometer registers 350ºF.

Meanwhile, whisk the flour, cornstarch, baking powder, and fleur de sel in a medium bowl to blend. Add the lager and whisk until the batter is almost smooth. Transfer the batter to a 2-cup glass measuring cup. This will make it easier to coat the tomatoes. Spoon the warm tomato puree into a pastry bag. Holding the pastry bag tip just inside the hole at the bottom of the hollowed tomatoes, pipe the tomato puree into the tomatoes. Return the quarter-size pieces of tomatoes to the tomato holes and press gently to secure. Place the bread crumbs in a small bowl. Roll the tomatoes in the bread crumbs to coat, leaving the top one quarter of the tomato uncoated. Holding the tomatoes by their stems, dip each tomato into the batter to cover the bread crumbs. Fry the tomatoes in the hot oil until the batter is deep golden brown, about 2 minutes.

TO ASSEMBLE AND SERVE

Arrange the mixed baby greens on 4 plates. Place 1 tomato beignet atop the baby greens on each plate and serve immediately.

ICE-COLD BROTH WITH SHELLFISH AND GINGER

This dish is about touch and sound. The vegetables and the partially frozen broth are crunchy, but the shellfish are soft and slightly mushy, making it a beautifully noisy dish. It's great to serve in summer. When purchasing the shellfish, make sure that their shells are closed. Another good rule to follow when buying shellfish: the heavier the better. Although this recipe is not labor intensive, you will need to start preparing it one day ahead. Buy the shellfish a day in advance and soak them in water overnight to remove any grit from the ocean. Then, prepare them the next day.

4 APPETIZER SERVINGS

Shellfish

20 littleneck clams (about 14 ounces), scrubbed

20 mussels (about 1¼ pounds), scrubbed

20 cockles (about 8 ounces), scrubbed

1 cup good-quality dry white wine

1 large onion, chopped (about 2¼ cups)

Icy Court Bouillon

1⅔ cups water

¾ cup good-quality dry white wine

2 pearl onions, peeled and cut crosswise into
    ⅛-inch-thin rounds

1 small carrot, peeled and finely diced (about ⅓ cup)

1 small leek (about 1 ounce; white and pale green parts only), halved lengthwise and thinly sliced crosswise (about ¼ cup)

1 tablespoon red wine vinegar

½ teaspoon sugar

3 tablespoons strained fresh lime juice

2 tablespoons soy sauce

2 teaspoons minced peeled fresh ginger

1 teaspoon oriental sesame seed oil

2 tablespoons chopped fresh basil

2 tablespoons fresh tarragon leaves

FOR THE SHELLFISH

Place the shellfish in a large bowl of cold water. Refrigerate overnight. Drain the water; rinse the shellfish. Remove the beards from the mussels.

Combine the wine and the onion in a heavy large pot. Bring to a boil over high heat. Stir in the clams. Cover and cook just until the clams open, about 4 minutes. Remove the pot from the heat. Using a slotted spoon, transfer the clams to a large bowl. Discard any clams that do not open. Return the cooking liquid to a boil. Add the mussels and cockles. Cover and cook just until the shellfish open, about 5 minutes. Transfer the shellfish to the large bowl with the clams (keep the meat in the shells). Discard any shellfish that do not open. Discard the cooking liquid. Refrigerate the shellfish until cold.

FOR THE ICY COURT BOUILLON

Freeze 4 shallow soup plates. Combine the first 7 ingredients in a medium saucepan. Bring to a boil. Reduce the heat and simmer until the carrots are crisp-tender, about 5 minutes. Strain the court bouillon into a shallow glass container. Transfer the vegetables to a small bowl; cover and refrigerate. Cover and freeze the court bouillon just until it becomes slushy, stirring occasionally, about 2 hours. Continue to freeze the icy bouillon, scraping it with a fork every 30 minutes until it is completely made up of ice crystals and resembles granité.

TO FINISH AND SERVE

Stir the lime juice, soy sauce, ginger, and ½ teaspoon of the sesame seed oil in a small bowl to blend. Stir the soy sauce mixture into the icy bouillon. Stir in the reserved chilled cooked vegetables.

Divide the shellfish equally among the 4 frozen soup bowls. Spoon ⅓ cup icy bouillon mixture over each serving. Drizzle each serving with ⅛ teaspoon sesame seed oil. Garnish with the basil and tarragon leaves. Serve immediately.

POTATO CAKE WITH ONIONS

This is my variation on the theme of tortilla de patata, the classic Spanish potato omelet, a rustic favorite. In this version, however, the potatoes are sliced paper thin and compressed into a charlotte mold, then cooked long and slow in a water bath until they melt in your mouth like butter.

6 SERVINGS

3 Maui onions, or Vidalia or other sweet onions (about 1 pound)
1 cup Clarified Butter (page 243)
11 Yukon Gold potatoes (about 7 pounds), peeled
Fleur de sel and freshly ground pepper
1 teaspoon freshly ground mace

Preheat the oven to 350ºF. Oil a 3-quart (8 x 4½-inch) charlotte mold. Using a mandoline, cut the onions into 1/16-inch-thin slices. Set the onions aside. Place the clarified butter in a large metal bowl. Set the bowl over a large saucepan of simmering water to keep the butter melted. Using a mandoline, cut the potatoes crosswise into ⅛-inch-thick slices. Toss the potato slices with the clarified butter to coat. Season the potato mixture to taste with fleur de sel and pepper.

Arrange enough potato slices over the bottom of the charlotte mold, overlapping slightly and in concentric circles, to create 1 layer. Sprinkle some of the onion slices over the potatoes. Sprinkle a pinch of the mace over the onions in the mold. Press the layers to compact. Repeat layering all of the potato and onion slices, sprinkling each layer with mace, alternating the direction of the circles to increase the stability of the cake, and creating about 20 layers total. Cover with aluminum foil.

Place the charlotte mold in a roasting pan. Fill the pan with enough hot water to come halfway up the sides of the mold. Bake until a skewer can be inserted into the center of the potatoes without resistance, adding more hot water to the roasting pan as needed, about 4 hours. Cool atop the stove for 15 minutes. Remove the foil. Place a platter atop the mold. Using oven mitts and holding the mold with one hand and the platter with the other hand, invert the mold onto the platter. Remove the mold and serve.

SEARED FOIE GRAS WITH PINEAPPLE, DRIED MINT, AND ROSE PETALS

The secret to preparing foie gras is very similar to that of scallops. The sauté pan must be very hot, and you should hear that strong sizzling sound when the foie gras hits the surface. The sense of touch, too, is very helpful. Press on the foie gras with your fingers. It should be brittle and crisp, but give way easily to pressure. Here, the earthiness of the foie gras is buoyed by the fruit and floral flavors of pineapple, mint, and rose petals.

4 APPETIZER SERVINGS

1 teaspoon dried mint leaves

1 teaspoon dried, pesticide-free rose petals

1 pineapple, peeled, quartered, and cored

¼ cup water

2 tablespoons plus 2 teaspoons granulated sugar

Fleur de sel and freshly ground pepper

1 tablespoon unsalted butter

2 tablespoons kirsch

2 tablespoons dark rum

4 ½-inch-thick slices grade A foie gras (about 4 ounces each)

Finely crumble the mint and rose petals into a small bowl. Set aside. Coarsely chop 2 pineapple quarters. Cut 1 pineapple quarter lengthwise into 4 equal slices. Reserve the remaining pineapple quarter for another use. Combine the chopped pineapple, water, and 2 tablespoons of the sugar in a heavy medium saucepan. Simmer, uncovered, over medium-low heat until the liquid evaporates and the pineapple is very tender, stirring occasionally, about 35 minutes. Do not allow the pineapple to caramelize. Puree the pineapple mixture in a blender. Season the pineapple puree to taste with fleur de sel and pepper.

DO AHEAD: *At this point, the mint and rose mixture and the pineapple puree can be prepared ahead. Store the mint and rose mixture in an airtight container at room temperature up to 2 days ahead. Cover the puree and refrigerate up to 1 day ahead.*

Melt the butter in a heavy large sauté pan over medium-high heat. Sprinkle the remaining 2 teaspoons sugar over the butter. Add the 4 pineapple slices and cook until caramelized, about 2 minutes per side. Add the kirsch and rum. Remove from the heat. Carefully ignite the liquid with a match. Simmer until the flames subside.

Sprinkle the foie gras with fleur de sel and pepper. Heat another heavy large sauté pan over high heat. Add the foie gras (do not add any oil) and cook until deep golden brown, pressing with a spatula, about 1 minute per side. Reduce the heat to low and cook just until crisp on the outside and warm in the middle, 2 minutes longer on each side. Transfer the foie gras to paper towels to absorb the excess oil.

TO ASSEMBLE AND SERVE

Place a small mound of pureed pineapple in the center of each of 4 large plates. Place 1 foie gras slice to one side of the puree. Place 1 caramelized pineapple slice on the other side of the puree. Sprinkle the mint and rose petal powder in a thin line alongside the pineapple slice near the rim of the plate. Sprinkle the foie gras and pineapple slice with fleur de sel and serve.

MELON AND PROSCIUTTO RISOTTO

Cantaloupe wrapped in prosciutto has long been a favorite Italian antipasto. So I decided to combine it with risotto, another Italian perennial. The first time I made this risotto, I served it to a large party of Italians. They loved it, and it soon caught on. It's wonderfully flavorful, and also texturally interesting, with the slightly chewy, al dente rice playing against the small chunks of melon. The challenge is to cook the rice perfectly; you'll need to test it constantly.

4 APPETIZER SERVINGS

1	2½-pound cantaloupe, peeled, halved, and seeded
1	cup heavy whipping cream
2	tablespoons extra virgin olive oil
1	tablespoon unsalted butter
¾	cup finely chopped onion
1¼	cups (about 8 ounces) Arborio rice
2	cups good-quality dry white wine
3	ounces ¼-inch-thick slices prosciutto, diced
⅓	cup freshly grated Parmigiano-Reggiano cheese
	Fleur de sel and freshly ground pepper

Coarsely chop half of the cantaloupe. Place the chopped cantaloupe in a blender and puree until smooth and thick (makes about 1⅔ cups). Using a small melon baller, scoop enough of the remaining cantaloupe to make 1 cup of cantaloupe balls. Set the cantaloupe puree and balls aside. Beat ½ cup of the cream in a large bowl until soft peaks form. Cover the whipped cream and refrigerate.

Heat the oil and butter in a heavy large saucepan over medium heat. Add the onion and sauté just until tender but not brown, about 2 minutes. Add the rice and stir until slightly translucent, about 2 minutes. Add the wine. Bring to a simmer. Reduce the heat to medium-low and simmer until the wine is absorbed, stirring frequently, about 8 minutes. Stir in the cantaloupe puree and the remaining ½ cup cream. Cook until the rice is tender but still firm to the bite, stirring frequently, about 20 minutes. Stir in the prosciutto, then the cheese. Stir in the reserved cantaloupe balls. Fold the whipped cream into the risotto. Season to taste with fleur de sel and pepper. Transfer the risotto to 4 shallow bowls and serve.

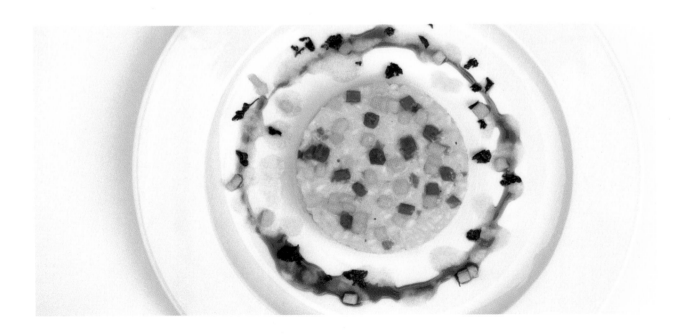

GRILLED FOIE GRAS WITH ROASTED PEARS AND SPICE SYRUP WITH SAUTERNES JELLY

Although I usually sear foie gras, grilling has its own advantages. The foie gras comes out exquisitely soft, so that it melts in your mouth. Here, the Sauternes jelly and the roasted pears contribute another dimension of softness.

4 APPETIZER SERVINGS

Sauternes Jelly

1 cup Sauternes wine
1 teaspoon unflavored gelatin

Roasted Pears and Syrup

1 vanilla bean, split lengthwise
1 cup water
½ cup sugar
½ red jalapeño chile, halved
1 tablespoon freshly ground star anise
¾ teaspoon freshly ground Ceylon
    cinnamon
2 Anjou pears, peeled

4 ½-inch-thick slices grade A foie gras
    (about 4 ounces each)
    Fleur de sel and freshly ground pepper
2 teaspoons extra virgin olive oil

FOR THE SAUTERNES JELLY

Place the Sauternes wine in a heavy small saucepan. Sprinkle the gelatin over the top. Let stand until the gelatin softens, about 5 minutes. Bring the mixture to a simmer. Whisk over low heat until the gelatin is dissolved, about 1 minute. Strain the wine mixture into a miniature loaf pan so that the mixture is about 1 inch deep. Cover and refrigerate until the mixture is softly set, at least 2 hours and up to 2 days.

FOR THE ROASTED PEARS AND SYRUP

Scrape the seeds from the vanilla bean into a heavy medium saucepan; add the bean. Add the water, sugar, chile, star anise, and cinnamon. Bring the liquid to a boil, stirring until the sugar dissolves. Add the pears. Reduce the heat to medium-low and simmer until a skewer pierces the pears easily, turning the pears occasionally, about 10 minutes. Using a slotted spoon, transfer the pears to a medium bowl. Cool the pears and poaching syrup separately. Strain the cooled poaching syrup through a fine-mesh strainer and into a small bowl. Cut the pears lengthwise in half. Using a melon baller, remove the core and seeds from the pears.

DO AHEAD: *The jelly, pears, and poaching syrup can be prepared up to 1 day ahead. Cover separately and keep refrigerated.*

TO FINISH AND SERVE

Sprinkle the foie gras with fleur de sel and pepper. Preheat the grill to high heat. Add the foie gras and cook until deep golden brown markings appear, pressing with a spatula, about 1 minute per side. Reduce the heat to low and cook until the center of the foie gras is warm, about 2 minutes longer per side. Transfer the foie gras to paper towels to absorb excess oil.

Meanwhile, heat the oil in a heavy large sauté pan over medium-high heat. Add the pears and cook until the pears are heated through and begin to brown, about 2 minutes per side.

Cut the jelly crosswise into ¾-inch-thick slices. Place 1 foie gras slice in the center of each of 4 wide shallow bowls. Place 1 pear half alongside each foie gras. Place 1 jelly slice along the opposite side of the foie gras. Drizzle the chilled poaching syrup around the foie gras and serve immediately.

SALAD OF TOMATO CONFIT WITH BASIL AND MINT AND VANILLA AND RASPBERRY BALSAMIC VINAIGRETTE

Here you will exercise your sense of touch in two ways. When shopping, press on the tomatoes to make sure they're firm and not overly ripe. When you eat the salad, though, the texture will be the opposite: wonderfully soft, like a balm on the tongue.

6 APPETIZER SERVINGS

Vinaigrette

3 tablespoons raspberry balsamic vinegar, or 1½ tablespoons each of raspberry vinegar
and balsamic vinegar

1 vanilla bean, halved lengthwise

2 tablespoons extra virgin olive oil
Fleur de sel and freshly ground black pepper

Tomato Confit

12 hothouse tomatoes (about 3 pounds)

2 tablespoons plus ⅓ cup extra virgin olive oil

Toast

12 ½-inch-thick French bread slices (each slice about 3 x 2 inches)

2 tablespoons extra virgin olive oil

10 fresh mint leaves, thinly sliced

10 fresh basil leaves, thinly sliced

FOR THE VINAIGRETTE

Place the vinegar in a large bowl. Scrape in the seeds from the vanilla bean; reserve the vanilla bean for another use. Gradually whisk in the olive oil. Continue whisking until the vinaigrette is well blended. Season the vinaigrette to taste with fleur de sel and black pepper.

FOR THE TOMATO CONFIT

Preheat the oven to 350°F. Submerge the tomatoes in a large pot of boiling water for 10 seconds. Using a slotted spoon, transfer the tomatoes to a large bowl of ice water to cool. Using a small sharp paring knife, peel off the tomato skins. Quarter each tomato. Remove the pulp and seeds from the tomato quarters. Arrange the tomato quarters, cut side down, on a heavy large baking sheet. Drizzle 2 tablespoons of the oil evenly over the tomatoes. Sprinkle with fleur de sel and pepper. Bake the tomatoes until they become tender but still hold their shape (do not allow tomatoes to become mushy), about 8 minutes. Drizzle the remaining ⅓ cup oil over the tomatoes. Let stand at room temperature.

DO AHEAD: *The vinaigrette and tomato confit can be prepared up to 4 hours ahead. Cover separately and keep at room temperature.*

FOR THE TOAST

Preheat the oven to 400°F. Brush the bread slices with the oil; arrange the bread on a large baking sheet. Sprinkle with fleur de sel and freshly ground pepper. Bake until the bread is toasted and beginning to color, about 8 minutes.

TO ASSEMBLE AND SERVE

Arrange the tomatoes on 6 plates. Drizzle the vinaigrette over. Sprinkle with the mint and basil. Season with fleur de sel and pepper. Serve the salad with the warm toast.

SEA URCHIN CRÈME BRÛLÉE

This crème brûlée is almost like a flan, but much lighter. It delivers pure flavor with no more gravity than a feather. Its texture is like the breath of a hummingbird. By itself, sea urchin has a very aggressive flavor, but the custard softens its normally briny taste.

6 APPETIZER SERVINGS

Carrot-Ginger Jelly

¾ cup fresh carrot juice
2   teaspoons fresh ginger juice
    (from a 2-inch piece of ginger)
½   teaspoon unflavored gelatin

Sea Urchin Custard

1   cup sushi-quality sea urchin roe
6   large egg yolks
2   cups heavy whipping cream
1   cup whole milk
¾   teaspoon fleur de sel
6   live sea urchins
12 ounces fresh crabmeat, preferably
    peeky toe
    Freshly ground white pepper

FOR THE CARROT-GINGER JELLY

Bring ¼ cup of the carrot juice and the ginger juice just to a simmer in a small saucepan. Sprinkle the gelatin over the top. Let stand until the gelatin softens, about 5 minutes. Stir over low heat until the gelatin is dissolved, about 2 minutes. Cool slightly. Combine the gelatin mixture and the remaining ½ cup carrot juice in a small bowl. Stir to blend. Cover and refrigerate until the mixture is gelatinous and resembles a loose jelly but is not firm, stirring occasionally, about 4 hours.

FOR THE SEA URCHIN CUSTARD

Position the oven rack in the center of the oven, and preheat the oven to 275ºF. Set six 6-ounce soufflé dishes in a 13 x 9 x 2-inch baking pan. Press the sea urchin roe through a fine-mesh strainer and into the workbowl of a food processor. Add the egg yolks and pulse to blend. Transfer the sea urchin mixture to a large bowl. Set aside.

Combine the cream and milk in a heavy medium saucepan. Bring to a simmer over medium heat. Gradually whisk the hot cream mixture into the sea urchin mixture. Mix in the fleur de sel. Strain the custard through a fine-mesh strainer and into a 4-cup glass measuring cup. Divide the custard equally among the prepared soufflé dishes. Transfer the pan to the oven. Carefully pour enough hot water into the baking pan to come halfway up the sides of the dishes.

Bake until the centers of the custards are gently set, about 50 minutes. Transfer the custards to a rack and cool. Refrigerate until cold, about 2 hours. Cover and refrigerate overnight.

Meanwhile, using a small sharp knife, neatly cut away the tops of the sea urchins, creating a 2½-inch opening. Using your fingers, gently loosen and remove the dark-colored viscera; discard the viscera. Loosen the orange-colored roe (also known as the tongues) from the shell and rinse them in a small bowl of cold water to remove any debris. Transfer 6 of the best-looking "tongues" to a small bowl; discard the remaining tongues. Cover and refrigerate the reserved tongues. Using a small firm brush, scrub the insides of the sea urchin shells to remove any remaining contents. Invert the shells onto a small baking sheet; cover and refrigerate.

DO AHEAD: *The carrot-ginger jelly, sea urchin custard, tongues, and sea urchin shells can be prepared 1 day ahead. Keep refrigerated.*

TO ASSEMBLE AND SERVE

Spoon off the crust from atop the custards. Whisk the carrot-ginger jelly until smooth. Spoon 3 tablespoons of the crabmeat into the bottom of each prepared sea urchin shell. Spoon the custard atop the crabmeat in the shells. Spoon 1 tablespoon of the carrot-ginger jelly neatly over each. Place 1 reserved sea urchin tongue atop each. Sprinkle with additional fleur de sel and freshly ground white pepper. Serve immediately.

TARTARE OF KOBE BEEF WITH POTATO CHIPS

There is no beef more tender than Kobe beef, which originated in Japan where, from my understanding, the cows are massaged with sake and given a lot of beer to drink while watching sports on ESPN. (Kobe is now produced in the United States; I get mine from Snake River Farms in Colorado.) Since the essence of tartare is softness, I thought it made sense to go for the most tender beef. For contrast, there's the accompanying dish of crisp, homemade potato chips. Verjus, the juice extracted from large, unripened grapes, adds an astringent note. You can find it in most specialty shops.

4 APPETIZER SERVINGS

Potato Chips

1 large russet potato (about 1 pound), peeled

Canola oil (for deep-frying)

Fleur de sel and freshly ground pepper

Beef Tartare

1½ tablespoons extra virgin olive oil

1½ tablespoons verjus

1 large egg yolk

1 teaspoon ketchup

½ teaspoon fleur de sel

¼ teaspoon freshly ground black pepper

Dash of hot pepper sauce (such as Tabasco)

8 ounces Snake River Farm Kobe beef tenderloin, fat removed, meat cut into ⅓-inch cubes

(see the Resource Guide, page 246)

2 tablespoons minced shallot

1 tablespoon minced white onion

1 tablespoon minced drained capers

2 teaspoons chopped fresh flat-leaf parsley

2 teaspoons extra virgin olive oil

FOR THE POTATO CHIPS

Using a mandoline, cut the potato lengthwise into ⅛-inch-thick slices. Rinse the potato slices under cold running water until the water runs clear. Pat the potato slices dry with paper towels.

Meanwhile, heat the canola oil in a deep fryer or a heavy large frying pan over medium heat, until a deep-fry thermometer registers 350°F. Working in batches and returning the oil to 350°F before adding each batch, fry the potato slices until golden, turning occasionally, about 4 minutes. Using a slotted spoon, transfer the chips to paper towels to drain. While still hot, sprinkle the chips with fleur de sel and pepper.

DO AHEAD: *At this point, the potato chips can be prepared up to 1 day ahead. Store the potato chips airtight at room temperature.*

FOR THE BEEF TARTARE

Whisk the first 7 ingredients in a medium bowl to blend. Stir in the beef, shallot, onion, capers, and parsley. Season to taste with more fleur de sel and pepper.

TO ASSEMBLE AND SERVE

Mound the tartare in the center of 4 plates, dividing equally. Drizzle ½ teaspoon olive oil around the tartare on each plate. Stack the potato chips atop the tartare. Serve immediately.

SWEETBREADS WITH GINGER, LICORICE, ROASTED PEARS, AND LEMON CONFIT

Sweetbreads, like foie gras, are at their best when they're crisp on the outside and soft within, and therefore should be flash-seared in a very hot sauté pan. Brushing them with cream and then dredging them lightly in flour produces an exquisite crust. Use your fingers to test them for doneness; they should feel crisp on the outside but should yield to pressure. The dried licorice roots and ginger are available in most spice shops.

4 MAIN-COURSE SERVINGS

Sweetbreads

2 6-inch pieces of dried licorice roots, crumbled

1 teaspoon dried coarsely grated ginger

4 8-ounce veal sweetbreads

½ cup (about) all-purpose flour
   Fleur de sel and freshly ground pepper

1 tablespoon heavy whipping cream

¼ cup extra virgin olive oil

Roasted Pears

4 Anjou pears, peeled

1 tablespoon unsalted butter

1 teaspoon sugar
   Lemon Confit (page 244)

FOR THE SWEETBREADS

Grind the licorice roots and ginger in a spice grinder to form a fine powder. Sift the spice powder through a fine-mesh sieve to remove the fibrous pieces. Set the spice powder aside.

Place the sweetbreads in a medium saucepan. Add enough water to cover completely. Bring the water to a boil over high heat. Drain the water; cool the sweetbreads completely. Using a small sharp knife, peel off the outer larger pieces of membrane, leaving the smaller connective membranes intact.

DO AHEAD: *At this point, the spice powder and sweetbreads can be prepared up to 1 day ahead. Store the spice powder airtight at room temperature. Cover and refrigerate the sweetbreads.*

Place the flour on a small baking sheet. Sprinkle the sweetbreads with fleur de sel and pepper. Brush the cream all over the sweetbreads. Roll the sweetbreads in the flour to coat lightly. Heat the oil in a heavy large sauté pan over medium-high heat. Add the sweetbreads and cook until crisp on the outside and just heated through, about 5 minutes per side. Lightly dust the spice powder over the sweetbreads.

FOR THE PEARS

Slice the pears lengthwise to remove two of the rounded sides and form a ¾-inch-thick pear fillet. Melt the butter in a heavy large sauté pan over medium-low heat. Sprinkle the sugar over the butter. Add the pear fillets and cook until crisp-tender, about 5 minutes per side. Remove the sauté pan from the heat. Using a 1-inch biscuit cutter, cut out the core of each pear fillet to remove the seeds and tough parts. Reserve the pear trimmings for another use.

TO ASSEMBLE AND SERVE

Place 1 sweetbread on the left side of each of 4 large plates. Place 1 pear fillet on the right side of each plate. Spoon 2 tablespoons of the lemon confit into the center of each pear fillet. Serve immediately.

WHOLE DOVER SOLE FILLED WITH FENNEL, APPLE, GINGER, AND LIME

This treatment of fish provides a nice range of textures, with the slightly crunchy fennel and apple playing against the delicate flesh of the sole. But the real reason I included it in the Touch chapter is that I want you to see what a difference cooking a whole fish on the bone makes compared to fillets: the fish is far moister, more tender, and more flavorful.

4 MAIN-COURSE SERVINGS

Fennel and Apple Filling

- 2 tablespoons extra virgin olive oil
- 2 shallots, minced
- 1 pound fennel bulbs, finely diced (about 3 cups)
- 1 Granny Smith apple (about 8 ounces), peeled, cored, and finely diced
- 1½ tablespoons minced peeled fresh ginger
- 2 teaspoons finely grated lime peel
- 2 tablespoons chopped fresh flat-leaf parsley
  Fleur de sel and freshly ground pepper

Fish and Sauce

- 4 20-ounce whole Dover soles, cleaned (head and fins removed, white skin left intact)
- 3 tablespoons extra virgin olive oil
- 1 cup Fish Stock (page 240)
- ¼ cup yellow onion juice (from 1 onion run through a juicer)
- 3 tablespoons unsalted butter

FOR THE FENNEL AND APPLE FILLING

Heat the oil in a large nonstick sauté pan over medium heat. Add the shallots and sauté just until translucent, about 2 minutes. Add the fennel and sauté until tender but not brown, about 15 minutes. Add the apple, ginger, and lime peel. Reduce the heat to low. Cover the pan and cook just until the apple is crisp-tender, about 5 minutes. Stir in the parsley. Season the mixture to taste with fleur de sel and pepper. Chill until cold. Transfer the filling to a pastry bag. Keep refrigerated.

FOR THE FISH AND SAUCE

Cut a 2-inch-wide incision into the white skin, 1 inch from the head end of the fish. With the fish lying flat on the work surface, hold down the sides of the fish with one hand. With the other hand, insert a frosting knife between the skin and the flesh, carefully loosening the skin from the flesh to form a pocket down the center of the fish. Do not tear the skin.

DO AHEAD: *At this point, the filling and fish can be prepared up to 4 hours ahead. Keep the filling refrigerated. Cover the fish and refrigerate.*

TO FINISH AND SERVE

Preheat the oven to 375°F. Slowly squeeze the fennel and apple filling into the pocket of the fish (do not overstuff it). Rub fleur de sel and pepper over the fish. Heat the oil in a large nonstick sauté pan over medium heat until hot but not smoking. If the sauté pan is too hot, the fish skin will burst. Working in batches, place 2 fish, stuffed side down, in the sauté pan and cook just until the skin is brown, about 2 minutes. Transfer the fish, skin side up, to a heavy large baking sheet (do not wipe out the sauté pan). Bake the fish just until the flesh is opaque, about 8 minutes.

Meanwhile, add the fish stock and onion juice to the same sauté pan. Simmer until the liquid is reduced to ½ cup, about 8 minutes. Reduce the heat to low. Whisk in the butter, forming a smooth sauce. Strain the sauce into a small bowl. Season the sauce to taste with fleur de sel and pepper.

Place 1 fish on each of 4 large plates. Spoon the sauce over the fish and serve.

FRENCH SEA BASS WITH CRISPY SKIN, POTATOES FONDANTE, MAUI ONION CONFIT, AND LEMON, CARDAMOM, AND COFFEE BEAN SAUCE

French sea bass is one of the softest fish you can find. This is another sensual dish: One side is very crisp, the other voluptuously soft, so that you have two different textures in your mouth. Note: Ask your fishmonger for the head of the fish; it will intensify the flavor of the sauce. If it is available, cut it in half and soak it in cold water for thirty minutes to clean it before using.

4 MAIN-COURSE SERVINGS

4　6-ounce French sea bass fillets with the skins

4　tablespoons extra virgin olive oil

2　tablespoons strained fresh lemon juice

1　teaspoon coarsely ground green cardamom seeds

½　teaspoon freshly ground coffee beans
Fleur de sel and freshly ground pepper

1　cup Fish Stock (page 240)
Potatoes Fondante (recipe follows)
Maui Onion Confit (recipe follows)

Coat the fish fillets with 1 tablespoon of the oil. Cover and refrigerate for 30 minutes. Whisk the lemon juice, cardamom, and ground coffee in a small bowl to blend. Season the sauce to taste with fleur de sel. Set aside.

Rub the fish with fleur de sel and pepper. Heat 2 tablespoons of the oil in a heavy large nonstick sauté pan over high heat. Place the fish, skin side down, in the pan and cook until the skin is crisp, about 2 minutes (if available, for more flavor, add the fish head to the pan along with the fillets). Reduce the heat to medium and cook the fish for 2 minutes longer. Turn the fish over and cook until just opaque in the center, about 3 minutes. Using a metal spatula, place each fish fillet, skin side up, on the left side of each of 4 large warm dinner plates (do not clean the pan). Add the fish stock to the same sauté pan. Scrape up any browned bits from the bottom of the pan. Simmer until the liquid is reduced to ⅓ cup, about 8 minutes. Strain the reduced pan juices into a small bowl. Stir in the remaining 1 tablespoon oil, then the reserved cardamom sauce.

TO SERVE

Place 1 serving of the potatoes fondante alongside the fish on each plate. Spoon an oval-shaped mound of the Maui onion confit alongside each fish. Drizzle the sauce around the fish and serve.

POTATOES FONDANTE

4 SIDE-DISH SERVINGS

2 large russet potatoes (about 2 pounds total), peeled

2 tablespoons extra virgin olive oil

1 cup Chicken Stock (page 239)

3 tablespoons unsalted butter

1 fresh thyme sprig

1 garlic clove, peeled

Fleur de sel and freshly ground pepper

Using a small sharp knife or vegetable peeler, trim each potato into a large cylinder shape. Cut the potato cylinders crosswise into 1-inch-thick rounds. Pat dry.

Heat the oil in a heavy large sauté pan over medium heat. Arrange the potatoes in a single layer in the pan. Cook until the potatoes are golden brown, turning once, about 5 minutes per side. Add the chicken stock, butter, thyme, and garlic. Simmer until the potatoes are tender when pierced with a knife and the cooking liquid reduces, basting the potatoes occasionally, about 5 minutes. Season to taste with fleur de sel and pepper.

MAUI ONION CONFIT

MAKES ABOUT 1 CUP

1 teaspoon extra virgin olive oil

1 large Maui onion (about 12 ounces), or other sweet onion
such as Vidalia, cut into ½-inch pieces

2 garlic cloves, peeled

Fleur de sel

Heat the oil in a heavy medium sauté pan over medium-low heat. Add the onion and whole garlic. Sprinkle with fleur de sel. Cover and cook until the onion is translucent but not brown, stirring occasionally, about 25 minutes.

DO AHEAD: *The onion confit can be prepared up to 4 hours ahead. Cool. Cover and refrigerate. Rewarm before serving.*

GENTLY COOKED AHI INFUSED WITH VANILLA

Many dishes appeal to our sense of touch by creating a clash of textures: the soft versus the crunchy, the chewy versus the mushy, and so on. Sometimes, however, it's nice to revel in just one texture. In this recipe, the ahi is almost like warm butter, and we luxuriate in its uninterrupted softness. Note: Vanilla powder is merely the finely ground seeds of the vanilla bean. If you can't find it at your local spice shop, dry one vanilla bean in the oven for one hour at 300ºF, then grind it to a fine powder.

4 MAIN-COURSE SERVINGS

Red Beet Essence

- 1 cup strained fresh beet juice
   (from about 1½ pounds beets)
- 1 tablespoon heavy whipping cream
- 1 tablespoon chilled unsalted butter
   Fleur de sel and freshly ground pepper

Tuna

- 1 tablespoon extra virgin olive oil
- 4 4 x 2-inch-long grade A ahi tuna loin
   fillets (about 6 ounces each)
- 2 cups Clarified Butter (page 243)
- 2 teaspoons vanilla powder
- ¼ teaspoon fleur de sel

Red Beet Cups

- 4 beets (4 ounces each), peeled
- 2 cups canola oil
- ½ cup finely diced peeled beet
- 2 tablespoons fresh beet juice
   (from 1 small beet)
- 1 teaspoon minced shallot
- 1½ teaspoons finely chopped fresh flat-leaf
   parsley
- ½ teaspoon Dijon mustard
- ¼ teaspoon minced anchovy fillet
   Fleur de sel and freshly ground pepper

FOR THE RED BEET ESSENCE

Simmer the beet juice and cream in a heavy medium saucepan over medium-high heat until reduced to ⅓ cup, about 5 minutes. Whisk in the butter to form a smooth sauce. Season to taste with fleur de sel and pepper. Set aside.

TO PREPARE THE TUNA

Heat the oil in a heavy large sauté pan over high heat. Add the tuna slices and cook just until brown on both sides, about 1 minute per side.

In a large saucepan, heat the clarified butter to 120ºF. Add the tuna fillets, vanilla powder, and the fleur de sel. Cook 6 minutes for medium-rare, turning once. Using a metal spatula, transfer the tuna to a work surface. Reserve 2 tablespoons of the butter mixture and keep it warm.

TO PREPARE THE RED BEET CUPS

Trim the ends of the whole peeled beets to form 2-inch-thick disks. Using a melon baller, hollow the centers of each beet disk, forming small cups. Heat the oil in a heavy small saucepan over medium heat to 200ºF. Submerge the beet cups in the hot oil and cook until tender but still holding their shape, about 10 minutes. Using tongs, remove the beet cups from the oil and invert onto a plate lined with paper towels to drain.

Meanwhile, combine the diced beet, beet juice, and shallot in another heavy small saucepan. Add enough water to cover the beets (about ½ cup). Boil over medium-high heat until the cooking liquid has almost evaporated and the beets are crisp-tender, about 7 minutes. Remove from the heat. Add the parsley, mustard, and anchovy; stir to blend. Season to taste with fleur de sel and pepper. Spoon the beet mixture into the beet cups and serve.

TO ASSEMBLE AND SERVE

Cut each tuna fillet in half against the grain. Arrange the fillet pieces, cut side up, on 4 large plates. Place the red beet cups on the plates alongside the fish. Drizzle the reserved warm butter mixture over and around the fish. Spoon 1 tablespoon of the red beet essence alongside each. Serve immediately.

CAKE OF APPLE CONFIT

This incredibly airy "cake" is another dish that all but defies gravity. Baked for six hours, the apples are extremely light and very sweet. You taste them, but barely feel them in your mouth.

8 SERVINGS

Zest Confit

 2 oranges

 2 lemons

 1 ruby red grapefruit

1¼ cups water

 ½ cup sugar

Apple Cake

 2 cups sugar

 3 tablespoons water

 15 Granny Smith apples
   (about 8½ pounds), peeled and cored

   Crème fraîche

FOR THE ZEST CONFIT

Using a vegetable peeler, remove the peel and white pith from the fruit. Using a small sharp knife, trim away all the pith from the peels. Cut the peels into julienne strips (makes about 1½ cups total). Place the peels in a small saucepan of water. Bring the water to a boil. Drain. Rinse the peels under cold water. Repeat this process once.

Combine the peels, 1¼ cups of water, and the sugar in the same saucepan. Simmer gently over medium-low heat until the juices evaporate and the peels become translucent, about 25 minutes.

FOR THE APPLE CAKE

Preheat the oven to 250°F. Oil a 3-quart (8 x 4½-inch) charlotte mold. Combine 1 cup of the sugar and the water in a heavy small saucepan. Stir over medium-high heat until the sugar dissolves. Boil without stirring over medium heat until the syrup turns a deep amber brown color and just begins to smoke, occasionally brushing down the sides of the pan with a wet pastry brush and swirling the pan, about 8 minutes. Carefully pour the caramel into the charlotte mold. Using oven mitts, swirl the mold to coat the interior completely with the caramel (the caramel will stick to the pan as it cools). Refrigerate until the caramel is cold and set.

Meanwhile, using a mandoline, cut the apples crosswise into ⅛-inch-thick slices. Arrange enough apple slices over the bottom of the charlotte mold, overlapping slightly and in concentric circles, to create 1 layer. Sprinkle 2 teaspoons sugar and 1 tablespoon zest confit over the apple slices in the mold. Repeat layering all of the apple slices with the sugar and the zest confit, alternating the direction of the concentric circles to increase the stability of the cake, pressing to compact the layers, and creating about 20 layers total. Cover with aluminum foil.

Place the charlotte mold in a roasting pan. Fill the pan with enough hot water to come halfway up the sides of the mold. Bake until a skewer inserted near the center of the apples does not meet resistance, about 6 hours. Refrigerate until cold.

Remove the foil. Place the mold in a sauté pan of simmering water to melt the caramel coating slightly and help loosen the apple cake, about 3 minutes. Place a platter atop the mold. Holding the mold with one hand and the platter with the other hand, invert the mold onto the platter. Remove the mold.

DO AHEAD: *The apple cake can be prepared up to 8 hours ahead. Cover and refrigerate.*

Cut the apple cake into wedges and transfer to dessert plates. Drizzle any accumulated juices around and serve with the crème fraîche.

CREPES WITH HOT AND COLD CHOCOLATE

Two experiences of chocolate, experienced two different ways each, equals four separate chocolate experiences, one hot and bitter, the other cold and sweet. This will give your taste buds and your sense of touch much to explore.

8 SERVINGS

Chocolate Sauce

- ½ cup heavy whipping cream
- 4 ounces good-quality bittersweet (not unsweetened) chocolate, chopped

Crepes

- 1 cup all-purpose flour
- ⅓ cup sugar
- 3 large eggs, room temperature
- ¼ teaspoon fleur de sel
- 1¾ cups whole milk, room temperature
- 2 tablespoons unsalted butter, melted
- 2 teaspoons finely grated orange peel
- 1 tablespoon (about) canola oil

Chocolate Sorbet (recipe follows)
Unsweetened cocoa powder

FOR THE CHOCOLATE SAUCE

Bring the cream to a simmer in a heavy small saucepan over medium-low heat. Remove from the heat. Add the chocolate and stir until melted and smooth, about 1 minute. Set aside.

FOR THE CREPES

Whisk the flour, sugar, eggs, and fleur de sel in a large bowl to blend. Add the milk, butter, and orange peel; whisk to blend. Cover the crepe batter and refrigerate until cold, about 1 hour.

DO AHEAD: *At this point, the chocolate sauce and crepe batter can be prepared up to 1 day ahead. Keep the crepe batter refrigerated. Cool the chocolate sauce, then cover and refrigerate. Rewarm the sauce over low heat before serving.*

Preheat the oven to 200°F. Lightly brush a 7- to 8-inch nonstick crepe pan with oil and heat over medium heat. Pour 2 tablespoons of the crepe batter into the pan and quickly swirl the pan to coat the bottom thinly and evenly until all of the batter is set. Cook until the edge of the crepe is light brown, about 1 minute. Loosen the crepe edges gently with a rubber spatula. Using your fingertips, carefully lift the crepe by the edge and turn the crepe over. Cook until the bottom begins to brown in spots, about 1 minute. Fold the crepe in half, then in half again, forming a triangle. Transfer to a baking sheet; keep warm in the oven. Repeat with the remaining batter, brushing the pan lightly with more oil if necessary before adding more batter, and making about 24 crepes total.

Arrange 3 crepes on each of 8 plates. Drizzle the warm chocolate sauce over the crepes. Spoon an oval-shaped scoop of the chocolate sorbet atop each serving. Dust with cocoa powder and serve immediately.

CHOCOLATE SORBET

MAKES ABOUT 3 CUPS

2²/₃ cups water

¹/₃ cup pure maple syrup

¹/₃ cup sugar

11 ounces good-quality bittersweet
(not unsweetened) chocolate, chopped

Combine the water, maple syrup, and sugar in a heavy medium saucepan. Bring to a boil over high heat. Place the chocolate in a large bowl. Gradually whisk the hot syrup mixture into the chocolate. Stir until the mixture is smooth and well blended. Place the chocolate mixture over another large bowl of ice water. Using a whisk, stir until the mixture is cold and well blended.

Transfer the mixture to an ice cream maker. Process according to the manufacturer's instructions. Transfer the sorbet to a container. Cover and freeze until firm, at least 4 hours. Let the sorbet soften slightly at room temperature before serving.

DO AHEAD: *The sorbet can be prepared up to 8 hours ahead. Keep frozen.*

CHOCOLATE SOUFFLÉS WITH BITTERSWEET CHOCOLATE SAUCE

This is the recipe most often requested by my dinner guests. What sets it apart is its fluffy, mousselike texture, which comes from the fact that it contains no flour or cream. It's also very easy to make. The batter can be prepared a couple of hours in advance and popped into the oven at the last minute.

4 SERVINGS

Bittersweet Chocolate Sauce

¼ cup heavy whipping cream
2 ounces good-quality bittersweet (not unsweetened) chocolate, chopped

Whipped Cream

⅔ cup heavy whipping cream
2 teaspoons granulated sugar

Chocolate Soufflés

2 tablespoons unsalted butter, melted
¾ cup granulated sugar
8 ounces good-quality bittersweet (not unsweetened) chocolate, chopped
12 large egg whites
Powdered sugar (for sifting)

FOR THE BITTERSWEET CHOCOLATE SAUCE

Stir the cream and chocolate in a heavy small saucepan over medium-low heat until melted and smooth, about 1 minute. Set aside.

FOR THE WHIPPED CREAM

Whisk the cream and sugar in a large bowl until soft peaks form. Cover and refrigerate.

FOR THE CHOCOLATE SOUFFLÉS

Preheat the oven to 350°F. Using a pastry brush, coat the interiors of four 9-ounce soufflé dishes with the melted butter; then coat with about ¼ cup of the sugar. Place the dishes on a heavy baking sheet. Stir the chocolate in a large wide bowl over a saucepan of simmering water until melted and smooth. Keep the bowl over the simmering water in order to keep it hot.

Meanwhile, using an electric mixer with the whisk attachment, beat the egg whites in another large bowl on medium-low speed until firm peaks form. Add the remaining ½ cup sugar and beat until blended. With the machine on low, gradually beat in the hot melted chocolate, mixing just until blended (the mixture will resemble chocolate mousse). Turn the machine off. Using a large flat rubber spatula, fold in any remaining chocolate from the bottom of the bowl. Divide the soufflé batter equally among the prepared soufflé dishes, mounding slightly.

DO AHEAD: *At this point, the chocolate sauce, whipped cream, and soufflés can be prepared up to 4 hours ahead. Cover and refrigerate the chocolate sauce, then stir over low heat to rewarm before serving. Keep the whipped cream refrigerated. Keep the soufflés at room temperature.*

TO FINISH AND SERVE

Bake the soufflés until they puff but are still moist in the center, about 14 minutes. Sift with powdered sugar. Serve immediately, passing the chocolate sauce and whipped cream separately.

WARM WAFFLES WITH CHESTNUT ICE CREAM

Waffles aren't just for breakfast anymore. In fact, in France, they never were; they are served strictly for dessert. Nothing could go better with the crunchy waffles than this soft, rich chestnut ice cream. You can find the chestnut puree for the ice cream at gourmet groceries and specialty shops. The ice cream is best when served soft, so I recommend freezing it for no longer than six hours.

6 SERVINGS

Chestnut Ice Cream

- ½ cup water
- ½ cup granulated sugar
- 1¼ cups heavy whipping cream
- 2 tablespoons light corn syrup
- ¾ cup prepared sweetened chestnut puree

Waffles

- 1 cup all-purpose flour
- 2 tablespoons granulated sugar
- 1 tablespoon active dry yeast
- ½ teaspoon fleur de sel
- 2 large eggs, separated
- 3 tablespoons unsalted butter, melted
- 1 cup whole milk

Powdered sugar (for sifting)

FOR THE CHESTNUT ICE CREAM

Bring the water and sugar to a boil in a heavy small saucepan, stirring to dissolve the sugar. Remove from the heat. Stir in the cream and corn syrup. Transfer the mixture to a small bowl. Cover and refrigerate at least 2 hours.

Transfer the cream mixture to an ice cream maker. Process according to the manufacturer's instructions. Spoon half of the ice cream into a container. Dollop half of the chestnut puree over the ice cream. Spoon the remaining ice cream over. Dollop the remaining chestnut puree over. Cover and freeze until semifirm, about 2 hours.

DO AHEAD: *The ice cream can be prepared up to 6 hours ahead. Keep frozen.*

FOR THE WAFFLES

Whisk the flour, sugar, yeast, and fleur de sel in a large bowl to blend. Add the egg yolks, melted butter, and ½ cup of the milk. Stir to blend. Mix in the remaining ½ cup milk. Using a clean whisk or an electric mixer, beat the egg whites in another large bowl until semifirm peaks form. Fold the egg whites into the batter. Cover and refrigerate until the batter has doubled, at least 2 hours and up to 2 days ahead.

Preheat the oven to 200°F. Preheat a Belgian waffle iron according to the manufacturer's instructions. Spoon ½ cup of the batter onto the iron for each individual waffle. Cover and cook until golden brown, crisp, and just cooked through, about 7 minutes (cooking times will vary and are based on the waffle iron used). Transfer the waffle to a baking sheet and keep warm in the oven. Repeat, making 6 waffles total.

Place a warm waffle in the center of each of 6 plates. Sift the powdered sugar over the waffles. Spoon a scoop of the chestnut ice cream atop the waffles and serve immediately.

CARAMEL FLAN

This is a classic dish that is the essence of simplicity, yet far from easy to get just right. The custard should walk a tightrope between firmness and lightness. When it does, it's a wonderful textural sensation. The flans can be prepared up to two days in advance. The important thing is to make sure they're cold before you serve them, so refrigerate them for at least six hours.

6 SERVINGS

2 cups sugar
¼ cup water
4 cups whole milk
1 vanilla bean, split lengthwise
6 large eggs

Position the oven rack in the center of the oven and preheat the oven to 325ºF. Set six 9-ounce soufflé dishes in a roasting pan. Combine 1 cup of the sugar and the water in a heavy small saucepan. Stir over medium-high heat until the sugar dissolves. Boil without stirring until the syrup turns a deep golden brown color, occasionally brushing down the sides of the pan with a wet pastry brush and swirling the pan, about 4 minutes. Immediately pour the caramel into the soufflé dishes, dividing equally. Set aside.

Meanwhile, pour the milk into a heavy medium saucepan. Scrape the seeds from the vanilla bean into the milk; add the bean. Bring to a simmer over medium heat. Remove from the heat.

Whisk the remaining 1 cup sugar and the eggs in a large bowl until the sugar is dissolved and the mixture is foamy, about 5 minutes. Gradually whisk in the hot milk mixture. Remove the bean. Pour the custard into the prepared soufflé dishes, dividing evenly. Transfer the roasting pan to the oven. Pour enough hot water into the pan to come halfway up the sides of the dishes.

Bake until the outer 1-inch perimeters of the flans are softly set but the centers are still loose, about 35 minutes (the custard will firm up after it is refrigerated). Transfer the flans to a rack and cool. Refrigerate until cold, about 2 hours. Cover and keep refrigerated overnight.

TO SERVE

Run a small sharp knife around each flan to loosen it from the dish. Working with 1 flan at a time, place a plate atop the flan; invert the flan onto the plate. Shake gently to release the flan from the dish (you will hear it being released). Carefully remove the dish, allowing the caramel syrup to run over the flan.

APPLE BEIGNETS WITH GREEN APPLE AND CALVADOS GRANITÉ

I like to eat this dish with my fingers! Spoon the granité onto the beignet and bite in. I think you'll enjoy the contrast between the crunchy beignet and the soft granité, as well as the dueling hot and cold sensations in your mouth.

4 SERVINGS

- ¾ cup all-purpose flour
- ½ cup cornstarch
- 1 teaspoon baking powder
- ½ teaspoon fleur de sel
- 1 cup ice-cold good-quality lager
  Canola oil (for deep-frying)
- 4 Fuji or Pink Lady apples, peeled and cored
  Powdered sugar (for sifting)
  Green Apple and Calvados Granité
  (recipe follows)

Whisk the flour, cornstarch, baking powder, and fleur de sel in a medium bowl to blend. Add the lager. Whisk until the batter is almost smooth.

TO FINISH AND SERVE

Add enough oil to a large wide frying pan to come 2 inches up the sides of the pan. Heat the oil over medium heat until a deep-fry thermometer registers 375ºF.

Meanwhile, line a large baking sheet with paper towels. Cut each apple crosswise into 3 rings. Arrange the apple rings in a single layer on the prepared baking sheet. Pat the apple rings dry with additional paper towels. Working in batches, sift the powdered sugar over both sides of the apple rings, then dip the apple rings into the batter to coat lightly; shake the excess batter back into the bowl. Add the apple rings to the hot oil and fry until the coating is golden brown, about 2 minutes per side. Using tongs, transfer the beignets to paper towels to drain.

Sift more powdered sugar over the beignets. Arrange 3 beignets on each of 4 plates. Spoon the granité into small dessert bowls. Serve immediately.

GREEN APPLE AND CALVADOS GRANITÉ

MAKES ABOUT 4 CUPS

4 Granny Smith apples (about 1½ pounds),
   cored and coarsely chopped
½ cup sugar
3 tablespoons strained fresh lemon juice
2 tablespoons Calvados or apple brandy

Place an 8-inch square glass container in the freezer. Combine all the ingredients in a food processor and blend until the apples are coarsely pureed. Strain the juice mixture through a fine-mesh strainer and into the frozen glass container. Cover and freeze, stirring occasionally, until the liquid just becomes slushy, about 2 hours. Keep the mixture in the freezer, scraping it every 30 minutes with a fork until it is completely made up of ice crystals, about 3 hours longer.

DO AHEAD: *The granité can be prepared up to 1 day ahead. Keep frozen.*

SMELL

HEAR
TASTE
SEE
TOUCH
SMELL
HEAR
TASTE
SEE
TOUCH
SMELL
HEAR
TASTE
SEE
TOUCH
SMELL
HEAR
TASTE
SEE
TOUCH
SMELL

SEE

TOUCH

SMELL

{ HEAR }

TASTE

+ CHAPTER 3 —

IN A LOT OF WAYS, IT'S HARD TO SEPARATE OUR
SENSE OF SMELL FROM OUR SENSE OF TASTE.

OUR TASTE BUDS CAN INTERPRET FOUR DIFFERENT TASTES—SWEET, SOUR, BITTER, AND SALT—

BUT IT'S OUR NOSE THAT FILLS IN ALL THE BLANKS IN BETWEEN AND ALLOWS US TO EXPERIENCE

FLAVOR IN THREE DIMENSIONS. IT'S NOT JUST THAT WE INHALE THE VAPOR WHEN THE DISH IS PUT

BEFORE US; OUR SINUS PASSAGES ARE TICKLED ONCE MORE JUST BEFORE WE SWALLOW, SENDING

BEAUTIFUL MESSAGES TO OUR BRAINS. EVERYONE HAS AT SOME TIME SAT DOWN TO A MEAL WITH

A NOSE PLUGGED UP FROM A BAD COLD. YOU CAN HARDLY TASTE A THING. THE FLAVORS ARE

MUTED, LIKE A MUFFLED CONVERSATION TAKING PLACE IN ANOTHER ROOM.

THE ARABS BELIEVED THAT FRAGRANCE WAS THE STRONGEST LINK BETWEEN

THE BODY AND THE SOUL, AND THAT AROMATICS FED THE BREATH, WHICH THEY EQUATED WITH THE

SPIRIT. THEY BELIEVED THAT STRONG FRAGRANCES POSSESSED GREAT MEDICINAL POWER, AND

FROM SPICES AND HERBS THEY CREATED MANY PUNGENT TONICS AND ELIXIRS TO CURE BODILY ILLS

AND SPIRITUAL MALAISE ALIKE. IN THE HIGH MIDDLE AGES, COOKING WAS STRONGLY LINKED TO

ALCHEMY, AND PEOPLE WERE OFTEN FAR MORE CONCERNED WITH THE WAY FOOD SMELLED THAN

THE WAY IT TASTED. (IT WASN'T UNTIL THE LATE SEVENTEENTH CENTURY THAT FRENCH CUISINE

BROKE AWAY FROM THIS EXTREME USE OF SPICES AND FOCUSED MORE ON HARMONIZING FLAVORS.)

AND TO THIS DAY, THE CHINESE CONTINUE TO USE HERBS AND SPICES AS MEDICINE.

One of the most soothing aromas is that of fresh bread coming straight from the oven.

Still, I believe that even after you sweep away all of these ancient ideas, smell is the sense that bonds us most profoundly to food on an emotional level. It is the sense that truly connects body and soul, and it is the sense that is most strongly connected to memory, and to emotion. We never forget the scent worn by our first true love; the minute someone walks into the room wearing the same fragrance, we're transported to another time and place.

The same thing happens with cooking. Certain dishes from childhood, when their perfume is emanating from a pot on the kitchen stove or a pan in the oven, have the power to make us feel comfortable and secure. To me, one of the most soothing aromas is that of fresh bread coming straight from the oven. It reminds me of my grandmother, who loved to bake.

One thing I've noticed from visiting spice shops is the incredible passion the people who run them have for their wares. Here, the spices aren't locked away in small glass bottles sealed in plastic, as they are in the supermarket. They're sold in bulk, and their perfume is incredibly pungent and seductive. I suspect that spice merchants spend much of their time in a beautiful state of benign intoxication. The moment the merchant notices your enthusiasm for this whole new universe of sensations, you can spend a half a day as he beckons you to inhale deeply from his wares. So it is with my friend Perry Doty, a spice expert, who had taught me volumes. "Here, check this out! Have you ever smelled anything like that in your life?" he'll ask, as excited as if he were fussing over a newborn son. "But what do you do with it?" I'll ask, and he'll reel off any number of suggestions. We've become good friends over this shared passion.

It's the same in the market. The pungent scent of fresh herbs, the sweet perfume of young strawberries—you don't even need to see the produce, because your nose tells you so much about it. Our sense of smell also tells us quite insistently when something is bad. It is impossible to get food that has spoiled past our nostrils.

Every now and then I like to design a dish that I know will work its way through the sinuses and lift you up by your sense of smell. Of course, some dishes infuse the house with their perfume while they're cooking, and sometimes I'll decide to prepare a certain dish, such as chicken in dried verbena and curry leaves, just to fill the house with its scent.

One way to create an intensely aromatic experience is to seal in the vapors while the dish is cooking. Your guests will be dazzled when you open the thing up and a cloud of intense aromatic vapor comes pouring out. There are a couple of techniques for this. One is to cook *à l'étouffée*. It's a classic technique that basically means cooking with a very tight lid to seal in the vapors, although I like to take it a step further and create a perfect seal by placing a strip of dough around the top of the pot. (See Chicken Etouffée in Dried Verbena and Curry Leaves, page 138.) The other is to cook *en papillote*, which means enclosing the food in paper and letting the steam puff it up. It's a little more work, but well worth it. (See Red Mullet en Papillote with Salted Butter and Citrus Zest, page 124.)

When your sense of smell has been awakened, it's amazing what can happen.

At home, I like to invite people into the kitchen before the meal is prepared. The fragrances emanating from the stove and oven always get them excited.

Nothing stimulates my appetite and my imagination like going out into nature and concentrating on its smells: the wind rustling through the leaves in the forest, the surf at the beach, the pine trees as they bake in the mountain sun. I'll never forget digging truffles in the winter in France. Their powerful, earthy bouquet cutting through the cold air never failed to arouse my imagination. (An aside on truffles: Lore has it that they're an aphrodisiac. I don't know if that's true, but I do know that in the restaurant, once I've sent out the first order of a white truffle risotto and its perfume has had a chance to permeate the room, the orders for it start to multiply immediately. The guests may not fall in love with each other, but they sure fall in love with the smell of truffles.)

MUSSEL VELOUTÉ WITH CURRY

The curry that infuses this wine-based velouté sauce is softer than most and has a distinctly floral character that sings the praises of the mussels without drowning out their flavor. (It also complements vegetables, fish, and chicken.)

6 APPETIZER SERVINGS

- 1 tablespoon unsalted butter
- 1 shallot, thinly sliced
- 1 cup good-quality dry white wine
- 2 pounds black mussels (about 60), scrubbed and debearded
- 1 cup heavy whipping cream
- 1½ teaspoons Curry Powder (page 241)
- 4 fresh chervil sprigs
- 4 fresh peppermint sprigs

Melt the butter in a heavy 5-quart pot over medium heat. Add the shallot and sauté until tender, about 2 minutes. Add the wine; bring to a boil over high heat. Stir in the mussels. Cover and cook just until the mussels open, about 2 minutes. Stir the mussels in the cooking liquid and cook for 2 minutes longer. Discard any mussels that do not open. Using tongs, transfer the mussels to a large bowl; cover loosely to keep them warm. Strain the cooking liquid through a fine-mesh strainer and into a large glass measuring cup; discard the shallots. Return the cooking liquid to the pot. Add the cream and the Curry Powder. Cover and steep for 5 minutes over low heat.

Divide the mussels and cooking liquid among 4 wide shallow bowls. Garnish with the chervil and peppermint. Serve immediately.

RED MULLET EN PAPILLOTE WITH SALTED BUTTER AND CITRUS ZEST

En papillote is a traditional cooking method in which food is enclosed in parchment paper and baked. It intensifies the taste by compressing aromatic steam within the paper, sealing in flavor. It's also part magic act: The paper puffs up and, when slit open to reveal the red mullets dusted with citrus zest, an aromatic cloud of vapor unfurls that's sure to whet your appetite.

4 APPETIZER SERVINGS

8 teaspoons salted butter

8 1-ounce red mullet fillets with the skin, scales removed

1 teaspoon finely grated orange peel

1 teaspoon finely grated lemon peel

1 teaspoon extra virgin olive oil

Position the oven rack in the lower third of the oven and preheat the oven to 400°F. Cut out four 15 x 12-inch pieces of parchment paper. Fold one piece of parchment paper in half to make a 12 x 7½-inch rectangle, then unfold the paper on a work surface. Spread 1 teaspoon of the butter in the center of half the paper, covering an area the size of 2 fillets. Place 2 fillets, side by side and skin side up, atop the buttered area. Dot the fillets with 1 teaspoon butter. Sprinkle ¼ teaspoon of the orange peel and ¼ teaspoon of the lemon peel over the fillets. Sprinkle with freshly ground white pepper. Fold the second half of the paper over the fish. Beginning at one end of the folded corners, seal the package by folding the edges of the paper at 1-inch increments, overlapping the folds along the edges and tapering the paper inward at the corner to form a crescent-shaped package. Repeat to form 4 packages total.

DO AHEAD: *The fish packages can be prepared up to 4 hours ahead. Cover and refrigerate.*

TO FINISH AND SERVE

Drizzle the olive oil over a heavy large rimmed baking sheet. Place the baking sheet in the preheated oven just until the oil begins to smoke, about 5 minutes. Arrange the packages on the hot baking sheet. Bake until the packages puff and the fish is just cooked through, about 5 minutes. Transfer 1 package to each of 4 plates. Serve immediately, then cut the top of the packages open.

ESCARGOTS WITH SHALLOT MOUSSE
AND PARSLEY COULIS

Escargots (okay, snails, let's face it) are a favorite in my native Burgundy, where they're usually loaded up with so much garlic you can't really taste—or smell—much else. But good escargots, with their intriguingly earthy flavor, are worth tasting. I still like garlic with escargots, but I've found a way to soften it by adding a dollop of shallot mousse, which adds a high note but isn't too domineering. Also, the sharpness of the shallots is muted by the parsley coulis.

6 APPETIZER SERVINGS

Shallot Mousse

6 ounces shallots (about 12 medium), peeled

⅓ cup heavy whipping cream

Fleur de sel and freshly ground pepper

Parsley Coulis

2 large bunches fresh flat-leaf parsley, stems removed (about 4 cups)

1 tablespoon unsalted butter

Escargots

3 tablespoons extra virgin olive oil

6 dozen canned cooked tiny escargots (about 4 ounces), drained and rinsed

6 garlic cloves, finely chopped

¼ cup chopped fresh flat-leaf parsley

Pea shoots or watercress (for garnish)

FOR THE SHALLOT MOUSSE

Cook the shallots in a medium saucepan of boiling water until very soft, about 8 minutes. Drain the water. Transfer the shallots to a food processor and puree until smooth. Press the shallot puree through a fine-mesh strainer and into a small bowl. Cover and refrigerate until cold.

Beat the cream in a large bowl until stiff. Fold the cold shallot puree into the cream. Season the shallot mousse to taste with fleur de sel and pepper. Cover and refrigerate.

DO AHEAD: *The mousse can be prepared up to 4 hours ahead. Keep refrigerated.*

FOR THE PARSLEY COULIS

Cook the parsley in a large pot of boiling salted water until the leaves are very soft but still green, about 3 minutes. Drain. Transfer the parsley to a large bowl of ice water to cool. Drain again. Transfer the parsley to a food processor and puree with 3 ice cubes until smooth. Stir the parsley coulis in a small saucepan over medium-high heat until hot but not boiling. Whisk in the butter. Season the coulis to taste with fleur de sel and pepper.

FOR THE ESCARGOTS

Heat the oil in a large sauté pan over medium-high heat. Add the escargots and sauté just until heated through, about 3 minutes. Remove the pan from the heat. Add the garlic and parsley; toss to coat the escargots. Season to taste with fleur de sel and pepper.

TO ASSEMBLE AND SERVE

Using two small spoons, form the shallot mousse into 4 oval-shaped quenelles. Place 1 quenelle in the center of each of 4 pasta bowls. Spoon the parsley coulis around the quenelles. Arrange the escargots atop the coulis. Garnish with the pea shoots or watercress and serve immediately.

SCALLOPS ON THE HALF SHELL
WITH CITRUS GRATIN

This is my twist on an American classic, Oysters Rockefeller, except that instead of oysters, we use scallops, and instead of spinach, citrus gratin. (Well, they both have bread crumbs.) Part of the fun is the way the citrus gratin tickles your nose.

4 APPETIZER SERVINGS

1 cup unsalted butter, room temperature
$\frac{1}{2}$ cup dried bread crumbs
1$\frac{1}{2}$ tablespoons finely grated orange peel
1$\frac{1}{2}$ tablespoons finely grated lemon peel
3 tablespoons strained fresh orange juice
3 tablespoons strained fresh lemon juice
Fleur de sel and freshly ground pepper
24 fresh small scallops on the half shell
2 cups (about) rock salt

Using an electric mixer, beat the butter, bread crumbs, orange peel, and lemon peel in a large bowl until light and fluffy. Gradually beat in the orange juice and lemon juice. Season the citrus butter to taste with fleur de sel and freshly ground white pepper.

DO AHEAD: *The citrus butter can be prepared up to 1 day ahead. Cover and refrigerate. Bring to room temperature before using.*

Preheat the broiler. Arrange the scallops in their half shells on a heavy baking sheet. Using 1 generous tablespoon of citrus butter for each scallop, spread an even layer of the citrus butter atop the scallops, covering the meat and shell completely. Broil until the citrus butter browns on top, about 5 minutes.

Cover 4 large plates with the rock salt. Arrange 6 scallops in their shells on each plate atop the salt. Serve immediately.

SAUTÉED VEGETABLES WITH CURRY

This versatile side dish goes particularly well with simple entrees. I like to serve it on top of mashed potatoes.

6 SIDE-DISH SERVINGS

Curry Spices

- 1 tablespoon coriander seeds
- 1½ teaspoons cumin seeds
- 1½ teaspoons brown or yellow mustard seeds
- 1 teaspoon ground cayenne pepper
- ¾ teaspoon fenugreek seeds
- ¾ teaspoon ground turmeric

Vegetables

- 16 fingerling potatoes, cut crosswise into ⅛-inch-thick slices (about 2 cups)
- 8 ounces cauliflower florets, trimmed into very small individual florets (about 1 cup)
- 2 small turnips, peeled, cut into ⅛-inch-thick 1-inch squares (about 1 cup)
- 2 carrots, peeled, cut crosswise into ⅛-inch-thick rounds (about 1 cup)
- 1 small celery root, peeled, cut into ⅛-inch-thick 1-inch squares (about 1 cup)
- ¼ head of Savoy cabbage (about 8 ounces), thinly sliced (about 2 cups)
- ¼ cup Clarified Butter (page 243)
- 1 onion, very thinly sliced
- 1 garlic clove, finely chopped
- 4 dried curry leaves
- 1 cup canned unsweetened coconut milk
  Fleur de sel and freshly ground pepper

FOR THE CURRY SPICES

Combine all the spices in a spice grinder. Blend until the spices are very finely ground. Set aside.

FOR THE VEGETABLES

Blanch the potatoes, cauliflower, turnips, carrots, and celery root in a large pot of boiling water until crisp-tender, about 2 minutes. Strain the vegetables out from the boiling water. Transfer the vegetables to a large bowl of ice water to cool completely. Drain the vegetables well. Using the same boiling water, blanch the cabbage. Drain, then cool the cabbage separately in another bowl of ice water. Drain the cabbage well.

Heat the clarified butter in a heavy large wok over medium-high heat. Add the onion and sauté until tender and the edges begin to brown, about 5 minutes. Add the garlic; sauté until fragrant, about 30 seconds. Add the curry spices and curry leaves; sauté until fragrant, about 30 seconds. Add the potatoes, cauliflower, turnips, carrots, and celery root. Sauté 1 minute. Add the coconut milk. Simmer until the vegetables are heated through, about 2 minutes. Add the cabbage. Simmer until the cabbage is tender, adding a small amount of water to thin the sauce if desired, about 1 minute longer. Season to taste with fleur de sel and pepper.

Divide the vegetable curry equally among 4 shallow soup plates. Serve immediately.

RUM VINEGAR

This aromatic condiment goes particularly well with seafood; drizzle a bit of it on grilled fish after it's cooked. It's also a nice complement to fruit salads, and an easy way to add pizzazz when you're cooking simple dishes.

MAKES ABOUT 2 CUPS

8 long peppers

1 Ceylon cinnamon stick, broken into pieces

4 whole cloves

2 vanilla beans, cut into 1-inch pieces

¼ cup whole coriander seeds

¼ cup finely shredded mace

¼ cup toasted peanuts

¼ cup unsalted butter

4 carrots, peeled and finely chopped

¼ cup ¼-inch pieces of peeled fresh ginger

2 cups cane vinegar or Japanese-style rice vinegar

1 cup Fish Stock (page 240)

1 cup Chicken Stock (page 239)

½ cup dark rum

4 2-inch pieces of sugar cane

Mix the first 7 ingredients together in a spice grinder until coarsely ground. Set the spice powder aside.

Melt the butter in a heavy large saucepan over medium heat. Add the carrots and ginger. Sauté until the carrots are crisp-tender (do not allow the carrots to brown), about 8 minutes. Mix in ½ cup of the spice powder. Add the vinegar; bring to a boil. Add the fish stock and chicken stock. Cover and simmer gently over low heat to infuse the vinegar mixture, about 30 minutes. Remove from the heat. Keep the mixture covered and let stand for 1 hour.

Strain the vinegar mixture through a fine-mesh strainer and into a 2-cup glass measuring cup, pressing on the solids with the back of a ladle to extract as much liquid as possible. Discard the solids. Using a funnel, transfer the vinegar to a jar. Add the rum and sugar cane. Seal the bottle with the lid. Refrigerate at least 2 days and up to 1 week before using so that the flavorings will have a chance to infuse the rum. The vinegar should keep, refrigerated, for at least 3 months.

VEGETABLE TART WITH DRIED FRUIT

This combination of savory and sweet is sure to get anyone's mouth watering.

4 APPETIZER SERVINGS

Tarts

- 2 vine-ripened tomatoes, each cut crosswise into 4 rounds
- 2 tablespoons plus 4 teaspoons extra virgin olive oil
   Fleur de sel and freshly ground pepper
- 8 baby carrots, peeled and blanched
- 4 shallots, peeled and blanched
- 4 pearl onions, blanched and peeled
- 8 fresh shiitake mushrooms, stems removed
- 2 tablespoons unsalted butter
- 1 tablespoon sugar
- 1 Granny Smith apple, peeled, cored, and cut crosswise into 1/8-inch-thick rounds
- 8 toasted whole pecans
- 2 dried black Mission figs, halved
- 2 dried apricots, halved
- 2 tablespoons golden raisins
- 1 large egg, beaten to blend
- 2 10-ounce pieces of Puff Pastry Dough (page 242)

Sauce

- 2 2-ounce mackerel fillets, sliced
- 1 cup Fish Stock (page 240)
- 1/4 cup heavy whipping cream
   Pinch of saffron threads

FOR THE TARTS

Preheat the oven to 375°F. Arrange the tomato slices on a heavy small baking sheet. Drizzle 1 tablespoon of the oil over the tomatoes. Season with fleur de sel and pepper. Bake the tomatoes until they are tender but still hold their shape, about 8 minutes.

Meanwhile, drizzle 1 teaspoon oil into each of four 9-inch pasta bowls. Distribute the carrots, shallots, and pearl onions among the bowls. Heat 1 tablespoon olive oil in a heavy medium sauté pan over medium heat. Add the mushrooms and sauté until tender, about 2 minutes per side. Transfer 2 mushrooms to each bowl.

Melt the butter in a heavy large sauté pan over medium-high heat. Sprinkle in the sugar. Working in batches, add the apple slices in a single layer and cook just until golden brown, about 30 seconds per side. Transfer the apples to the bowls. Top with the pecans, figs, apricots, raisins, and tomato slices. Season with fleur de sel and pepper.

Cut each piece of pastry dough in half. Roll out each piece into a 12-inch round (about 1/8 inch thin). Transfer 2 pastry rounds to a baking sheet. Cover with wax paper. Top with the remaining 2 pastry rounds. Cover and refrigerate until the pastry rounds are very cold, about 30 minutes.

Brush the edges of the bowls with the beaten egg. Lightly coat 1 side of each pastry with the egg. Place 1 pastry round, coated side up, atop each bowl. Press the dough firmly to the outside of each bowl.

MEANWHILE, PREPARE THE SAUCE

Bring the mackerel and fish stock to a boil in a heavy small saucepan over medium-high heat. Reduce the heat to medium and simmer until the liquid is reduced by half, about 12 minutes. Whisk in the cream, and simmer for 3 minutes longer. Transfer the fish mixture to a food processor and puree until almost smooth. Strain the sauce through a fine-mesh strainer and into the same saucepan, pressing to extract as much liquid as possible; discard the solids. Whisk in the saffron. Season the sauce with fleur de sel and pepper. Keep warm.

DO AHEAD: *At this point, the tarts and sauce can be prepared up to 8 hours ahead. Cover the tarts and keep them refrigerated. Cool the sauce, then cover and refrigerate it. Rewarm the sauce before serving.*

TO FINISH AND SERVE

Preheat the oven to 400°F. Place the tarts on 2 heavy large baking sheets. Bake until the pastry puffs and is golden brown, about 25 minutes. Cut an incision around the rim of the crust. Transfer the crusts to 4 side plates. Spoon the sauce over the filling and serve with the crusts alongside.

WHITE SEA BASS WITH ROASTED FIGS AND FOUR SPICES

This incredibly fragrant dish is almost as much fun to smell as it is to eat. The fish is sautéed with fresh bay leaves, the sauce is redolent of cinnamon and figs, and the four powdered spices—cloves, white pepper, ginger, and nutmeg—make it wonderfully aromatic. Inhale! Fresh figs are usually available from June to October.

4 MAIN-COURSE SERVINGS

Sauce

2 cups good-quality dry red wine
½ cup ruby port
4 fresh black Mission or honey figs, stemmed and coarsely chopped
1 Ceylon cinnamon stick
2 tablespoons chilled unsalted butter, cut into pieces
  Fleur de sel and freshly ground pepper

Roasted Figs

16 fresh black Mission or honey figs, stemmed
2 tablespoons unsalted butter
1 tablespoon sugar

Fish

4 6-ounce white sea bass fillets
2 tablespoons extra virgin olive oil
6 fresh bay leaves, scored
1 cup Creamed Leeks (page 135)
1 teaspoon Four Spices Powder (page 241)

FOR THE SAUCE

Combine the wine, port, figs, and cinnamon stick in a heavy medium saucepan. Boil over medium-high heat until reduced by half, about 5 minutes. Discard the cinnamon stick. Transfer the mixture to a blender and puree. Strain the sauce through a fine-mesh strainer and into the saucepan. Whisk in the butter to form a smooth sauce. Season the sauce to taste with fleur de sel and pepper. Set aside and keep warm.

FOR THE ROASTED FIGS

Preheat the oven to 375°F. Trim the tops and bottoms of the figs. Cut an X 1 inch down the tops of the figs. Arrange the figs on a heavy rimmed baking sheet. Dab each fig with butter, then sprinkle with sugar. Bake until the figs are tender but still hold their shape, about 8 minutes.

FOR THE FISH

Sprinkle the fish fillets with fleur de sel and pepper. Heat the oil in a heavy large sauté pan over medium heat. Add the bay leaves and sauté until fragrant, about 30 seconds (do not allow the leaves to brown). Transfer the leaves to a paper towel to drain; set aside. Add the fish to the sauté pan and cook over medium heat until opaque in the center, about 4 minutes per side.

TO ASSEMBLE AND SERVE

Spoon the creamed leeks in the center of 4 large dinner plates. Top with the fish. Spoon the sauce around the fish and leeks. Place 1 roasted fig in each corner on the plates. Sift the four spices powder over the figs. Place the sautéed bay leaves atop the fish and serve immediately.

CHANTERELLES WITH VINEGAR
AND GREEN CARDAMOM

Sweet, sour, and fragrant, these preserved mushrooms go well with both shellfish and prime rib. They need at least two days to mature, and are best after two weeks. When mushroom season arrives, you may want to prepare three pounds or so; they'll keep for three months in the refrigerator.

MAKES ABOUT 3 CUPS

8 ounces fresh chanterelle mushrooms, brushed clean of any grit
¾ cup honey, preferably acacia
¾ cup distilled white vinegar
15 whole coriander seeds
4 whole green cardamom pods

Cut the smaller chanterelle mushrooms lengthwise in half, and quarter the larger mushrooms lengthwise. Cook the honey in a heavy large saucepan over medium heat until amber brown, about 4 minutes. Remove from the heat. Add the vinegar (the mixture will bubble vigorously); stir to blend. Mix in the coriander seeds and cardamom pods. Add the mushrooms; toss to coat.

Transfer the mixture to two 12-ounce preserving jars. Seal the jar. Refrigerate for at least 2 days before using to let the flavors mingle. The mushrooms should keep for up to 3 months.

CREAMY PUMPKIN SOUP

This is a wonderful dish for autumn, particularly in November, when Thanksgiving comes around and pumpkins are in season. You'll love the smell of the bacon mingling with the spiced white bread, and of course the sweet, savory aroma of the pumpkin itself.

6 APPETIZER SERVINGS

2 tablespoons extra virgin olive oil

1 onion, chopped

1 leek (white and pale green parts only), chopped

1 3-pound sugar pumpkin, peeled, seeded, and coarsely chopped into 1-inch pieces (about 6 cups)

4 cups Chicken Stock (page 239)

1/2 cup heavy whipping cream

2 tablespoons unsalted butter
   Fleur de sel and freshly ground pepper

2 ounces thick-sliced bacon, cut crosswise into 1/8-inch-wide strips

1 slice Spiced White Bread (page 243), crust trimmed, cut into 1/2-inch cubes

Heat the oil in a heavy large pot over medium heat. Add the onion and leek; sauté until tender but not brown, about 10 minutes. Add the pumpkin and chicken stock. Bring to a boil over medium-high heat. Reduce the heat to medium and cook until the pumpkin is very tender, stirring occasionally, about 15 minutes. Working in batches, transfer the pumpkin mixture to a blender and puree until smooth. Return the soup to the pot. Whisk in the cream and butter. Season the soup to taste with fleur de sel and pepper.

DO AHEAD: *The soup can be prepared up to 8 hours ahead. Cool. Cover and refrigerate. Rewarm over medium-low heat before serving.*

Sauté the bacon in a heavy small sauté pan over medium-low heat until brown and crisp, about 5 minutes. Using a slotted spoon, transfer the bacon to paper towels to drain. Add the bread cubes to the pan drippings and sauté until golden brown, about 4 minutes. Using a slotted spoon, transfer the croutons to paper towels to drain. Season the croutons to taste with fleur de sel and pepper.

Ladle the soup into 6 wide shallow bowls. Garnish with the bacon and croutons. Serve immediately.

JOHN DORY IN HERB-FENNEL BOUILLON WITH VEGETABLES, LEMON CONFIT, AND CREAMED LEEKS

I was at the farmers' market, gathering produce for the week's menu, when an incredible mélange of aromas tickled my nose. I stopped in my tracks and turned toward the stall, where bundles of fresh tarragon, basil, cilantro, dill, and other herbs filled the air with their tantalizing scents. I wanted to make a dish that would capture that same sensation of standing over a table heaped with farm-fresh herbs and inhaling their essence. I decided to pack the flavor of the herbs themselves into a light bouillon, which is served around the John Dory. In this way, the forestlike perfume of the herbs still allows the delicate flavor of the fish to come through.

4 MAIN-COURSE SERVINGS

Herb-Fennel Bouillon

2 small fresh sprigs each of basil, cilantro, dill, parsley, sage, tarragon, thyme, and rosemary

2 cups Fish Stock (page 240)

1 fennel bulb, sliced

¼ cup Ricard or Pernod liqueur

Fish and Vegetables

4 4-ounce John Dory fillets

6 baby carrots, peeled, cut diagonally into ¼-inch-thick rounds and blanched

4 asparagus stalks, cut diagonally into ¼-inch-thick rounds and blanched

2 sweet baby Maui onions, blanched and thinly sliced crosswise

2 shallots, thinly sliced crosswise

1 fennel bulb, thinly sliced

1 tablespoon Ricard or Pernod liqueur
   Fleur de sel and freshly ground pepper

4 tablespoons Lemon Confit (page 244)
   Creamed Leeks (recipe follows)

FOR THE HERB-FENNEL BOUILLON

Remove the leaves from the stems of the herb sprigs. Cover and refrigerate the leaves. Place the stems in a heavy medium saucepan; add the fish stock, fennel, and Ricard. Bring to a boil. Remove the bouillon from the heat. Cover and let steep for 15 minutes. Strain the bouillon into a small bowl; discard the solids. Allow the bouillon to cool to 140°F.

DO AHEAD: *The bouillon can be prepared up to 1 day ahead. Cool completely. Cover and refrigerate. Rewarm before continuing.*

FOR THE FISH AND VEGETABLES

Preheat the oven to 400°F. Arrange the fish fillets in a 13 x 9-inch roasting pan. Pour 1 cup of the warm (140°F) bouillon over the fish. Bake until the fish is just opaque in the center and beginning to flake, about 8 minutes. Discard the poaching liquid.

Meanwhile, combine the remaining 1 cup bouillon, carrots, asparagus, baby onions, shallots, fennel, and Ricard in a medium saucepan. Bring the bouillon to a simmer. Season to taste with fleur de sel and pepper.

TO ASSEMBLE AND SERVE

Place a fillet in the center of each of 4 large shallow soup plates. Spoon the vegetable and bouillon mixture around the fish. Brush the top of each fillet with 1 tablespoon lemon confit. Serve with the warm creamed leeks. Sprinkle the reserved herb leaves over the fillets and serve immediately.

CREAMED LEEKS

MAKES ABOUT 1 CUP

2 large leeks (white and pale green parts only), sliced crosswise

1 cup heavy whipping cream

Fleur de sel and freshly ground pepper

Cook the leek slices in a large saucepan of boiling water until crisp-tender, about 30 seconds. Drain. Transfer the leek slices to a bowl of ice water to cool. Drain again.

Combine the leek slices and cream in a heavy medium saucepan. Cook over low heat until the mixture thickens and the leek slices become very tender, stirring occasionally, about 30 minutes. Season the mixture to taste with fleur de sel and pepper.

DO AHEAD: *The creamed leeks can be prepared up to 6 hours ahead. Cover and refrigerate. Rewarm over low heat before using.*

ROASTED VEAL TENDERLOIN WITH CARAMEL SAUCE AND BELGIAN ENDIVE TARTE TATIN

Making the caramel sauce that accompanies this veal tenderloin is a high-wire act for your nostrils. The aroma is sweet but salty, and you may fear you're on the verge of disaster as the sugar begins to burn. But don't worry: the result is beautifully bittersweet.

4 MAIN-COURSE SERVINGS

Caramel Sauce

- 6 tablespoons sugar
- 2 tablespoons water
- 6 tablespoons sherry vinegar
- 2/3 cup Veal Stock (page 238)
- 1/2 cup fresh Belgian endive juice (from about 5 whole Belgian endives)
- 6 tablespoons unsalted butter
- 6 tablespoons strained fresh lemon juice
  Fleur de sel and freshly ground pepper

Veal

- 4 6- to 8-ounce veal tenderloins
- 2 tablespoons extra virgin olive oil

- 4 Belgian Endive Tartes Tatin (recipe follows)

FOR THE CARAMEL SAUCE

Combine the sugar and water in a heavy small saucepan. Stir over medium-high heat until the sugar dissolves. Boil without stirring until the syrup turns a deep golden brown, occasionally brushing down the sides of the pan with a wet pastry brush and swirling the pan, about 3 minutes. Remove from the heat. Add the vinegar (the mixture will bubble vigorously), then the veal stock and the endive juice. Boil until the sauce is reduced to 1/2 cup and thick, about 10 minutes. Whisk in the butter, then the lemon juice. Season the sauce to taste with fleur de sel and pepper. Keep warm.

FOR THE VEAL

Preheat the oven to 450°F. Sprinkle the veal with fleur de sel and pepper. Heat the oil in a large ovenproof sauté pan over medium-high heat. Add the veal and cook just until brown all over but not cooked through, about 8 minutes. Transfer the sauté pan to the oven and roast until an instant-read meat thermometer inserted into the center of the veal registers 130°F for medium-rare, about 8 minutes. Transfer the veal to a work surface; tent with aluminum foil, and let rest for 5 minutes.

TO ASSEMBLE AND SERVE

Cut each veal tenderloin crosswise into 4 equal pieces. Spoon the caramel sauce over the center of each of 4 large plates. Invert 1 Belgian endive tarte tatin atop the sauce on each plate. Arrange 4 veal pieces around the perimeter of each tart. Serve immediately.

BELGIAN ENDIVE TARTES TATIN

4 SIDE-DISH SERVINGS

2½ pounds Belgian endive (about 8 large
   endives)

2 tablespoons extra virgin olive oil

2 tablespoons sugar

½ cup strained freshly squeezed orange
   juice
   Fleur de sel and freshly ground pepper

1 10-ounce piece of Puff Pastry Dough
   (page 242)

Trim the core ends of the endives and peel away the leaves. Discard the cores (or reserve for making Belgian endive juice). Heat 1 tablespoon of the oil in a heavy large sauté pan over medium heat. Add 1 tablespoon of the sugar and stir until the sugar browns, about 2 minutes. Add half of the endive leaves and sauté until they are golden brown and crisp-tender, about 8 minutes. Add half of the orange juice and simmer until the juice is reduced by half, about 2 minutes. Transfer the cooked endive mixture to a baking sheet to cool. Repeat with the remaining oil, sugar, endive leaves, and orange juice. Season the mixture to taste with fleur de sel and pepper.

Butter four 4-inch nonstick cake pans. Arrange the most attractive endive leaves over the bottoms of the prepared cake pans, overlapping slightly. Then, evenly distribute the remaining leaves among the pans.

Roll out the puff pastry on a lightly floured work surface into a 20 x 5-inch rectangle that is about ¼ inch thick. Using a small sharp knife, cut out four 4½-inch rounds of puff pastry; remove the pastry trimmings. Transfer the pastry rounds to a small baking sheet. Cover and refrigerate until cold.

DO AHEAD: *At this point, the tartes and pastry rounds can be prepared up to 8 hours ahead. Cover separately and refrigerate.*

TO FINISH AND SERVE

Preheat the oven to 400°F. Place 1 puff pastry round atop the endive leaves in each pan; tuck in the edges. Place the pans on a baking sheet. Bake until the pastry puffs, about 20 minutes. Reduce the oven temperature to 350°F and continue baking until the endive leaves around the edges of the pans are caramelized and the pastry is golden brown, about 15 minutes longer. Let stand in the pans for 5 minutes.

Run a small sharp knife around the edges of the pans to loosen the tartes. Set 1 plate upside down on each tarte. Turn the tartes and plates over together to invert the tartes onto the plates. Remove the pans. Replace any endive leaves that may have become dislodged.

CHICKEN ÉTOUFFÉE IN DRIED VERBENA AND CURRY LEAVES

A l'étouffée is one of my favorite methods for preparing chicken. The term generally refers to any dish cooked with a tightly covered lid, but I like to take it a step further and seal the pot with a strip of dough, which locks in the flavor and renders an incredibly soft texture. In this case, dried verbena and curry leaves create an intense perfume within the pot. When unleashed in a cloud of vapor, you'll think a genie has escaped from a bottle. Don't be afraid to re-create this dish with other herbs and spices of your choice.

4 MAIN-COURSE SERVINGS

Chicken Étouffée

1½ cups all-purpose flour
⅔ cup plus 1 cup water
1 cup dried lemon verbena leaves
1 cup dried curry leaves
1   4-pound whole chicken (liver, heart, gizzard, and neck removed)
    Fleur de sel and freshly ground pepper
2 teaspoons extra virgin olive oil

Porcini Mushrooms

1 tablespoon extra virgin olive oil
1 pound fresh porcini mushrooms, brushed clean of any grit, halved lengthwise
2 garlic cloves, minced
1 tablespoon chopped fresh flat-leaf parsley

FOR THE CHICKEN ÉTOUFFÉE

Preheat the oven to 375°F. Using a wooden spoon, stir the flour and ⅔ cup water in a large bowl until a dough forms. Roll out the dough on a lightly floured work surface into a 30-inch-long rope (or long enough to wrap around the perimeter of a 5½-quart Dutch oven). Cover and set aside. Combine the verbena leaves, curry leaves, and 1 cup water in a 5½-quart Dutch oven. Tie the chicken legs together to hold its shape. Rub the chicken all over with fleur de sel, pepper, and oil. Place the chicken atop the leaf mixture. Cover with the lid. Moisten the edges of the pot and lid with water. Wrap the dough rope around the edge of the pot and lid. Press the dough to adhere and seal well. Bake the chicken for 1 hour and 20 minutes. Remove the pan from the oven and let rest for 15 minutes (do not remove the dough crust).

MEANWHILE, FOR THE PORCINI MUSHROOMS

Heat the oil in a heavy large nonstick sauté pan over high heat. Add the mushrooms and the garlic. Sauté until the mushrooms are golden brown and crisp-tender, about 4 minutes. Remove the pan from the heat. Stir in the parsley. Season the mushrooms to taste with fleur de sel.

TO FINISH AND SERVE

Using a knife, cut the dough crust away from the pot. Remove the string from the chicken. Cut the legs, breasts, and thighs from the chicken. Cut the breasts in half. Place 2 pieces of chicken on each of 4 dinner plates. Surround with the sautéed mushrooms. Drizzle the pan juices from the Dutch oven over the chicken and serve.

NOTE: *If the chicken is not cooked through after the dough crust is removed, then cut the chicken into pieces as directed and return the chicken pieces to the pot. Cover and bake in the oven just until the chicken is cooked through.*

RED WINE-POACHED BEEF WITH STAR ANISE, LONG PEPPER, AND CARDAMOM INFUSION

Here's a refinement of the French classic beef à la bourguignon. I decided to poach the beef without searing it, as is usually done. Sliced very thin, the meat is as soft as butter. As much as the flavor, you'll enjoy the aroma of the wine and spices as they perfume your house.

4 MAIN-COURSE SERVINGS

Beef

1   750-ml bottle good-quality dry red wine
2   whole star anise
2   teaspoons coarsely ground long pepper
1   teaspoon coarsely ground green cardamom seeds
1   1¹/₂- to 2-pound (large end) piece of prime beef tenderloin, trimmed

Port Reduction Sauce

2   cups ruby port
1   cup Beef Stock (page 236)
2   tablespoons chilled unsalted butter, cut into pieces
    Fleur de sel and freshly ground black pepper

Additional freshly ground star anise, long pepper, and green cardamom (for garnish)
Caramelized Belgian Endive with Lemon (recipe follows)

FOR THE BEEF

Combine the wine, star anise, long pepper, and cardamom in a heavy large saucepan. Bring to a boil over high heat. Remove the cooking liquid from the heat and cool to 185°F. Add the beef to the cooking liquid. Place the saucepan over low heat so that the cooking liquid barely simmers. Cook, uncovered, until an instant-read meat thermometer inserted into the center of the beef registers 135°F for medium-rare, about 25 minutes.

MEANWHILE, PREPARE THE PORT REDUCTION SAUCE

Combine the port and beef stock in a heavy medium saucepan. Boil over high heat until the liquid thickens slightly and is reduced to ¹/₂ cup, about 25 minutes. Whisk in the butter to form a smooth sauce. Season the sauce to taste with fleur de sel and pepper. Keep warm.

TO ASSEMBLE AND SERVE

Cut the beef crosswise into 12 slices. Arrange the beef slices in the center of 4 large plates, overlapping slightly and dividing equally. Sprinkle the beef with fleur de sel and black pepper. Drizzle the port sauce around the beef. Sprinkle with the additional ground star anise, long pepper, and cardamom. Serve the caramelized belgian endive with lemon alongside.

CARAMELIZED BELGIAN ENDIVE WITH LEMON

4 SIDE-DISH SERVINGS

4 heads of Belgian endive

1 cup strained fresh lemon juice

1 cup water

   Fleur de sel and freshly ground pepper

2 tablespoons extra virgin olive oil

2 tablespoons sugar

Combine the endive, lemon juice, and water in a heavy medium saucepan. Cover and cook over low heat until the endive is tender, about 20 minutes. Using tongs, transfer the endive to a plate. Cool for 5 minutes. Cut each endive lengthwise in half. Using a small melon baller, trim the tough center core of the endive halves. Season the endive with fleur de sel and ground pepper.

Meanwhile, boil the cooking liquid until it is reduced to ¼ cup, about 12 minutes. Keep the lemon reduction warm.

TO FINISH AND ASSEMBLE

Heat the oil in a large nonstick sauté pan over medium-high heat. Sprinkle the sugar over the oil. Place the endive halves, cut side down, in the pan. Cook until the sugar begins to caramelize and the endive halves are golden brown, about 2 minutes per side.

Arrange 2 caramelized endive halves on each of 4 plates. Drizzle the warm lemon reduction over the endive and serve.

DUCK DUSTED WITH GRAND CARAVAN SPICES WITH CARAMELIZED SPICED PEARS AND BABY ROOT VEGETABLES

The duck is cooked two different ways: on the stove and in the oven, rendering crispy skin and moist, juicy flesh. However, the essence of this dish is its aromatic quality. I've chosen these spices in tribute to the caravans that traversed the Middle East in early medieval times.

4 MAIN-COURSE SERVINGS

Duck

- 1 5-pound duck (neck, heart, and gizzard removed)
   Fleur de sel and freshly ground white pepper
- 2 tablespoons extra virgin olive oil
- 1 teaspoon each freshly ground Ceylon cinnamon, coriander, dried ginger, green cardamom, mace, and nutmeg

Sauce

- 2 tablespoons sugar
- 2 tablespoons honey
- 3 tablespoons sherry vinegar
- ½ cup Duck Stock (page 239)
- 2 tablespoons strained fresh orange juice
- 2 tablespoons strained fresh lemon juice
- 2 tablespoons chilled unsalted butter

   Caramelized Spiced Pears and Baby Root Vegetables (recipe follows)

FOR THE DUCK

Preheat the oven to 400°F. Rinse the duck inside and out and pat it dry with paper towels. Rub it inside and out with fleur de sel and pepper. Heat 1 tablespoon of the oil over medium heat in a heavy large roasting pan that is just large enough to fit the duck. Add the duck to the roasting pan and roast until the duck is dark brown on all sides, about 45 minutes. Using tongs, lift the duck out of the roasting pan and slide a roasting rack under it and into the roasting pan. Set the duck, breast side up, on the rack. Roast it in the oven until an instant-read meat thermometer inserted into the innermost part of the thigh registers 140°F, about 20 minutes. Cover the pan loosely with aluminum foil. Set the pan atop the rear of the stove to allow the meat to absorb the juices, about 20 minutes.

Mix all the spices together in a heavy small sauté pan. Stir the spice mixture over medium-low heat until fragrant, about 2 minutes. Transfer the spice mixture to a fine-mesh shaker; set aside.

MEANWHILE, PREPARE THE SAUCE

Combine the sugar and honey in a heavy small saucepan. Stir over medium-high heat until the sugar dissolves. Boil without stirring until the syrup turns a deep golden brown, occasionally brushing down the sides of the pan with a wet pastry brush and swirling the pan, about 2 minutes. Remove from the heat. Carefully add the vinegar (the caramel will bubble vigorously), then the duck stock, orange juice, and lemon juice. Return to the heat. Boil until the sauce is reduced by half, about 6 minutes. Whisk in the butter until the sauce is smooth. Season the sauce to taste with fleur de sel and freshly ground white pepper. Keep warm.

TO FINISH AND SERVE

Return the duck to the oven just to rewarm, about 5 minutes. Brush the duck with the remaining 1 tablespoon oil. Generously dust the duck all over with the spice mixture. Transfer the duck to a serving platter. Spoon the caramelized spiced pears and baby root vegetables and any of their cooking liquid around the duck. Serve, passing the duck sauce alongside in a small bowl.

CARAMELIZED SPICED PEARS AND BABY ROOT VEGETABLES

4 SIDE-DISH SERVINGS

2 cups water

¾ cup plus 2 teaspoons sugar

1 Ceylon cinnamon stick

4 whole cloves

1 vanilla bean, split lengthwise

2 firm but ripe Bartlett pears, peeled and stemmed

8 baby turnips, peeled

8 baby red beets, peeled

1 tablespoon extra virgin olive oil

¾ cup Duck Stock (page 239)

Fleur de sel and freshly ground pepper

Stir the water, ¾ cup sugar, cinnamon, and cloves in a heavy medium saucepan to blend. Scrape the seeds from the vanilla bean into the sugar mixture; add the bean. Bring to a boil over medium-high heat, stirring until the sugar dissolves. Add the pears. Reduce the heat to medium-low and simmer until the pears are crisp-tender, about 15 minutes. Using a slotted spoon, transfer the pears to a bowl; cool. Cut the pears lengthwise in half. Using a melon baller, remove the core. Discard the poaching liquid.

Cook the turnips in a large saucepan of boiling salted water until just crisp-tender, about 5 minutes. Using a slotted spoon, transfer the turnips to a bowl of ice water to cool. Transfer the turnips to a plate; set aside. Cook the beets in the same saucepan of boiling salted water until crisp-tender, about 7 minutes. Using a slotted spoon, transfer the beets to the bowl of ice water to cool. Drain.

DO AHEAD: *At this point, the pears, turnips, and beets can be prepared up to 1 day ahead. Cover separately and refrigerate.*

Heat the oil in a heavy large sauté pan over medium-high heat. Sprinkle the remaining 2 teaspoons sugar over the oil. Add the pear halves, turnips, and beets. Cook until the pears and vegetables begin to brown, about 8 minutes. Add the duck stock. Reduce the heat to medium-low and simmer until the liquid is reduced by half, about 5 minutes. Season to taste with fleur de sel and freshly ground pepper.

HOT CHOCOLATE GALETTES

If you love the smell of hot chocolate, you'll love these miniature treats—you'll think there's a hot chocolate factory in your kitchen. They're all but pure chocolate, crispy on the outside and molten within.

4 SERVINGS

3   ounces good-quality bittersweet (not
    unsweetened) chocolate, chopped
1   tablespoon unsalted butter
¼   cup sugar
1   large egg
1   large egg yolk
2   tablespoons all-purpose flour

Line 4 cupcake molds with paper or foil cupcake liners; set aside. Stir the chocolate and butter in a heavy small saucepan over medium-low heat until melted and smooth, about 1 minute. Remove from the heat.

Using an electric mixer, beat the sugar, egg, and egg yolk in a large bowl until thick ribbons form on the surface of the batter when the beater is lifted, about 5 minutes. Sift the flour over the egg mixture, then fold in the flour. Fold in the melted chocolate mixture. Using a trigger ice cream scoop, spoon the batter into the prepared cupcake liners. Cover and refrigerate until cold, at least 1 hour or overnight.

Preheat the oven to 400°F. Remove the "cupcakes" from the molds and place them in their papers on a heavy baking sheet. Bake until the tops of the galettes puff and crack and a tester inserted into the center comes out with moist batter attached, about 10 minutes. Transfer 1 galette to each of 4 dessert plates and serve warm.

BRIOCHE

MAKES 1 LOAF

¾   cup warm whole milk (105° to 110°F)
2   tablespoons active dry yeast
3½ cups all-purpose flour
3   large eggs, stirred to blend
2   tablespoons sugar
4   teaspoons fleur de sel
12 ounces unsalted butter,
    room temperature

Stir the warm milk and yeast in a small bowl. Let stand until the yeast dissolves, about 10 minutes. Using an electric mixer with a paddle attachment, mix the flour, eggs, sugar, and fleur de sel in a large bowl to blend well; add the yeast mixture. Beat on medium speed until the dough is elastic, about 2 minutes (the dough will be sticky). With the machine running, gradually add the butter; beat until well blended. Cover the dough and refrigerate until cold, about 2 hours (this will make the dough easier to work with).

Preheat the oven to 150°F. Lightly oil a 9¼ x 5 x 2¾-inch loaf pan. Transfer the dough to a lightly floured work surface. Divide the dough into 4 equal pieces. Roll each piece into a 5 x 2 x 2-inch oval-shaped ball. Place the balls side by side in the prepared pan. Bake until the dough rises slightly, about 20 minutes. Increase the oven temperature to 375°F and continue baking the brioche until it is dark brown on the outside and an instant-read thermometer registers 200°F when inserted into the center of the loaf, about 1 hour longer. Cool the brioche in the pan for 5 minutes. Turn the bread out and cool completely on a rack.

FRIED CANDIED MILK WITH GREEN CARDAMOM

This is a sweet, spongy dessert with a texture similar to that of a baba. The syrup is infused with green cardamom, which adds a little sitar music to the background. Almond flour and almond milk can be found at Indian and Middle Eastern groceries.

6 SERVINGS

Almond Sauce

¾ cup almond milk
¼ cup whole milk
1 tablespoon almond flour

Cardamom Syrup and Candied Milk

3½ cups water
1¼ cups sugar
2 tablespoons smashed green cardamom pods
   Canola oil (for coating the baking sheet and your hands, and for deep-frying)
¾ cup powdered milk
2 tablespoons all-purpose flour
½ teaspoon baking powder
   Pinch of fleur de sel
1 tablespoon canned sweetened condensed milk
3 tablespoons (or more) whole milk
   Cardamom Sorbet (page 147)

FOR THE ALMOND SAUCE

Blend all the ingredients in a blender until smooth. Transfer the almond milk to a small bowl. Cover and refrigerate until very cold, at least 1 hour.

FOR THE CARDAMOM SYRUP AND CANDIED MILK

Combine the water, sugar, and cardamom in a heavy medium saucepan. Bring to a boil over high heat. Strain the cardamom syrup into a wide bowl. Cool to room temperature.

Lightly grease a small baking sheet with canola oil. Using an electric mixer, mix the powdered milk, flour, baking powder, and fleur de sel in a large bowl to blend. Mix in the sweetened condensed milk. Add the whole milk, 1 tablespoon at a time, mixing until a smooth, sticky dough forms. Oil the palms of your hands. Working with about 1 teaspoon of dough at a time, gently roll the dough between your palms to form twenty-four ¾-inch balls. Transfer the balls to the oiled baking sheet.

Pour enough canola oil into a deep fryer, or in a heavy large wok, to reach a depth of 3 inches. Heat the oil to 220°F over medium-low heat. Add all the candied milk balls to the warm oil and cook until golden brown, stirring frequently and allowing the temperature of the oil to rise gradually to 250°F, about 25 minutes. Using a slotted spoon, transfer the candied milk balls to the cardamom syrup. Submerge until the balls are soaked through and spongy, about 2 minutes. Using a slotted spoon, transfer the balls to a container in a single layer.

DO AHEAD: *The almond milk and soaked candied milk balls can be prepared up to 1 day ahead. Keep the almond milk refrigerated. Cover and refrigerate the candied milk balls.*

TO ASSEMBLE AND SERVE

Pour 2 tablespoons of the almond milk into each of 6 small dessert bowls. Spoon an oval-shaped scoop of the cardamom sorbet into the center of each bowl. Place the candied milk balls around the sorbet, dividing equally. Serve immediately.

CARDAMOM SORBET

The sorbet is best when made no more than eight hours before serving. If you must freeze it longer, let it melt back to a liquid in a bain-marie and return it to the ice cream maker until soft-solid.

MAKES ABOUT 2 CUPS

1½   cups water
¼   cup light corn syrup
3   tablespoons sugar
1   tablespoon whole green cardamom pods

Combine all the ingredients in a heavy medium saucepan over high heat. Bring to a boil. Remove from the heat. Cover and steep for 30 minutes. Transfer the cardamom mixture to a small bowl. Cover and refrigerate the mixture until cold, at least 2 hours.

Strain the mixture to remove the cardamom pods and pieces. Transfer the mixture to an ice cream maker. Process according to the manufacturer's instructions. Transfer the sorbet to a container; whisk to blend well. Cover and freeze until the sorbet is firm, stirring occasionally, about 4 hours.

DO AHEAD: *The sorbet can be prepared up to 8 hours ahead. Keep frozen.*

JUBILEE OF CHERRIES WITH KIRSCH, MINT, AND VANILLA ICE CREAM

A new twist on an old classic, this version is perked up with citrus zest and lavender honey. When the kirsch is set aflame, though, the basic appeal of the dish remains the same: Its bouquet fills your nose in a delightful way.

4 SERVINGS

¼ cup honey, preferably lavender

12 ounces fresh cherries, pitted (about 2 cups)

2 tablespoons kirsch (clear cherry brandy)

4 teaspoons grated orange peel

2 teaspoons grated lemon peel

2 tablespoons very thinly sliced fresh mint leaves

Vanilla Ice Cream (page 245)

Bring the honey to a boil in a heavy large sauté pan over medium-high heat. Add the cherries. Reduce the heat to medium and cook until the juices form and boil, about 5 minutes. Add the kirsch. Carefully ignite the kirsch with a long match. Simmer until the flames subside, about 2 minutes. Continue cooking until the liquid thickens slightly, stirring occasionally, about 1 minute. Add the orange peel and lemon peel.

Spoon the cherries and sauce into 4 wide soup plates. Sprinkle the mint over. Spoon an oval-shaped scoop of vanilla ice cream atop each serving. Serve immediately.

LOST BREAD WITH SAUTÉED PEARS
AND VANILLA AND CARAMEL SAUCES

When I first came to California and saw people ordering French toast for breakfast, I was puzzled. In France we don't call it French toast. We call it "lost bread" (pain perdu), which in this case basically means day-old brioche, and we eat it for dessert. (For breakfast we have nutritious cigarettes and espresso, which, combined, form a perfect protein.) This version is a little more elaborate, as it has two different sauces, but you'll love the way it perfumes the air with the scents of vanilla and rum.

4 SERVINGS

Custard

½ cup whole milk

½ cup heavy whipping cream

½ cup sugar

6 large egg yolks

1 tablespoon dark rum

4 1-inch-thick slices Brioche (page 145),
    or use store-bought brioche

2 tablespoons unsalted butter

Caramelized Pears

1 tablespoon unsalted butter

1 tablespoon sugar

2 ripe but firm Anjou pears, peeled, each cut
    into 8 wedges, and cored

⅓ cup Caramel Sauce (recipe follows)

⅓ cup Vanilla Sauce (recipe follows)

FOR THE CUSTARD

Whisk the first 5 ingredients in an 8 x 8 x 2-inch glass baking dish. Using a 3½-inch biscuit cutter, cut the brioche slices into rounds; discard the trimmings. Add the brioche rounds to the egg mixture and let soak until the mixture is absorbed and the brioche is soaked through, about 8 minutes per side.

Melt the butter on a heavy griddle over medium-low heat. Add the soaked brioche to the griddle. Cook until golden brown and just cooked through, about 6 minutes per side.

FOR THE CARAMELIZED PEARS

Melt the butter in a heavy large sauté pan over medium-high heat. Stir in the sugar. Add the pears and sauté until crisp-tender and golden brown, about 8 minutes.

TO ASSEMBLE AND SERVE

Place 1 brioche round in the center of each of 4 large plates. Drizzle the caramel sauce and vanilla sauce around the brioche. Arrange the pear wedges alongside and serve immediately.

CARAMEL SAUCE

MAKES ¾ CUP

¼ cup sugar
2 tablespoons water
½ cup heavy whipping cream

Combine the sugar and water in a heavy small saucepan. Stir over medium-high heat until the sugar dissolves. Boil without stirring until the syrup turns a deep golden brown, occasionally brushing down the sides of the pan with a wet pastry brush and swirling the pan, about 3 minutes. Remove from the heat. Add the cream (the mixture will bubble vigorously). Using a whisk, stir over low heat until smooth. Cool to lukewarm before serving.

DO AHEAD: *The caramel sauce can be prepared 1 day ahead. Cool completely. Cover and refrigerate. Rewarm before using.*

VANILLA SAUCE

MAKES 1¾ CUPS

1¼ cups whole milk
¼ cup heavy whipping cream
½ vanilla bean, split lengthwise
4 large egg yolks
⅓ cup sugar

Combine the milk and cream in a heavy medium saucepan. Scrape the seeds from the vanilla bean into the milk and cream mixture; add the bean. Bring to a simmer over medium-high heat. Remove from the heat.

Meanwhile, whisk the egg yolks and sugar in a medium bowl to blend. Gradually whisk in the hot milk mixture. Return the mixture to the saucepan. Using a heat-resistant rubber spatula, stir just until the custard thickens and leaves a path on the back of the spatula when a finger is drawn across, about 4 minutes (do not boil). Strain the custard sauce through a fine-mesh strainer and into a medium bowl set over a large bowl of ice water. Stir until the sauce is cold. Cover and refrigerate. Discard the vanilla bean before using. Serve the sauce cold.

DO AHEAD: *The vanilla sauce can be prepared 1 day ahead. Keep refrigerated.*

CARAMEL SOUFFLÉS

Coming out of the oven, most soufflés don't give off much of an aroma. This one is a fragrant exception; its lovely, bittersweet smell will perfume the whole house.

6 SERVINGS

2½ cups whole milk
5 large eggs, separated
2¼ cups sugar
⅓ cup all-purpose flour
¼ cup water
3 oranges, peeled and segmented

Bring the milk to a boil in a heavy medium saucepan. Using an electric mixer, beat the egg yolks and 6 tablespoons of the sugar in a large bowl until light and fluffy, about 5 minutes. Mix in the flour. Gradually mix in the hot milk. Return the mixture to the saucepan. Stir with a whisk over medium-low heat until the pastry cream thickens and bubbles begin to break on the surface of the cream, about 2 minutes. Remove from the heat. Press plastic wrap directly onto the surface of the pastry cream. Set aside and keep warm.

Combine 1½ cups of the sugar and the water in a heavy small saucepan. Stir over medium heat until the sugar dissolves, about 3 minutes. Boil without stirring until the syrup turns a deep amber brown color and just begins to smoke, occasionally brushing down the sides of the pan with a wet pastry brush and swirling the pan, about 8 minutes longer. Immediately whisk the hot caramel into the pastry cream. Transfer the caramel cream to a large bowl. Press plastic wrap directly onto the surface of the caramel cream. Refrigerate until cool, at least 3 hours.

Preheat the oven to 400°F. Butter six 9-ounce soufflé dishes; coat with sugar. Place the dishes on a heavy baking sheet. Whisk the caramel cream to loosen. Using an electric mixer on medium-low speed, beat the egg whites in another large bowl until soft peaks form. Gradually beat in the remaining 6 tablespoons sugar. Continue beating just until firm peaks form. Fold the egg whites into the caramel cream just until blended (do not overmix). Divide the soufflé batter equally among the prepared soufflé dishes.

Bake the soufflés until they puff but are still moist in the center, about 20 minutes. Serve immediately with the orange segments alongside.

TASTE SEE TOUCH SMELL HEAR TASTE SEE TOUCH SMELL HEAR TASTE SEE

HEAR

SEE

TOUCH

SMELL

{ HEAR }

TASTE

+ CHAPTER 4

TASTE SEE TOUCH SMELL HEAR TASTE SEE TOUCH SMELL HEAR TASTE

YOU MUST COOK WITH YOUR EARS!

LEARN TO LISTEN WHEN YOU COOK! WHAT'S THE PROBLEM, DID YOU GO DEAF? CAN'T YOU HEAR

WHAT THAT FISH IS TELLING YOU? HE'S TELLING YOU HE'S SUFFERING! HE'S SUFFERING

BECAUSE YOU ARE NOT COOKING HIM PROPERLY! USE YOUR EARS! LISTEN TO HIM!"

  I WAS TWENTY YEARS OLD, AND THESE WERE THE WORDS OF PASSARD, MY

MENTOR. I WAS LOST. MAYBE I WAS MISSING SOMETHING, BUT I PRETTY MUCH DECIDED THAT

PASSARD HAD GONE CRAZY. WHO BUT A MADMAN HEARS VOICES FROM A FILLET OF COD COOKING

AWAY IN A 400-DEGREE OVEN? NEXT HE'D BE TELLING ME THAT THE PRIME RIB SIZZLING ON THE

GRILL HAD LODGED AN OFFICIAL COMPLAINT ABOUT BEING OVERLY SALTED. WHAT WAS NEXT?

REBELLIOUS BROCCOLI? CLEARLY, PASSARD HAD SNAPPED.

  BUT AS I STAYED ON WITH HIM, I CAME TO APPRECIATE HIS CRAZY WISDOM. I

LEARNED THAT MY EARS COULD BE A POWERFUL TOOL IN THE KITCHEN.

If I'd stopped to think about it sooner, it would have been obvious. When we prepare food and eat it, our ears are with us from start to finish. Certainly in France, a considerably more vocal culture than America, your sense of hearing comes alive the minute you come within a block of the market. The barking voices of farmers hawking their wares ring in your ears, but their cries are much more than appeals for a financial transaction. Their energy springs from genuine passion. *Tomatoes! Green beans! These are the best in the market! Get the juiciest strawberries of all! Pay no attention to him—my green beans are better!* They aren't just selling their wares, they're putting their children up for adoption, and they are very proud of their children of the harvest. The sound of their raw voices alone is enough to make you hungry, to make you want to buy more than you could possibly carry away.

Our sense of hearing also comes into play when we are actually eating. Pay attention to the sound food makes when you bite into it—there is music to be heard. When I was a kid, my dad would take me out to the country on weekends. We would find our way to a certain apple tree from which hung the most beautiful, green Granny Smith apples. I loved to pluck one from the branches, and I always sat down on the spot and ate it right under the tree. Those country-fresh apples were delicious—sweet and tart—but for me the truest pleasure of eating them was auditory: the crunch of the apple as I bit into it, the wind rustling through the leaves, the creaking of the branches above. I would close my eyes and just listen and eat, enveloped in a cocoon of pure *appleness*.

This enchantment with sound extends into the smallest nooks and crannies of the kitchen. The kitchen to me is like a symphony in miniature. I love the *whisp* sound the knife makes when I sharpen it and the thud when it hits the cutting board; the crackle of the oil when potatoes are plunged into the deep fryer; the whirring of the mixer as it whips cream. It is the same when the food is served: the whack of the knife handle shattering the hard shell encasing a lobster cooked in salt, the slapping sound when you bite into the brittle crust of vanilla crème brûlée, the crunch of a crispy soft-shell crab—all of these auditory sensations deepen our appreciation of food.

I suppose that hearing, applied to cooking, could well be the sense that takes the most time to develop. But with attention and alertness, you may be surprised at how listening enhances your culinary judgment. For me, the thermostat on the oven has become like the volume control on a stereo. The fish is alive in the oven and he is communicating with me. Sometimes I even talk back to him (or her, as the case may be). Learn to cook with your ears. When you drop foie gras into the skillet for searing, the sizzling sound should be immediate and intense. When you cook the prime rib with brown sugar, the sound should be fierce; that way you know you're creating a good crust. When you prepare crayfish *à la nage,* you should hear the water boiling, but not too strongly or else the meat of the crayfish will become mealy and break up. In so many cases when you can't really see the cooking process, your ears can lead the way.

"Cook with love, Ludo, so that the fish hasn't died for nothing!" Passard told me. And when you do anything with love, naturally you have to listen.

ZUCCHINI AND ACACIA BLOSSOM BEIGNETS

This is a good recipe for testing your ears. The oil should be heated to 375°F. Use a deep-fry thermometer, but listen closely for the rolling sputter that indicates you've got the right temperature, and next time try using only your ears. Take care not to overbatter the flowers; they should be light and delicate. Also, avoid dropping too many flowers in the oil at a time. If the oil temperature drops, they'll become soggy. As you might expect, both the zucchini and acacia blossoms are a gift of springtime. If you can't find acacia, the zucchini blossoms are still delightful by themselves.

4 APPETIZER SERVINGS

Canola oil (for deep-frying)
1¼ cups all purpose flour
¾ cup cornstarch
2 teaspoons fleur de sel
1½ teaspoons baking powder
2 cups ice-cold good-quality lager
20 fresh zucchini blossoms
8 fresh acacia blossoms

Preheat the oven to 200°F. Pour enough oil into a heavy wide pot to measure 3 inches in depth. Heat the oil over medium heat until a deep-fry thermometer registers 375°F.

Mix the flour, cornstarch, fleur de sel, and baking powder in a large bowl to blend. Add the lager and whisk until the batter is almost smooth. Working in batches and using tongs, dip each zucchini and acacia blossom into the batter; allow the excess batter to fall back into the bowl. Fry the blossoms in the hot oil until the coating is crisp and golden brown, maintaining the oil temperature so that the flowers do not become soggy, about 1½ minutes per side. Using a slotted spoon, transfer the beignet blossoms to a plate lined with paper towels to drain. Season the beignets to taste with fleur de sel. Transfer the beignet blossoms to a baking sheet; keep warm in the oven while frying the remaining blossoms.

Arrange 5 zucchini blossom beignets and 2 acacia blossom beignets on each of 4 large plates. Serve immediately.

CRISPY SOFT-SHELL CRABS WITH BUTTER NOISETTE AND AGED BALSAMIC VINEGAR

Munching on these crabs, you'll hear a sound like stepping on chestnuts that have fallen from the tree in autumn. Also, when searing the crabs, you should pay attention to the strong sizzling sound of the hot oil.

8 APPETIZER SERVINGS

6 tablespoons Clarified Butter (page 243)
8 2-ounce soft-shell crabs
  Fleur de sel and freshly ground pepper
  All-purpose flour (for coating)
¼ cup unsalted butter
¼ cup strained fresh lemon juice
3 tablespoons minced peeled fresh ginger
2 tablespoons aged balsamic vinegar
2 tablespoons chopped drained capers
2 tablespoons chopped fresh flat-leaf
  parsley
2 tablespoons seeded, finely diced tomato

Preheat the oven to 200ºF. Heat 3 tablespoons of the clarified butter in a heavy large sauté pan over medium-high heat. Sprinkle the crabs with fleur de sel and pepper. Dredge 4 of the crabs in the flour; shake off the excess flour. Add the coated crabs to the clarified butter and cook until golden brown and crisp, about 2 minutes per side. Transfer the crabs to a baking sheet and keep warm in the oven. Wipe out the sauté pan. Repeat with the remaining 3 tablespoons clarified butter and 4 crabs.

Add the unsalted butter to the sauté pan. Stir over medium-low heat until the butter melts and is golden brown, about 2 minutes. Whisk in the lemon juice, ginger, vinegar, capers, parsley, and tomato. Season the sauce to taste with fleur de sel and pepper.

Place 2 crabs on each of 4 plates. Spoon the sauce over the crabs and serve immediately.

EGGS CAVIAR

This is one of my guests' favorite appetizers. The hardest part is mastering the egg topper when removing the crowns of the eggs. I recommend deep breathing exercises to avoid stress when you hear the shells breaking the wrong way. But keep at it. The payoff makes it worthwhile. I suggest using brown eggs because their shells are stronger and less likely to shatter when you cut off their tops.

4 APPETIZER SERVINGS

4 large brown eggs
1 tablespoon unsalted butter
2 tablespoons finely diced onion
1 tablespoon sliced fresh chives
   Fleur de sel and freshly ground pepper
4 teaspoons caviar, preferably osetra

Line a small cookie sheet with paper towels. Arrange the eggs, pointed side down, in the egg carton. Using an egg topper, neatly perforate the top of each egg and remove the top portion of each eggshell. Set the tops of the shells aside. Empty the egg yolks and whites into a large bowl and set aside. Gently submerge the top and bottom portions of the eggshells into a large bowl of very hot water until any remaining egg contents coagulate, about 5 minutes. Using your forefinger and thumb, gently remove the thin membrane lining from the eggshells. Arrange the eggshells, cut side down, on the prepared cookie sheet to dry.

DO AHEAD: *The eggshells can be prepared up to 8 hours ahead. Cover the eggshells and egg contents separately and refrigerate.*

Set the bottom portion of the eggshells in egg holders. Whisk the reserved egg yolks and whites together, then strain to remove any pieces of eggshell. Melt the butter in a heavy small saucepan over medium-low heat. Add the onion and sauté until translucent, about 3 minutes. Whisk in the egg liquids. Cook until the eggs just become creamy and thicken slightly (the eggs should not be lumpy), whisking constantly and briskly, about 3 minutes. Remove from the heat. Whisk in the chives. Season the creamed eggs to taste with fleur de sel and pepper.

Using a small spoon, neatly fill each eggshell with the warm creamed eggs, leaving room for the caviar. Spoon 1 teaspoon of caviar atop each. Set the top portion of the eggshells askew atop the filled eggs. Serve immediately.

YOUNG GARLIC SOUP WITH THYME, SCALLOPS, AND GOLD LEAF

Learning to listen to food as it cooks is one of the best ways to improve your skill. Use your sense of hearing when cooking the scallops. The sauté pan should be very hot before adding them, so when they hit the surface you should hear a strong sizzling sound. Cook the scallops until they're lightly browned, crisp on the outside, and medium-rare on the inside. The gold leaf is purely decorative, but it adds a nice touch if it is available.

6 APPETIZER SERVINGS

- 1 quart whole milk
- 4 young garlic bulbs (about 7 ounces total), cloves separated and peeled
- 2 teaspoons minced peeled fresh ginger
- 1 small bunch fresh thyme
  Fleur de sel and freshly ground pepper
- 2 teaspoons unsalted butter
- 2 teaspoons extra virgin olive oil
- 12 large sea scallops
- 1 small bunch fresh pepper cress leaves or small watercress leaves
- 3 3¾-inch-square sheets of edible gold leaf (optional)

Combine the milk, garlic cloves, and ginger in a heavy medium saucepan. Tie all but 12 small, tender sprigs of the thyme into a bundle with kitchen twine. Add the thyme bundle to the milk mixture. Bring to a simmer. Simmer gently, uncovered, over low heat until the garlic is very tender and the liquid is reduced by one fourth, stirring occasionally, about 35 minutes. Discard the thyme bundle. Working in batches, puree the milk mixture in a blender until smooth. Return the soup to the saucepan. If necessary, simmer the soup over low heat until it is reduced to 3½ cups. Season the soup to taste with fleur de sel and pepper.

DO AHEAD: *At this point, the soup can be prepared up to 8 hours ahead. Cool. Cover and refrigerate. Rewarm before serving.*

Melt the butter and oil in a heavy large sauté pan over high heat. Sprinkle the scallops with fleur de sel and pepper. Working in batches, add the scallops to the pan and sear until golden brown and just cooked through, about 2 minutes per side.

TO ASSEMBLE AND SERVE

Mound the cress in the center of each of 6 wide shallow soup bowls. Place 2 scallops atop the cress in each bowl. Surround the cress with the reserved small thyme sprigs. Tear the gold leaf, if using, into large nonuniform strips and arrange it around the scallops; the gold leaf is delicate and will tear easily. Ladle enough soup into the bowls to come halfway up the sides of the scallops.

WHOLE LOBSTER COOKED IN SALT AND TARRAGON

This may sound crazy, but yes, you're going to bury your lobster in sea salt, which, when baking, will form a coat of armor around the lobster to seal in moisture and flavor. To me, the moment of glory is the sharp, percussive sound of the salt shell cracking beneath the blow of the knife handle—which of course you'll want to perform in front of your guest! If you want to prepare 2 lobsters, use a rectangular roasting pan just large enough to fit both lobsters without crowding them, and increase the salt enough to encase the lobsters completely.

2 APPETIZER SERVINGS

1   1½- to 2-pound live lobster

6   cups (about) coarse-grained sea salt

1   tablespoon extra virgin olive oil

8   ounces fresh porcini mushrooms, brushed
    clean of any grit, halved lengthwise

3   teaspoons finely chopped fresh tarragon
    Fleur de sel and freshly ground pepper

1   tablespoon cold unsalted butter, thinly
    sliced

Preheat the oven to 350ºF. Plunge the lobster headfirst into a large pot of boiling water and cook until the lobster is bright red, about 2 minutes. Using tongs, cool the lobster under cold running water. Pat dry with paper towels.

DO AHEAD: *At this point, the lobster can be prepared up to 8 hours ahead. Cover and refrigerate.*

Using an oval-shaped roasting pan just large enough to fit the lobster, cover the bottom of the pan with ½ cup of the sea salt. Set the lobster atop the sea salt. Pour enough remaining sea salt over to cover the lobster completely. Bake for 30 minutes.

Meanwhile, heat the oil in a heavy medium sauté pan over medium-high heat. Add the mushrooms and sauté until the mushrooms are golden brown, about 2 minutes per side. Remove from the heat. Stir in 2 teaspoons of the tarragon. Season the mushrooms to taste with fleur de sel and pepper.

TO FINISH AND SERVE

Using the handle of a heavy large knife, break the salt crust covering the lobster. Transfer the lobster to a cutting board. Remove the lobster tails and claws from the body. Crack the shells and carefully remove the tail and claw meat from the shells. Cut the tail lengthwise in half.

Place 1 lobster tail half and 1 claw on each of 2 plates. Top with the butter slices. Sprinkle with the remaining 1 teaspoon tarragon. Surround with the sautéed mushrooms and serve immediately.

CRAYFISH À LA NAGE

When I was a boy, my friends and I loved to scramble for crayfish along the banks of the river near our home. They were such strange, exotic creatures that we were happy enough just to play with them. It didn't occur to us that they'd be wonderful to eat—at least not until we were a little older. One day my friend Jacques' mom told us to round up a batch of them for her, which she cooked for us à la nage. I couldn't believe the incredible perfume that came out of her kitchen, let alone the wonderful taste, and the sound of the crayfish rattling against the pot as they boil still transports me back to those days. Nage in French means "swimming" and, in specific culinary terms, in a court bouillon. Figuratively speaking, that is what the crayfish do in this recipe—they swim in flavor!

4 MAIN-COURSE SERVINGS

5 quarts water

½ cup white wine vinegar

4¼ teaspoons fleur de sel

3 pounds live crayfish (about 80)

3 tablespoons unsalted butter

1 Maui, Vidalia, or other sweet onion, cut into ¼-inch-thick rounds

2 small carrots, peeled and cut into ¼-inch-thick rounds

1 bouquet garni (made of 1 bay leaf, 2 fresh rosemary sprigs, 2 fresh thyme sprigs, and 2 fresh flat-leaf parsley sprigs)

6 whole cloves

½ teaspoon freshly cracked white pepper

1 cup Sancerre

¼ cup heavy whipping cream

2 tablespoons fresh tarragon leaves

1 tablespoon strained fresh lemon juice

Combine 4 quarts of the water, the vinegar, and 4 teaspoons of the fleur de sel in a large pot. Bring to a boil over high heat. Working in batches, add the crayfish and boil for 2 minutes. Drain. Discard the cooking liquid. Pull the tail away from the body of each crayfish; discard the body. Peel and devein the tails. Cover and refrigerate the tail meat.

Melt the butter in a 5-quart pot over medium heat. Add the onion, carrots, bouquet garni, cloves, white pepper, and remaining ¼ teaspoon fleur de sel. Sauté until the onion begins to soften, about 4 minutes. Add the remaining 1 quart water to just cover the vegetables. Boil until the vegetables are crisp-tender, about 4 minutes. Strain the cooking liquid; return the liquid to the pot. Set the vegetables aside. Discard the bouquet garni and whole cloves. Add the Sancerre to the cooking liquid. Boil, uncovered, over high heat until the liquid is reduced to 2 cups, stirring occasionally, about 20 minutes.

DO AHEAD: *At this point, the crayfish tail meat, vegetables, and cooking liquid can be prepared up to 8 hours ahead. Cover separately and refrigerate.*

Add the cream to the cooking liquid. Boil until the liquid is reduced to 1½ cups, about 5 minutes. Add 1 tablespoon of the tarragon and the reserved crayfish tail meat to the cooking liquid. Simmer over low heat to rewarm the crayfish and infuse the cooking liquid, about 2 minutes.

Using a slotted spoon, divide the crayfish equally among 4 wide soup bowls. Add the reserved vegetables to the cooking liquid to rewarm, about 2 minutes. Using tongs, transfer the vegetables to the bowls, dividing equally and placing atop the crayfish. Add the lemon juice to the cooking liquid. Season the liquid to taste with fleur de sel and pepper. Drizzle the cooking liquid around the vegetables. Sprinkle with the remaining 1 tablespoon tarragon and serve.

ROAST BEEF WITH LONG PEPPER AND SPICED FRENCH FRIES

Here's another test for your ears while you preside over the furious sputter of the beef as it cooks in caul fat, the fatty stomach lining of the pig, which renders a wonderful crust. You should be able to obtain caul fat from specialty butchers, but if you can't find it, the recipe will work just fine without it. The French fries are dredged in flour for added crispness.

4 MAIN-COURSE SERVINGS

Roast Beef

1	4-ounce piece caul fat
2	tablespoons Szechwan peppercorns
6	whole long peppers
1	tablespoon fleur de sel
2	tablespoons extra virgin olive oil
1	2-pound (large end) piece of prime beef tenderloin, trimmed)
½	cup Beef Stock (page 236)

Spiced French Fries

¼	cup all-purpose flour
2	tablespoons onion powder
1	tablespoon paprika
1	tablespoon fleur de sel
1	tablespoon garlic powder
1½	teaspoons cayenne pepper
1½	pounds russet potatoes, peeled
	Grapeseed oil (for deep-frying)

FOR THE ROAST BEEF

Preheat the oven to 450°F. Soak the caul fat in a large bowl of water for 15 minutes. Rinse the caul fat under cold running water; squeeze to remove the excess water.

Coarsely grind the Szechwan peppercorns, long peppers, and fleur de sel in a spice grinder. Rub the beef with the olive oil. Roll the beef in the pepper mixture, then wrap with the caul fat. Tie the beef with kitchen string to maintain its shape. Transfer the beef to a heavy rimmed baking sheet. Roast until an instant-read meat thermometer inserted into the center of the beef registers 135°F for medium-rare, about 35 minutes. Transfer the beef to a cutting board. Tent loosely with aluminum foil and let rest for 10 minutes.

Add the beef stock to the baking sheet. Stir to scrape up the pan drippings. Transfer the pan juices to a small saucepan. Cover and set aside.

MEANWHILE, PREPARE THE SPICED FRENCH FRIES

Mix the first 6 ingredients in a medium bowl to blend. Set the spice mixture aside. Line a large baking sheet with paper towels. Using a mandoline, cut the potatoes lengthwise into strips about 5 x ½ x ¼ inches. Rinse the potato strips under cold running water until the water runs clear. Pat the potato strips dry with paper towels.

Pour enough grapeseed oil into a heavy wide pot to come 2 inches up the sides of the pot. Heat the oil over medium-high heat to 350°F. Toss the potato strips in a large bowl with 1 tablespoon of the oil to coat. Working in batches, toss the potatoes with the spice mixture to coat, then fry in the hot oil until crisp and golden, about 2 minutes. Using tongs, transfer the fries to the prepared baking sheet. Return the oil to 350°F before adding each batch of potatoes.

TO FINISH AND SERVE

Rewarm the pan juices in the small saucepan over medium heat. Remove from the heat. Cover and keep warm.

Remove the caul fat from the beef. Cut the beef crosswise into 12 slices. Arrange 3 beef slices in the center of each of 4 plates. Surround with the spiced French fries. Drizzle the warm pan juices over the beef and serve immediately.

ARCTIC CHAR WITH SAFFRON SAUCE AND WHOLE TURNIPS FILLED WITH OLIVES AND FRESH HARISSA

Arctic char may be my favorite fish. Quite versatile, it's denser than trout and lighter than salmon, with a flavor robust enough to stand up to saffron. Here, the fun is in the sizzle you'll hear as you crisp up the skin in the sauté pan, along with the brittle ripping sound the skin makes as you eat it.

4 MAIN-COURSE SERVINGS

Turnips

¼ cup pitted Niçoise olives, finely chopped
1 garlic clove, finely chopped
1 red jalapeño chile, seeded and finely chopped
1½ tablespoons chopped fresh mint
1 tablespoon chopped fresh flat-leaf parsley
1 tablespoon chopped fresh cilantro
2 tablespoons extra virgin olive oil
4 3- to 4-ounce whole small turnips, peeled
Fleur de sel and freshly ground pepper

Fish and Sauce

2 cups Fish Stock (page 240)
¼ cup heavy whipping cream
Pinch of saffron
1 tablespoon strained fresh lemon juice
2 tablespoons extra virgin olive oil
4 6-ounce arctic char fillets with skin
2 lemons, halved

FOR THE TURNIPS

Preheat the oven to 425°F. Stir the first 6 ingredients in a medium bowl to blend. Stir in 1 tablespoon of the olive oil.

Using a melon baller, scoop out the centers of the turnips. Coat the turnips with the remaining 1 tablespoon oil. Using about 1 tablespoon of the olive mixture for each, fill the turnips, mounding slightly. Arrange the turnips in an 8-inch square baking dish. Sprinkle with fleur de sel and pepper. Bake, uncovered, until the turnips are crisp-tender and the filling is hot, about 35 minutes.

FOR THE FISH AND SAUCE

Boil the fish stock and cream in a heavy small saucepan over high heat until reduced to ⅔ cup, about 25 minutes. Remove from the heat. Add the saffron and steep for 10 minutes. Add the lemon juice. Season the sauce to taste with fleur de sel and pepper.

Heat 1 tablespoon oil in each of 2 heavy large sauté pans over medium-high heat. Sprinkle the char with fleur de sel and pepper. Add 2 char fillets, skin side down, to each pan and cook until golden brown and crispy on the bottom, about 6 minutes. Remove the pans from the heat. Turn the fillets over and let rest in the pans until just cooked through, about 2 minutes.

TO ASSEMBLE AND SERVE

Place the char fillets, skin side up, on the left-hand side of each of 4 large dinner plates. Spoon the saffron sauce around the char. Place the turnips on the right-hand side. Serve immediately with the lemon halves.

SALMON EN CROUTE WITH RED WINE-SHALLOT REDUCTION, POTATOES, AND CLAMS

I love crust in any form. After playing around with several different versions, I eventually discovered that nothing encases salmon and complements its soft texture better than phyllo dough, which makes almost a spattering sound when you cut into it.

4 MAIN-COURSE SERVINGS

Salmon

4 6-ounce salmon fillets
   Fleur de sel and freshly ground pepper
6 17½ x 13½-inch sheets fresh phyllo pastry
   or frozen phyllo dough, thawed
½ cup Clarified Butter, melted (page 243)

Sauce

1 cup dry red wine
1 cup ruby port
¼ cup minced shallots
2 tablespoons cold unsalted butter

Potatoes with Clams (recipe follows)

FOR THE SALMON

Sprinkle the salmon fillets with fleur de sel and pepper. Place 1 phyllo sheet on the work surface so that the long edge lines up with the work surface (keep the remaining phyllo sheets covered with plastic wrap and a clean, slightly damp kitchen towel so that they do not dry out). Brush the phyllo sheet with some melted clarified butter. Repeat layering the phyllo sheets and clarified butter 2 times. Place two salmon fillets on the left half of the stacked phyllo sheets, spacing evenly. Fold the other half of the phyllo stack over the salmon. Press the edges of the phyllo stacks together to enclose the salmon completely. Using a small sharp knife, trim the phyllo to extend 1 inch beyond the edges of the salmon, making 2 separate salmon packets. Transfer the salmon packets to a heavy large baking sheet. Repeat with the remaining phyllo sheets, clarified butter, and salmon fillets to make 4 salmon packets total. Cover the packets and refrigerate until they are firm, about 15 minutes (this will make them easier to handle).

DO AHEAD: *At this point, the salmon packets can be prepared up to 1 day ahead. Keep them refrigerated.*

FOR THE SAUCE

Bring the wine, port, and shallots to a boil in a heavy small saucepan. Reduce the heat to medium-low and simmer until the liquid thickens slightly and is reduced to ⅓ cup, about 15 minutes. Whisk in the butter to blend well. Season the sauce to taste with fleur de sel and freshly ground pepper.

TO FINISH AND SERVE

Preheat the oven to 400°F. Oil another large baking sheet. Heat a heavy large sauté pan over medium-high heat. Working in batches, add the salmon packets and cook until the phyllo directly over the salmon is golden brown, about 2 minutes per side. Transfer the salmon packets to the oiled baking sheet. Bake the salmon packets until the salmon is just cooked through, about 8 minutes for medium doneness.

Place 1 salmon packet in the center of each of 4 large plates. Spoon the sauce around the perimeter of the plates. Surround the packets with the warm potatoes with clams. Serve immediately.

POTATOES WITH CLAMS

4 SIDE-DISH SERVINGS

20 live Manila clams (about 12 ounces total),
   scrubbed

16 fingerling potatoes (about 8 ounces total),
   unpeeled

1 tablespoon extra virgin olive oil
  Fleur de sel and freshly ground pepper

1 tablespoon chopped fresh flat-leaf parsley

Steam the clams in a medium saucepan containing 1 inch of boiling salted water just until the clams open, about 2 minutes. Discard any clams that do not open. Remove the saucepan from the heat. Using a slotted spoon, transfer the clams to a large bowl. Remove the clam meat from the shells; discard the shells. Set the clam meat aside.

Meanwhile, boil the potatoes in a large saucepan of boiling lightly salted water until tender, about 7 minutes.

DO AHEAD: *At this point, the clam meat and boiled potatoes can be prepared up to 8 hours ahead. Cover them separately and refrigerate.*

Cut the potatoes crosswise into ½-inch-thick rounds. Heat the oil in a heavy medium sauté pan over medium heat. Add the potatoes. Cover and cook to rewarm the potatoes (do not allow the potatoes to brown), stirring occasionally, about 4 minutes. Add the reserved clam meat. Season the mixture to taste with fleur de sel and freshly ground pepper. Mix in the parsley.

WHOLE DORADE WITH SALT CRUST, YELLOW WINE SAUCE, AND SORREL SALAD

In this recipe, the delicate flesh of the dorade is protected by a brittle crust of heavily salted dough; the sound it makes when shattered is exquisite! The sauce includes vin jaune, or "yellow wine," made from grapes that are dried and fermented on top of hay, which gives it a pungent, earthy essence. You can all but taste the fields in the French countryside. If you can't find vin jaune, Sauternes will do nicely.

2 MAIN-COURSE SERVINGS

Fish

3½ cups all-purpose flour
¾ cup coarse-grained sea salt
1⅓ cups water
1 2-pound whole dorade, cleaned and scaled

Sauce

2 cups Fish Stock (page 240)
1⅓ cups vin jaune or Sauternes
4 tablespoons chilled unsalted butter, cut into pieces
Fleur de sel and freshly ground pepper

Salad

3 tablespoons argan oil or good-quality extra virgin olive oil
1 tablespoon Banyuls vinegar or good-quality sherry vinegar
3 cups fresh sorrel, stems removed

FOR THE FISH

Preheat the oven to 450°F. Butter a heavy large rimmed baking sheet. Using an electric mixer with a hook attachment, or a wooden spoon, mix the flour, sea salt, and water in a large bowl until blended. Knead on medium-low speed until the dough is moist but not sticky, about 2 minutes. Transfer the dough to a lightly floured work surface. Gather the dough; flatten into a square shape. Roll out the dough into a triangular shape ¼ inch thick and large enough to encase the fish, about 20 inches long and 18 inches wide at the widest end. Place the fish atop the dough with the head at the widest end. Fold the dough over the fish, smoothing the dough over the fish to remove any air pockets and encase the fish completely. Using a small sharp knife, trim the dough to contour the fish, leaving a 1-inch edge of dough. Seal any holes in the dough with the dough scraps; the fish must be encased completely. Transfer the encased fish to the prepared baking sheet.

Bake until the crust is pale but firm and an instant-read thermometer registers 135°F when inserted near the center of the fish, about 25 minutes. Transfer the baking sheet to a cooling rack. Let stand for 5 minutes. Carefully cut around the edge of the crust and remove the top layer of crust. Carefully remove the fillets from the fish.

MEANWHILE, PREPARE THE SAUCE

Boil the fish stock in a heavy medium saucepan over high heat until reduced to 1 cup, about 10 minutes. Add the wine and boil until the liquid thickens and is reduced to ½ cup, about 20 minutes. Whisk in the butter to form a smooth sauce. Season the sauce to taste with fleur de sel and pepper.

FOR THE SALAD

Whisk the oil and vinegar in a medium bowl to blend. Season the vinaigrette to taste with fleur de sel and pepper. Toss the sorrel in a large bowl
with enough vinaigrette to coat. Season the salad to taste with fleur de sel
and pepper.

TO FINISH AND SERVE

Mound the salad in the center of 2 large plates. Place a fish fillet atop
each. Spoon the sauce around the fish and serve immediately.

CÔTE DE BOEUF WITH BROWN SUGAR, HERB SALAD, AND POMMES SOUFFLÉS

Basting the prime rib with brown sugar dissolved in olive oil renders a truly magnificent crust. The beef must be cooked over high heat, producing a fierce sizzling sound, like a torrential rain falling on a tin roof.

2 MAIN-COURSE SERVINGS

Prime Rib

¼ cup (packed) golden brown sugar
3 tablespoons extra virgin olive oil
1 2- to 2½-pound prime rib beef roast

Herb Salad

1 tablespoon extra virgin olive oil
2 teaspoons strained fresh lemon juice
¼ cup fresh flat-leaf parsley leaves
¼ cup fresh chervil leaves
¼ cup 1-inch pieces fresh chives
2 tablespoons fresh tarragon leaves
2 tablespoons fresh thyme flowers
 or 1 tablespoon fresh tender thyme leaves
 Fleur de sel and freshly ground pepper

Pommes Soufflés (recipe follows)

FOR THE PRIME RIB

Stir the brown sugar and 2 tablespoons of the oil in a small bowl to blend. Place the prime rib in a roasting pan. Spread the sugar mixture all over the prime rib. Cover and refrigerate overnight, basting occasionally.

Preheat the oven to 375°F. Heat the remaining 1 tablespoon oil in a heavy large ovenproof frying pan over medium-high heat. Add the prime rib and cook just until brown and crisp on all sides, but not cooked through, about 2 minutes per side. Transfer the pan to the oven and roast until an instant-read meat thermometer registers 135°F for medium-rare, about 20 minutes. Let stand for 15 minutes before slicing.

FOR THE HERB SALAD

Whisk the oil and lemon juice in a large bowl to blend. Add the herbs; toss to coat. Season the salad to taste with fleur de sel and pepper.

TO ASSEMBLE AND SERVE

Cut the prime rib into ½-inch-thick slices. Arrange the prime rib slices and pommes soufflés on 2 large dinner plates. Mound the herb salad on the plates alongside the prime rib. Serve immediately.

POMMES SOUFFLÉS

These aren't soufflés in the conventional sense; they're leaf-thin slices of potatoes puffed up with air in the middle through a trick of thermodynamic conversion, which renders them crispy and delicate. I have to warn you, these may take some practice. But once you've mastered them, the effort is well worth it.

2 SERVINGS

1 large russet potato, scrubbed

8 cups canola oil (for deep-frying)

Fleur de sel and freshly ground pepper

Line a large baking sheet with paper towels. Using a vegetable peeler, trim the potato into a long, oval shape. Using a mandoline, cut the potatoes lengthwise into 1/8-inch-thick slices. Dry the potato slices very well with paper towels.

Fill each of 2 heavy large frying pans with 4 cups of the oil. Heat the oil in 1 pan over medium-low heat to 275°F. Heat the oil in the second pan over medium heat to 350°F. Working in batches, add the potato slices to the 275°F oil and fry until the potato slices begin to bubble, swirling occasionally and maintaining the oil temperature, about 4 minutes. Using a slotted spoon, carefully transfer the potato slices from the pan with 275°F oil to the pan with 350°F oil; fry just until they puff. They will puff immediately. Using a slotted spoon, transfer the puffed potato slices to the prepared baking sheet to drain (the potatoes will deflate).

DO AHEAD: *At this point, the potatoes can be prepared up to 8 hours ahead. Cover and refrigerate. Cool the 350°F oil; cover and keep at room temperature. Return the oil to 350°F before continuing.*

Just before serving, cook the potato puffs in the 350°F oil until they puff again and become crisp and pale golden, about 30 seconds per side. Using a slotted spoon, remove the potato slices from the oil and drain on the paper towel–lined baking sheet. Season the potato slices with fleur de sel and pepper and serve immediately.

VANILLA CRÈME BRÛLÉE

Who doesn't love crème brûlée, especially that delicate cracking sound it makes when you break its thin crust of caramelized sugar and hear it crunch in your mouth. Here, the vanilla bean enhances its nearly perfect flavor.

Position the rack in the center of the oven and preheat the oven to 180ºF. Place six 4-inch crème brûlée dishes with 1-inch-high sides on a heavy large baking sheet. Combine the cream and milk in a heavy medium saucepan. Using a small sharp knife, scrape the seeds from the vanilla bean into the milk mixture; add the bean. Bring the cream mixture to a boil.

Meanwhile, whisk the egg yolks and 6 tablespoons sugar in a large bowl to blend. Gradually whisk in the hot cream mixture. Strain the custard through a fine-mesh strainer and into a 4-cup glass measuring cup. Divide the custard equally among the prepared dishes. Carefully transfer the dishes on the baking sheet to the oven.

Bake until the custards are almost set in the center when the dishes are gently shaken, about 2 hours. Using a metal spatula, transfer the custards in the dishes to a cooling rack; cool for 30 minutes. Cover and refrigerate for at least 3 hours and up to 2 days.

TO FINISH AND SERVE

Working with 1 custard at a time, sprinkle 2 teaspoons sugar evenly over each custard. Holding a blowtorch so that the flame is 2 inches above the surface of the custard, slowly wave the flame over the custards to evenly melt and brown the sugar, about 2 minutes. Refrigerate until the caramelized sugar topping is firm and the custards are cold, at least 1 hour but no longer than 4 hours so that the topping doesn't soften.

6 SERVINGS

1²⁄₃ cups heavy whipping cream

½ cup whole milk

1 vanilla bean, split lengthwise

5 large egg yolks

6 tablespoons plus 12 teaspoons sugar

NAPOLEONS OF PUFF PASTRY
WITH VANILLA-WHISKEY CREAM

There are all kinds of reasons to love napoleons, but at the top of my list is their flaky texture and the sound they make when you saw into them with a knife (not to mention the delicate crunch when you bite into those multiple layers of puff pastry). A little bourbon and vanilla add character to the usual crème patissière.

6 SERVINGS

Vanilla-Whiskey Cream

  2 cups whole milk
  1 vanilla bean, split lengthwise
  6 large egg yolks
  ½ cup granulated sugar
  ½ cup all-purpose flour
  ¼ cup bourbon
  2 tablespoons unsalted butter

Puff Pastry

  2 10-ounce pieces of Puff Pastry Dough
     (page 242)
     Powdered sugar (for dusting)

FOR THE VANILLA-WHISKEY CREAM

Place the milk in a heavy medium saucepan. Scrape the seeds from the vanilla bean into the milk; add the bean. Bring the milk to a boil. Meanwhile, using an electric mixer, beat the egg yolks and sugar in a large bowl until light and fluffy, about 5 minutes. Mix in the flour. Gradually mix in the hot milk mixture. Return the mixture to the saucepan. Stir with a whisk over medium-low heat until the pastry cream thickens and bubbles begin to break on the surface of the cream, about 5 minutes. Remove from the heat. Add the whiskey and butter; whisk to blend. Transfer the vanilla-whiskey cream to a small bowl. Press plastic wrap directly onto the surface of the cream. Refrigerate until cold, at least 3 hours and up to 2 days.

FOR THE PUFF PASTRY

Preheat the oven to 375°F. Line a heavy large baking sheet with parchment paper. Roll out 1 piece of the puff pastry dough into a 12-inch square (about ⅛ inch thin). Trim the edges slightly. Using a large sharp knife, cut the pastry square crosswise into 3 equal strips. Transfer the strips to the prepared baking sheet. Cover with a sheet of parchment paper. Refrigerate until the dough is cold, about 20 minutes.

Place a second baking sheet atop the paper covering the pastries. Bake the pastries until they puff slightly and are golden brown, turning the pastries over after the first 20 minutes of baking, and baking a total of about 35 minutes.

Using a metal spatula, transfer the pastries to a cutting board. Using a large serrated knife, trim the warm pastries, if necessary, so that they are of equal dimensions (each should now be about 9 x 3 inches). Cut each pastry strip crosswise in half (there will be 6 pastry pieces total). Repeat with the remaining piece of puff pastry dough. Cool the pastry pieces completely.

TO FINISH AND SERVE

Remove the vanilla bean from the pastry cream. Transfer the pastry cream to a pastry bag fitted with a large round tip.

Split each pastry piece horizontally in half. Arrange 1 pastry half on each of 6 plates. Pipe the cream lengthwise over the pastries in 4 even rows; top each with a second pastry half. Repeat layering the cream and remaining pastries. Dust with powdered sugar and serve.

BUGNES WITH ORANGE FLOWER WATER

Bugnes are sort of like the French version of tortillas, except they're sweet. At any rate, they give you the same satisfying crunch you get from eating a tortilla chip. They make a wonderful accompaniment to strong coffee.

MAKES 32

2 large eggs, room temperature

1 tablespoon finely chopped grated orange peel

1 tablespoon orange flower water

½ tablespoon extra virgin olive oil

1¾ cups all-purpose flour

¼ cup powdered sugar

½ teaspoon fleur de sel

2 tablespoons unsalted butter, room temperature

Canola oil (for deep-frying)

Additional powdered sugar

Stir the eggs, orange peel, orange flower water, and olive oil in a medium bowl to blend. Using an electric mixer with a paddle attachment, or a wooden spoon, mix the flour, powdered sugar, and fleur de sel in a large bowl to blend. Mix in the egg mixture. Gradually beat in the butter. Mix until a smooth dough forms. Divide the dough into 4 equal pieces. Form each piece into a disk. Cover and refrigerate until the dough is cold, about 1 hour (this will make the dough easier to work with).

DO AHEAD: *The dough can be prepared up to 8 hours ahead. Keep refrigerated.*

Heat the canola oil in a deep fryer or in a heavy wide pot over medium heat to 375°F. Working with 1 piece of dough at a time, roll out the dough into an 8-inch round. Cut the round into 8 triangles. Fry the triangles in the oil until puffed and golden brown, about 1 minute per side. Using tongs, transfer the bugnes to a plate lined with paper towels to drain.

Arrange the bugnes on plates. Sift the additional powdered sugar over and serve hot.

FIG PASTILLA WITH ROSE FLOWER WATER

Pastilla is a Moroccan pastry that usually contains pigeon or other fowl and is served as a first course. This version, made with two kinds of figs and fresh almonds, makes for a nice, light dessert. I love how it sounds when you cut it with a knife, and the way the crust crunches in your mouth. This dish is best in September, when figs are in peak season. If you can't find the Italian honey figs, substitute an equal number of the Black Mission variety.

4 SERVINGS

½ cup Pastry Cream (page 73)

2 tablespoons rose flower water

8 17½ x 13½-inch sheets fresh phyllo pastry

½ cup (about) Clarified Butter (page 243)

⅓ cup (about) sugar

4 teaspoons freshly ground
   Ceylon cinnamon

4 tablespoons sliced fresh almonds, toasted

8 fresh figs, preferably 4 black Mission figs
   and 4 Italian honey figs, quartered
   Vanilla Ice Cream (page 245)

Position the rack in the center of the oven and preheat the oven to 400°F. Line a heavy large baking sheet with parchment paper. Whisk the pastry cream and rose flower water in a small bowl to blend. Set aside.

Place 1 phyllo sheet on the work surface so that the long edge is even with the work surface (cover the remaining phyllo sheets with plastic wrap and a slightly damp clean kitchen towel so that they do not dry out). Brush with some clarified butter. Sprinkle with 2 teaspoons of the sugar. Repeat layering with 3 more phyllo sheets, clarified butter, and sugar. Cut the phyllo stack crosswise into two 13 x 8-inch rectangles. Sprinkle 1 teaspoon cinnamon over each rectangle. Sprinkle 1 tablespoon almonds in the center of the bottom half of each phyllo stack. Arrange 4 Black Mission fig quarters and 4 Italian honey fig quarters alternately and in concentric circles atop the almonds on each phyllo stack. Spoon 2 tablespoons of the rose flower pastry cream atop each. Fold the top side of the phyllo stack over the figs. Brush with more clarified butter. Fold the edges to enclose the fillings completely. Using a large metal spatula, invert the pastries onto the prepared baking sheet. Brush the tops with the clarified butter. Repeat to make 4 pastries total.

Bake until the pastry is crisp and brown, about 25 minutes. Transfer the warm pastries to large plates and serve immediately with vanilla ice cream.

ALMOND PITHIVIER

Named for the French town of Pithiviers, where it was created, this classic treat is usually reserved for the celebration of the Magi's visit to the baby Jesus, which is observed during the first week of January. It's very crunchy on the outside but soft and creamy within. If you want to follow tradition, place a miniature trinket in the dough before baking (in France, it's a little crown made of porcelain or sometimes gold; needless to say, we chew very carefully). Whoever gets the slice with the crown has to pay a dollar to everyone else.

6 SERVINGS

1¾ cups sliced almonds (about 6 ounces)

¾ cup powdered sugar

¼ cup unsalted butter

1 large egg

2 teaspoons dark rum

2 tablespoons Pastry Cream (page 73)

2 10-ounce pieces of Puff Pastry Dough (page 242)

1 large egg yolk

1 teaspoon plus 2 tablespoons water

2 tablespoons granulated sugar

Blend the almonds in a food processor until they are very finely ground. Add the powdered sugar and blend until the mixture forms a fine powder. Add the butter, egg, and rum. Blend until a thick batter forms. Mix in the pastry cream. Transfer the almond cream to a bowl. Cover and refrigerate until the almond cream is semifirm, about 30 minutes.

Preheat the oven to 425°F. Line a heavy large baking sheet with parchment paper. Roll out each piece of the puff pastry dough on a lightly floured work surface into a 10-inch square. Transfer 1 pastry square to the prepared baking sheet. Gently spread the almond cream over the center of the pastry square on the baking sheet, leaving a 2-inch border around the edges. Brush the pastry edges with water. Top with the second pastry square. Press the edges firmly together to enclose the filling and seal the pastries well, taking care to remove any air bubbles. Using a sharp knife and the bottom of a 10-inch tart-pan bottom as an aid, cut the pastry into a 10-inch round. Mix the egg yolk with 1 teaspoon water in a small bowl to blend. Brush the top of the pastry with the egg wash. Using the knife tip, decoratively score the surface of the pastry. Bake until the pastry puffs and is golden brown on top, about 35 minutes. Reduce the heat to 350°F and continue baking until the pastry is cooked through and golden brown all over, about 35 minutes.

Meanwhile, stir the remaining 2 tablespoons water and granulated sugar in a small saucepan over medium-high heat until the sugar dissolves and the mixture is syrupy, about 2 minutes. Brush the warm sugar syrup over the warm pithivier (this will make the pastry crispy) and serve.

TASTE

HEAR TASTE SEE TOUCH SMELL HEAR TASTE SEE TOUCH SMELL HEAR TASTE SEE TOUCH

5

CHAPTER

SEE

TOUCH

SMELL

HEAR

{ TASTE }

IN REGARD TO FOOD,
TASTE IS THE MOTHER OF ALL SENSES.

BUT IT'S ASTONISHING TO CONTEMPLATE THE FACT THAT OUR MOUTHS ARE EQUIPPED WITH

THESE TINY, INCREDIBLY POWERFUL SENSORS (TASTE BUDS) THAT NOT EVEN NASA COULD REPLI-

CATE! THEY NOT ONLY ENABLE US TO IDENTIFY FOODS (OR OTHER SUBSTANCES) BY INTERPRET-

ING THEIR MOLECULAR STRUCTURE AND READING THEIR NUTRITIONAL VALUE, BUT ARE SO POW-

ERFULLY LINKED TO HUMAN SENSUAL GRATIFICATION THAT THEY HAVE SET OFF MASSIVE WAVES

OF MIGRATION AND TRADING PATTERNS, NOT TO MENTION WARS. THINK, FOR EXAMPLE, OF THE

RIGORS ENDURED BY THE ANCIENT SPICE CARAVANS TRAVELING THE SILK ROAD. YOU COULD

MAKE A CASE THAT THE SPICE TRADE THAT AROSE IN LATE MEDIEVAL TIMES WAS AS INSTRU-

MENTAL AS ANY OTHER MOVEMENT IN PULLING EUROPE OUT OF A CENTURIES-OLD SULK, DUR-

ING WHICH NOTHING MUCH MORE INTERESTING THAN TURNIPS WAS CONSUMED. CINNAMON,

CARDAMOM, SALT, AND PEPPER . . . THE INTOXICATING EFFECTS OF THESE EARTH-GROWN ITEMS

WERE ENOUGH TO INSPIRE PEOPLE TO UNDERTAKE GREAT VOYAGES AND UNDERGO MONUMENTAL

RISKS.

Theoretically, our sense of taste registers four different flavor sensations—sweet, sour, salty, bitter—and anything you put into your mouth will exude one or more of those sensations. While it is certainly useful to categorize flavors in this way, I believe that the sense of taste is much more vast, subtle, and nuanced. When you try to capture the sense of taste in terms of some chemo-neurological paradigm, something gets lost. Flavor is like emotion; it is better experienced than described, and when you are cooking, it is better to rely more on your sensual imagination than your analytical skills.

Having said that, one of the most important aspects of taste is the balancing of flavors. A few years ago, a lot of chefs designed dishes to encompass all four flavor sensations at once. Frankly, it was too much, and the resulting concoctions were cluttered and confusing to the palate. I think that most successful dishes contain two or three of them—occasionally four, but not very often (although my recipe for squab in chocolate sauce hits all four). Personally, my favorite combination is sweet and sour. There is something beautiful about creating a gentle tug of war between these two polarities. Think, for example, about eating an apple: Here is the perfect combination of sweet and sour.

Furthermore, we have to strive for balance within each of the individual flavor categories themselves. A dessert that is too sweet is cloying on the tongue and soon grows tiresome; too much salt can ruin anything, just as too much sugar can. Sometimes you can find balance by playing one flavor off another. Something overly sweet can be made delightful by balancing it with something sour, or even something salty.

I try to taste every dish before it's sent to the dining room (although, obviously, that's not practical in certain cases). Any dish, or for that matter any herb, vegetable, or spice, can look or smell one way, but surprise you by the way it tastes. You can be easily fooled. Black cardamom, for instance, has a smoky fragrance but tastes strongly of chlorophyll. If I hadn't tasted it first, I might have been misled. Some herbs may have quite pungent aromas, but little taste. Or their scent may be pallid to the nose, but their flavor may be overpowering to the tongue. Tomatoes may be sweet or acidic, but you won't know this unless you taste them first. I sometimes play a game with myself. I like to challenge myself to create dishes limited to no more than five ingredients, while incorporating no more than three flavors; that is, you may have more than one variation on the theme of, say, sweet, salty, or sour, but you don't want to engage all four tastes or the dish becomes cluttered.

As always, the essence of good cooking lies in the produce itself. Whether by complementing it with sauce or punching it up with spice, we want to enhance the flavor of the produce rather than to mask it. (Believe it or not, this approach is quite a departure from French cooking of a century ago. It used to be that the sauce was all that counted; if the sauce was good, it didn't much matter what lay underneath it.)

The fact is, you can sharpen your sense of taste with practice. When I worked in Saint-Etienne with Pierre Gagnaire, he and other chefs around town would put on what they'd call la *semaine du gout*—"The Week of Tastes." Schoolchildren would make the rounds to various restaurants every day, and these sophisticated, high-strung chefs would put simple flavors before them—chocolate, lemon, vanilla—and challenge them to taste deeply, to remember the sensation. In doing so, these chefs believed they were not only ushering them into our tradition of gastronomy. They also believed that

learning to taste strengthened all of one's senses, and made for a more alert, fully developed human being.

And it's true, I believe. You can sharpen your sense of taste when you're eating out. When you dig into a dish of some complexity, roll the flavors in your mouth and write down the ingredients. What do you taste? Oregano. Garlic. But what is that licorice flavor? Pernod! Okay, but there's some herb you just can't seem to identify. When the meal is over, ask your server. If he or she doesn't know, ask to speak to the chef if he's not too busy. Chefs are always pleased when people find their food intriguing enough to inspire further inquiry. If you have a friend who's similarly inclined, play games with each other. Fix each other meals and do your initial tasting with your eyes closed. Soon you'll find yourself able to visualize the whole tray of ingredients, which helps when you're inventing dishes of your own. The more you can identify ingredients by using only your sense of taste, the better you'll be in the kitchen. You can be blind but still able to see with your tongue.

SPICED OIL

With a flavor poised delicately between floral, tangy, and nutty, this oil will add punch to any simply prepared fish or meat after it's cooked. You can drizzle the oil over steamed vegetables, or even sear vegetables in it. It's also good for dressing salads. The oil should last for at least three months.

MAKES ABOUT 2 CUPS

2 cups canola oil

1½ tablespoons coarsely ground nutmeg

1½ tablespoons coarsely ground juniper berries

4 teaspoons coarsely ground green cardamom pods

Pinch of saffron

Place the oil in a heavy medium saucepan. Cook over low heat until the oil registers 180ºF, about 8 minutes. Remove from the heat. Add the spices to the oil. Cover and steep for 30 minutes. Cool the oil to room temperature, about 2 hours. Using a funnel, pour the oil mixture into a bottle. Seal the lid. Store at room temperature for 2 weeks before using. Leave the sediment at the bottom of the bottle when using (do not shake before using).

DO AHEAD: *The oil can be made 3 months ahead. Keep airtight at room temperature.*

SPICED VINEGAR

Excellent for dressing salad, especially those composed of sweeter vegetables, such as carrots, beets, and turnips (but don't pair it with, say, daikon radish, because they'll only get into a fight). It's also good for punching up mayonnaise and finishing sauces, and works nicely with simple grilled fish and meat. This vinegar should be good for at least three months.

MAKES ABOUT 2 CUPS

2 cups red wine vinegar

6 shallots, thinly sliced

1 whole nutmeg

1 whole clove

1 tablespoon brown or yellow mustard seeds

1 tablespoon finely grated orange peel

1 teaspoon coarsely ground long pepper

1 teaspoon coarsely ground mace

Bring the vinegar to a simmer in a heavy medium saucepan. Add all the remaining ingredients. Using a funnel, carefully pour the hot vinegar mixture into a bottle. Seal with the lid. Store at room temperature for 3 to 4 weeks before using.

DO AHEAD: *The vinegar can be made 3 months ahead. Store airtight at room temperature.*

ONION JAM

2 8-ounce Maui, Vidalia, or other sweet onions
1/3 cup grenadine
1/4 cup distilled white vinegar
1/4 cup red Burgundy
1/4 cup sugar
1 tablespoon unsalted butter
Fleur de sel and freshly ground pepper

Using a mandoline, cut the onions into 1/16-inch-thin round slices. Combine the sliced onions and all the remaining ingredients in a heavy medium saucepan. Cook, uncovered, over low heat until the liquid is absorbed and the onions are very tender, stirring occasionally, about 1 hour and 15 minutes. Season the jam to taste with fleur de sel and pepper.

DO AHEAD: *The jam can be prepared up to 2 days ahead. Cool. Cover and refrigerate. Rewarm before serving.*

CARROT CONFIT WITH STAR ANISE

Carrots and oranges are a match made in heaven. Both are sweet, but in different ways. Add the pungency of star anise, and you've got a real winner.

3 pounds carrots (about 10), peeled
1 1/2 cups strained fresh orange juice
3 whole star anise
Fleur de sel and freshly ground pepper
2 cups extra virgin olive oil
1 fresh thyme sprig
1 fresh rosemary sprig
1 teaspoon coarsely ground star anise
1/4 teaspoon fleur de sel

Coarsely chop half of the carrots. Combine the chopped carrots, orange juice, and whole star anise in a heavy medium saucepan. Cover partially and simmer over medium-low heat until the carrots are very tender and the liquid is reduced to about 1/3 cup, stirring occasionally, about 30 minutes. Discard the star anise. Transfer the carrot mixture to a food processor and puree until smooth. Press the puree through a fine-mesh strainer. Season the puree to taste with fleur de sel and pepper.

DO AHEAD: *The carrot puree can be prepared up to 8 hours ahead. Cool, then cover and refrigerate. Rewarm before serving.*

Meanwhile, cut the remaining carrots crosswise into 4-inch pieces. Heat the oil, thyme, and rosemary in a heavy medium saucepan over low heat until aromatic, about 10 minutes. Add the carrot pieces and cook until very tender but not brown, about 40 minutes. Using tongs, transfer the carrots to a cutting board and cut them lengthwise in half.

TO ASSEMBLE AND SERVE

Spoon the warm carrot puree into 4 wide shallow soup bowls. Arrange the carrot pieces atop the puree, dividing equally. Sprinkle with the ground star anise, fleur de sel, and freshly ground pepper.

CHILLED ASPARAGUS SOUP WITH ARGAN OIL

The argan tree grows in Morocco, and while the oil made from its fruit is just now becoming available in the U.S., I predict that it will soon make a big splash. Certainly it's a worthy addition to your pantry. Its flavor is hard to describe: nutty, but with subtle floral undertones. This recipe for asparagus soup is pretty basic, but I think you'll find that drizzling it with this exotic oil (it takes 100 pounds of the fruit to make one liter) will add both body and a note of complexity that mystically enhances the taste of the asparagus.

4 APPETIZER SERVINGS

4   pounds fresh asparagus, trimmed,
    cut into 2-inch lengths

⅓   cup plus 2 teaspoons argan oil or
    good-quality extra virgin olive oil
    Fleur de sel

Cook the asparagus in a large pot of boiling salted water until very tender but still green, about 6 minutes. Drain. Transfer the asparagus to a large bowl of ice water to cool. Cut off the asparagus tips. Place half of the tips in a small bowl; cover and refrigerate. Working in 4 batches, puree the remaining tips and pieces in a blender until smooth, adding about 3 tablespoons of the ice water to each batch to help form a puree. With the machine running, drizzle ⅓ cup oil through the feed tube into the soup. Process until well blended. Season the soup to taste with fleur de sel. Cover and refrigerate until cold.

DO AHEAD: *The soup and reserved asparagus tips can be prepared 4 hours ahead. Cover the soup and refrigerate. Keep the tips refrigerated.*

Ladle the soup into 4 soup bowls. Cut the reserved asparagus tips lengthwise in half and float them atop the soup. Sprinkle each serving with a pinch of fleur de sel. Drizzle each serving with ½ teaspoon oil. Serve immediately.

BITTER ALMOND CAULIFLOWER SOUP

The addition of bitter almond paste transforms what would otherwise be the librarian of soups into a sultry vixen. If you don't have bitter almond paste, substitute six tablespoons of finely ground almonds.

4 APPETIZER SERVINGS

Soup

1 tablespoon extra virgin olive oil
¼ cup minced onion
8 cups cauliflower florets
(from about one 2½-pound head)
2 cups Chicken Stock (page 239)
1 cup heavy whipping cream
3 tablespoons bitter almond paste
3 tablespoons unsalted butter
½ cup crème fraîche
Fleur de sel and freshly
ground white pepper

Spiced Croutons

1 ½-inch-thick slice Spiced White Bread
(page 243)
1 tablespoon extra virgin olive oil
2 tablespoons fresh chervil sprigs
4 almonds, thinly sliced, toasted

FOR THE SOUP

Heat the oil in a heavy large saucepan over medium-low heat. Add the onion and sauté until tender but not brown, about 3 minutes. Add the cauliflower, chicken stock, and cream. Bring to a simmer over medium-high heat. Reduce the heat to medium and simmer until the cauliflower is tender, stirring occasionally, about 6 minutes. Working in batches, transfer the cauliflower mixture and almond paste to a blender and puree until smooth, adding the butter while blending, about 1 minute. Return the soup to the saucepan. Whisk in the crème fraîche. Season the soup to taste with fleur de sel and white pepper.

FOR THE SPICED CROUTONS

Trim the crust from the bread slice. Cut the bread slice into ½-inch cubes. Heat the oil in a heavy medium sauté pan over medium-low heat. Add the bread cubes and sauté until golden brown, about 5 minutes. Season the croutons with fleur de sel and pepper. Transfer the croutons to a paper towel.

TO SERVE

Ladle the soup into 4 wide shallow soup bowls, dividing equally. Garnish with the croutons, chervil sprigs, and almonds.

FRENCH GREEN BEAN SALAD WITH COCONUT, APPLE, HORSERADISH MOUSSE, AND LEMONGRASS OIL

This salad hits a lot of different flavor notes. It's sweet, spicy, and tangy all at once. I created it for a wine pairing in Hawaii, where coconut was used abundantly. It goes particularly well with pink champagne.

6 FIRST-COURSE SERVINGS

Lemongrass Oil

- ½ cup extra virgin olive oil
- 2 lemongrass stalks, cut crosswise into 1-inch pieces

Salad

- ½ cup heavy whipping cream
- 3 tablespoons minced grated peeled fresh horseradish (from one 2-inch piece) Fleur de sel and freshly ground pepper
- 1 pound French green beans (haricots verts), trimmed and blanched
- 1 Granny Smith apple, peeled, cored, halved, and cut lengthwise into ⅛-inch slices
- 6 baby Maui onions or pearl onions, blanched, peeled, and thinly sliced into rings
- ⅓ cup shaved fresh coconut

FOR THE LEMONGRASS OIL

Heat the oil and lemongrass in a small saucepan over low heat until the lemongrass becomes pale golden and infuses the oil, about 30 minutes. Cool completely. Remove the lemongrass. Set the oil aside.

FOR THE SALAD

Using an electric mixer, beat the cream and horseradish in a large bowl until firm peaks form. Season the horseradish mousse to taste with fleur de sel and pepper. Cover and refrigerate.

DO AHEAD: *The lemongrass oil can be prepared, covered, and stored at room temperature up to 2 days ahead. The horseradish mousse can be prepared and refrigerated up to 2 hours ahead.*

TO FINISH AND SERVE

Toss the green beans with 2 tablespoons lemongrass oil in a large bowl. Season to taste with fleur de sel and pepper. Using about 2 tablespoons for each serving, spoon an oval-shaped scoop of the horseradish mousse into the center of 6 large plates. Surround the mousse with the green beans. Insert 2 apple slices vertically into the mousse for each serving. Garnish with the onion slices and coconut.

SEARED FOIE GRAS IN REDUCTION OF CHOCOLATE, RED WINE, AND POMEGRANATE WITH ONION JAM AND JUNIPER BERRIES

This version of foie gras hearkens back to French cooking at the dawn of the twentieth century—in other words, it's one of those rich, hearty dishes fit for a royal banquet. Because the sauce (a powerhouse combination of red wine, chocolate, and a little veal stock) takes center stage, it's not necessary to use the most expensive foie gras.

4 APPETIZER SERVINGS

½ cup good-quality dry red wine

½ cup ruby port

¼ cup Veal Stock (page 238)

3 ounces good-quality bittersweet
(not unsweetened) chocolate, chopped
Fleur de sel and freshly ground pepper
Four ½-inch-thick slices foie gras
(about 4 ounces each)

1 cup Onion Jam (page 193)

2 teaspoons freshly ground juniper berries

¼ cup pomegranate seeds

Boil the wine, port, and veal stock in a heavy small saucepan over high heat until reduced to ¼ cup, about 9 minutes. Remove from the heat. Add the chocolate and whisk until melted and the sauce is smooth. Season to taste with fleur de sel and pepper.

DO AHEAD: *The chocolate sauce can be prepared up to 1 day ahead. Cool. Cover and refrigerate. Rewarm before serving.*

Sprinkle the foie gras with fleur de sel and pepper. Heat a heavy large sauté pan over high heat. Add the foie gras (do not add any oil) and cook until deep golden brown, pressing with a spatula, about 1 minute per side. Reduce the heat to low and cook until the center of the foie gras is warm, about 1 minute per side. Transfer the foie gras to paper towels to absorb the excess oil.

TO ASSEMBLE AND SERVE

Spoon 3 tablespoons of the warm onion jam into the center of each of 4 large plates. Top with the foie gras. Spoon 2 tablespoons of the chocolate sauce over each slice of foie gras. Dust with the ground juniper berries. Place the pomegranate seeds around the perimeter of the plates. Serve immediately.

AHI AND HAMACHI IN VERJUS WITH DAIKON RADISH AND MUSTARD OIL

Verjus, the juice extracted from large, unripened grapes, had long fallen out of favor for use in cooking. Now it's been justly rediscovered for its ability to add a sour, slightly acidic high note to dishes. You should be able to find it in quality wine shops. Here, the tartness of the verjus is softened with a little honey, but given a dash of fiery astringency by a drizzling of mustard oil, all of which enhances the fresh flavor of the ahi and hamachi.

4 APPETIZER SERVINGS

¼ cup verjus

2 tablespoons mustard oil

1 tablespoon honey
   Fleur de sel and freshly ground pepper

1 cup finely diced sashimi-grade ahi tuna

½ cup finely diced hamachi (Japanese yellowtail)

¼ cup finely diced peeled daikon radish

2 tablespoons crème fraîche

1 teaspoon brown or yellow mustard seeds, coarsely ground

12 fresh chives

Whisk the verjus, mustard oil, and honey in a medium bowl to blend. Season the sauce to taste with fleur de sel and pepper.

DO AHEAD: *The sauce can be prepared up to 4 hours ahead. Cover and refrigerate. Return to room temperature before using.*

TO FINISH AND SERVE

Add the tuna and hamachi to the sauce; toss to coat. Season the seafood mixture to taste with fleur de sel and pepper. Place one 4-inch ring mold with ¾-inch-high sides in the center of each of four plates. Spoon the seafood mixture into the rings, pressing lightly to compact. Sprinkle the daikon radish atop the seafood mixture. Drizzle the crème fraîche around the perimeter of the plates, and then sprinkle the mustard seeds over the crème fraîche. Carefully remove the ring molds. Lay 3 chives atop each and serve immediately.

CAESAR GREEN BEAN SALAD
WITH BABY ROMAINE LETTUCES

I'd never even heard of Caesar salad before coming to the United States, but I fell in love with it the first time I ate it. I had a feeling that fresh green beans would be a fantastic addition, providing a sweet note to contrast with the slightly tart-salty dressing, and the popularity of this version has proven me right!

4 APPETIZER SERVINGS

Salad Dressing

- 2 anchovy fillets in oil, drained and minced
- 1 large egg yolk
- 1 garlic clove, minced
- 1 teaspoon Dijon mustard
- 1 teaspoon freshly grated Parmesan cheese
- 2 tablespoons strained fresh lemon juice
- 1 tablespoon Lobster Stock (page 240), optional
- 1 teaspoon chopped fresh tarragon
  Dash of hot pepper sauce (such as Tabasco)
- 6 tablespoons extra virgin olive oil
  Fleur de sel and freshly ground pepper

Salad

- 8 ounces French green beans (haricot verts), trimmed
- 1 tablespoon extra virgin olive oil
- ½ cup ½-inch-cubes of crustless white bread
- 2 heads of baby red romaine lettuce
- 2 heads of baby green romaine lettuce
- 2 ounces sliced bacon, cut crosswise into ⅛-inch-thin strips and blanched
- 1 garlic clove, cut lengthwise into paper-thin slices
- 1 tablespoon fresh tarragon leaves
- 2 Meyer lemons, segmented

FOR THE SALAD DRESSING

Whisk the first 5 ingredients in a large bowl to blend. Whisk in the lemon juice, lobster stock (if using), chopped tarragon, and hot pepper sauce. Gradually add the oil, whisking constantly until the mixture thickens slightly and is well blended. Season the dressing to taste with fleur de sel and pepper. Cover and refrigerate.

FOR THE SALAD

Cook the green beans in a medium pot of boiling water until crisp-tender, about 2 minutes. Drain. Transfer the green beans to a large bowl of ice water to cool; drain again. Pat dry with paper towels. Refrigerate until cold.

Heat the oil in a heavy small sauté pan over medium heat. Add the bread cubes and sauté until golden brown, about 3 minutes. Season the croutons to taste with fleur de sel and pepper. Drain on a paper towel.

DO AHEAD: *The dressing, green beans, and croutons can be prepared up to 8 hours ahead. Keep the dressing and green beans refrigerated. Store the croutons in an airtight container at room temperature.*

TO ASSEMBLE AND SERVE

Toss the romaine lettuces in a large bowl with enough of the dressing to coat lightly. Season to taste with fleur de sel and pepper. Arrange the lettuces in the center of 4 plates, dividing equally. Toss the green beans with enough of the dressing to coat lightly. Season to taste with fleur de sel and pepper. Arrange the green beans atop the lettuces. Sprinkle the croutons, bacon, garlic, and tarragon leaves around. Garnish with the lemon segments and serve immediately.

GREEN LENTILS WITH CINNAMON

A savory, aromatic treatment of lentils that whispers of Arabia, this dish goes well with white meats such as chicken and veal, as well as foie gras.

4 SIDE-DISH SERVINGS

1 white onion, halved

1 whole clove

6 cups purified water (such as Evian)

8 ounces dried petite green lentils (about
  1¼ cups), rinsed and drained

1 carrot, peeled and quartered

1 celery rib, quartered

1 bouquet garni (made of 2 fresh rosemary
  sprigs,
  2 fresh thyme sprigs, 2 fresh flat-leaf
  parsley sprigs, and 1 bay leaf)

1 teaspoon freshly ground Ceylon
  cinnamon

¼ cup unsalted butter
  Fleur de sel and freshly ground pepper

1 English hothouse cucumber, peeled,
  seeded, and cut diagonally into ¼-inch-
  thick slices

Pierce one onion half with the clove. Place the onion halves in a heavy large saucepan. Add the purified water and the next 5 ingredients. Bring to a boil. Reduce the heat to medium and simmer gently, uncovered, until the lentils are tender, stirring occasionally, about 30 minutes. Discard the cooked vegetables and bouquet garni. Stir the butter into the lentils. Season to taste with fleur de sel and pepper.

Meanwhile, cook the cucumber slices in a medium saucepan of boiling water until crisp-tender, about 30 seconds. Drain. Transfer the cucumber slices to a large bowl of ice water to cool. Drain again.

Stir the cucumber slices into the lentils. Cook over medium heat until the cucumbers are heated through, about 2 minutes. Ladle the lentil mixture into 4 shallow soup plates and serve.

RACK OF LAMB WITH BROTH, BABY VEGETABLES, AND CARAWAY SEEDS

A favorite classic of French country cooking is navarin, a hearty (and heavy) mutton stew with small onions, potatoes, peas, and carrots. I thought it would be fun to refine a rustic staple, and while this is a stylized version of the original, it's quite satisfying. Instead of the traditional, heavily floured sauce, I've substituted lamb broth, a much less aggressive stand-in that still reinforces the flavor of lamb without making it too strong.

4 MAIN-COURSE SERVINGS

Broth and Vegetables

3 cups Lamb Stock (page 237)

2 large ripe tomatoes, quartered

4 shallots, halved

4 garlic cloves, halved

2 tablespoons tomato paste

4 fresh thyme sprigs

Fleur de sel and freshly ground pepper

8 fingerling potatoes, unpeeled

8 baby turnips, peeled

16 snow peas, stringed

¼ cup shelled fresh English peas

4 baby onions or pearl onions

Lamb

2 1½- to 2-pound racks of lamb
(about 8 ribs per rack), trimmed

1 tablespoon extra virgin olive oil

1 teaspoon coarsely ground caraway seeds

FOR THE BROTH AND VEGETABLES

Combine the first 6 ingredients in a heavy medium saucepan. Bring to a boil over high heat. Reduce the heat to medium-low and simmer until the liquid is reduced to 1 cup, stirring occasionally to break up the tomatoes, shallots, and garlic, about 30 minutes. Strain the broth into a 2-cup glass measuring cup, pressing on the solids to extract as much liquid as possible. Return the broth to the saucepan. Season the broth to taste with fleur de sel and pepper.

Meanwhile, cook the vegetables separately in a large saucepan of boiling salted water until they are crisp-tender, about 7 minutes for the potatoes, 2 minutes for the turnips, 30 seconds for the snow peas and English peas, and 20 seconds for the onions. Place the vegetables in a large bowl of ice water to cool. Drain again, and pat dry with paper towels. Cut the potatoes crosswise into ½-inch-thick slices. Peel the onions, then slice them crosswise into thin rings.

DO AHEAD: *At this point, the broth and vegetables can be prepared up to 8 hours ahead. Cover and refrigerate the broth. Rewarm the broth before continuing. Cover and refrigerate the precooked vegetables.*

FOR THE LAMB

Preheat the oven to 425ºF. Sprinkle the lamb with fleur de sel and pepper. Heat the oil in a heavy large sauté pan over high heat. Working in batches, cook the lamb in the pan until brown, about 4 minutes per side. Arrange the lamb, meat side up, on a large rimmed baking sheet. Roast until an instant-read meat thermometer inserted into the center of the lamb registers 135ºF for medium-rare, about 18 minutes. Transfer the lamb to a work surface. Tent loosely with aluminum foil and let stand for 5 minutes. Cut each lamb rack between the bones into 4 double chops.

TO FINISH AND SERVE

Add all the vegetables to the broth. Bring to a simmer. Using a slotted spoon, divide the vegetables equally among 4 wide shallow soup plates. Arrange 2 double chops atop the vegetables in each bowl. Ladle the broth over the lamb and vegetables. Sprinkle with the ground caraway seeds. Serve immediately.

LOBSTER POACHED IN VANILLA WITH MELON, MANGO, PAPAYA, AVOCADO, AND AGED BALSAMIC VINEGAR AND HONEY VINAIGRETTE

"What is it about vanilla that works so well with lobster?" a friend asked me. I huffed and said, "Well, of course it's . . . hmmm." I really had no idea, and I still don't. This recipe came about more or less by accident, and I can't really explain why. It's just one of those magical combinations that works. Sometimes it's better not to ask too many questions.

4 MAIN-COURSE SERVINGS

Lobsters

4 vanilla beans, split lengthwise

4 2-pound live lobsters

Salad

2 tablespoons aged balsamic vinegar

1 tablespoon fresh strained lemon juice

1 tablespoon honey

3 tablespoons extra virgin olive oil
Fleur de sel and freshly ground pepper

1/2 cantaloupe, halved and seeded

1 mango, pitted

1 papaya, halved and seeded

1 large avocado, halved and pitted

2 cups mixed baby greens

FOR THE LOBSTERS

Fill a large pot with water. Scrape the seeds from the vanilla beans into the water; add the beans. Bring the water to a boil. Working with 1 lobster at a time, submerge the lobsters headfirst into the boiling water, and cook until the shells are bright red and the meat is opaque, about 5 minutes. Using tongs, transfer the lobsters to a large bowl; cool. Remove the meat from the tails and claws. Cover and refrigerate until cold.

FOR THE SALAD

Whisk the vinegar, lemon juice, and honey in a large bowl to blend. Gradually add the oil, whisking until the vinaigrette is well blended. Season to taste with fleur de sel and pepper.

Using a melon baller, scoop out the flesh of each fruit to form small balls.

DO AHEAD: *The lobsters and vinaigrette can be prepared up to 8 hours ahead. Keep the lobsters refrigerated. Cover and refrigerate the vinaigrette; bring it to room temperature and rewhisk before using. All the fruit, except for the avocado, can be prepared up to 2 hours ahead (prepare the avocado just before serving to prevent it from discoloring). Cover the fruits separately and refrigerate.*

TO FINISH AND SERVE

Cut the lobster tails lengthwise in half. Toss the lobster tails and claw meat in a large bowl with enough vinaigrette to coat. Arrange 2 claw meat pieces in the center of each of 4 large plates. Arrange 2 lobster halves around the claw meat pieces. Toss the mixed baby greens in the same large bowl with enough vinaigrette to coat (about 2 tablespoons). Mound the greens atop the lobster pieces, dividing equally. Toss all the fruit with 1 tablespoon vinaigrette. Arrange the fruit around the greens and serve immediately.

CARAMELIZED COD WITH FIVE FLAVORS AND BABY SPINACH SALAD

Cod is a great fish for when you want to play around with flavors, as its taste is rather neutral. After trying this combination of flavors, consider experimenting with your own.

4 MAIN-COURSE SERVINGS

Five-Spice Powder

- 1 tablespoon grated orange peel, minced
- 1 tablespoon grated lime peel, minced
- ½ vanilla bean, halved lengthwise, coarsely chopped crosswise
- 1 6-inch piece of licorice root, broken into 1-inch pieces
- 2 tablespoons finely crumbled dried mint leaves

Fish and Salad

- 4 5-ounce cod fillets
  Fleur de sel and freshly ground pepper
- 1 teaspoon sugar
- 3 tablespoons extra virgin olive oil
- 3 tablespoons raspberry vinegar
- 2 cups baby spinach, stems removed
- 2 cups baby beet leaves, stems trimmed

FOR THE FIVE-SPICE POWDER

Preheat the oven to 200°F. Shake the orange peel, lime peel, vanilla, and licorice root in a small resealable plastic bag to combine. Sprinkle the mixture over a heavy baking sheet. Bake until the orange peel is dry and crisp, stirring occasionally, about 18 minutes. Transfer the dried mixture to a spice grinder. Add the dried mint and process into a powder. Sift the ground seasonings into a small bowl to remove any large pieces of licorice.

DO AHEAD: *The five-spice powder can be prepared up to 2 weeks ahead. Store airtight at room temperature.*

FOR THE FISH AND SALAD

Rub the cod fillets with fleur de sel and pepper. Sprinkle one side of each fillet with ¼ teaspoon sugar. Heat 1 tablespoon of the oil in a heavy large nonstick sauté pan over high heat. Add the cod and cook until golden brown on the outside and just opaque in the center, about 4 minutes per side.

Meanwhile, whisk the vinegar and remaining 2 tablespoons oil in a large bowl to blend. Add the spinach and the beet leaves; toss to coat. Season the salad to taste with fleur de sel and pepper.

TO ASSEMBLE AND SERVE

Arrange the salad in the center of 4 large dinner plates. Place the fillets atop the salad. Sift ¼ teaspoon of the five-spice powder over each fillet. Serve immediately.

GLAZED LANGOUSTINES WITH CEYLON CINNAMON AND FRIED ANGEL HAIR PASTA WITH CLAMS

What gave me the idea to match lobster with cinnamon? Just as with lobster and vanilla, I get tongue-tied trying to explain exactly why cinnamon brings out the best in lobster. All I know is that it has become one of my greatest hits. For the perfect accompaniment, serve this dish with fried angel hair pasta with clams. Langoustines are a petite species of the lobster family, known for their sweet, delicate flavor. If you can't find them, substitute an equal number of jumbo shrimp.

4 MAIN-COURSE SERVINGS

Glaze and Sauce

2 cups Lobster Stock (page 240)

3 cups good-quality dry white wine

4 shallots, sliced

6 tablespoons cold unsalted butter, cut into small pieces

1 3/4 teaspoons freshly ground Ceylon cinnamon

Fleur de sel and freshly ground pepper

Langoustines

4 quarts water

8 fresh bay leaves

4 fresh thyme sprigs

1 1/2 teaspoons coarse salt

20 3-ounce langoustines or jumbo shrimp

Additional freshly ground Ceylon cinnamon

Fried Angel Hair Pasta with Clams (recipe follows)

FOR THE GLAZE AND SAUCE

Boil the lobster stock in a heavy small saucepan over medium-high heat and boil until very dark amber brown and syrupy, about 12 minutes. Set the glaze aside.

Meanwhile, combine the wine and shallots in a heavy medium saucepan over medium-high heat and boil until reduced to 1/3 cup, about 18 minutes. Strain the sauce through a fine-mesh strainer into a small bowl, pressing gently on the shallots to extract the liquid. Discard the shallots. Return the sauce to the saucepan. Whisk in the butter to form a smooth sauce. Whisk in the cinnamon. Season the sauce to taste with fleur de sel and pepper. Set aside and keep warm.

FOR THE LANGOUSTINES

Combine the water, bay leaves, thyme, and coarse salt in a large pot. Bring to a boil over high heat. Working in 2 batches, add the langoustines to the boiling cooking liquid and cook for 5 minutes. Using tongs, transfer the langoustines to a work surface.

TO ASSEMBLE AND SERVE

Using a large sharp knife, cut the langoustines lengthwise in half. Arrange 10 langoustine halves on each of 4 very large plates. Spoon the sauce over the langoustines. Drizzle the glaze alongside. Sprinkle with the additional cinnamon. Serve the fried angel hair pasta with clams on plates alongside.

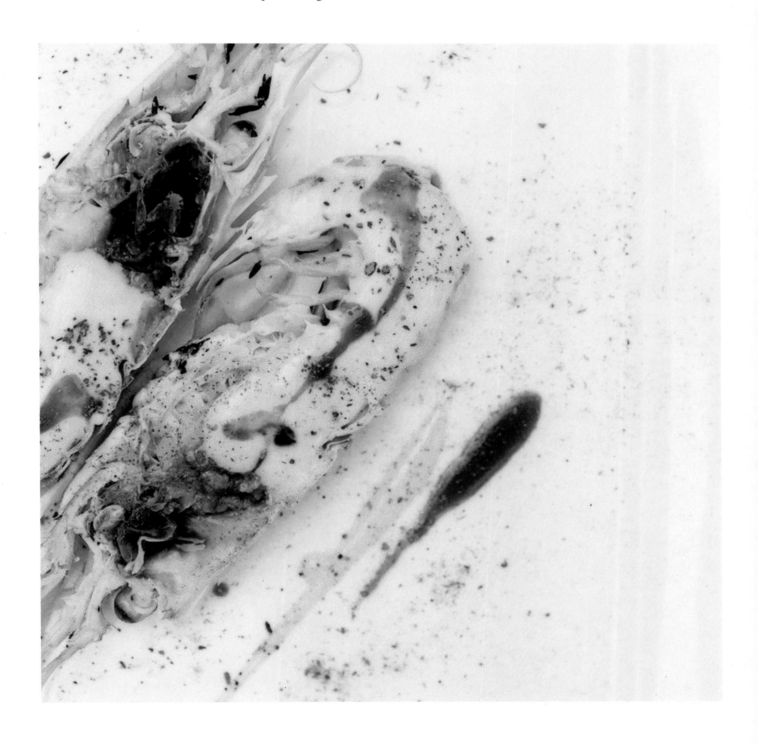

FRIED ANGEL HAIR PASTA WITH CLAMS

4 SIDE-DISH SERVINGS

20 live Manila clams (about 12 ounces total),
scrubbed

1 cup canola oil (for deep-frying)

1 cup dried angel hair pasta (vermicelli)
(6 ounces)

1½ cups Lobster Stock (page 240)
Fleur de sel and freshly ground pepper

Steam the clams in a large saucepan combining 1-inch of boiling salted water just until the clams open, about 2 minutes (discard any clams that do not open). Remove the saucepan from the heat. Using a slotted spoon, transfer the clams to a large bowl. Remove the clam meat from the shells; discard the shells. Set the clam meat aside.

Heat the oil in a heavy large sauté pan over medium heat. Add the pasta and sauté until golden brown, about 5 minutes. Using a slotted spoon, transfer the pasta to a paper towel–lined plate to drain.

Combine the lobster stock and pasta in a heavy medium sauté pan. Bring to a boil over medium-high heat. Reduce the heat to low and simmer gently until the pasta is tender and the mixture is creamy, stirring occasionally, about 6 minutes. Add the reserved clam meat and cook just until heated through, about 2 minutes. Season to taste with fleur de sel and pepper.

Spoon the pasta mixture onto 4 plates and serve immediately.

COD CRUSTED WITH GINGER, ALMONDS, AND SESAME SEEDS WITH BABY TOMATOES AND CANDIED GINGER

At some point early in my career, I fell in love with ginger. There is really nothing like it: Seductive yet petulant, it must be handled delicately (and lovingly) or it will overwhelm you with its power. I wanted to find a way to use it in a seafood dish, but after several failures, I almost decided it was too aggressive. With candied ginger, I finally found a way to tame it so that it allowed the flavor of the fish to come through. I also like this dish for the contrast between the supercrisp crust and the softness of the cod. Look for almond flour in Indian or Middle Eastern groceries, or see the Resource Guide on page 246.

6 MAIN-COURSE SERVINGS

Sauce

- 1 tablespoon extra virgin olive oil
- 2 tomatoes, coarsely chopped
- 1 onion, coarsely chopped
- 1 carrot, peeled and coarsely chopped
- 1 celery rib, coarsely chopped
- 4 cups Fish Stock (page 240)
- ½ cup coarsely chopped fresh lemongrass
- ¼ cup tomato paste
- ¼ cup peeled chopped fresh ginger
- 2 tablespoons heavy whipping cream
- 1 tablespoon sugar
  Fleur de sel and freshly ground pepper

Fish

- ½ cup almond flour
- 2 tablespoons unsalted butter, room temperature
- 2 tablespoons black sesame seeds
- 1 tablespoon all-purpose flour
- 1 teaspoon ground ginger
- ¾ teaspoon finely ground black pepper
- ¼ teaspoon fleur de sel
- 1 large egg yolk
- 6 5-ounce black cod or sable fish fillets

FOR THE SAUCE

Heat the oil in a heavy large saucepan over medium-high heat. Add the tomatoes, onion, carrot, and celery. Sauté until the onion is translucent, about 8 minutes. Add the fish stock. Simmer, uncovered, until the liquid is reduced by half, about 15 minutes. Add the lemongrass, tomato paste, and ginger. Simmer until the sauce is reduced by half again, about 15 minutes. Strain the sauce through a very fine-mesh strainer and into a small saucepan, pressing on the solids with the back of a spoon to extract as much liquid as possible. Whisk the cream and sugar into the sauce. Season to taste with fleur de sel and pepper.

FOR THE FISH

Using an electric mixer, beat the first 7 ingredients in a large bowl to blend. Beat in the egg yolk. Using an offset spatula, spread the sesame butter over a piece of wax paper, forming a 9-inch square with a ⅛-inch thickness. Cover with another piece of wax paper. Transfer to a small baking sheet. Refrigerate until firm, about 30 minutes. Using a sharp knife, cut the wrapped sesame butter into 6 squares with dimensions to resemble the fish fillets.

DO AHEAD: *The sauce and sesame butter can be prepared up to 8 hours ahead. Cover separately and refrigerate. Rewarm the sauce before serving.*

Preheat the oven to 500°F. Oil a heavy rimmed baking sheet. Arrange the fish fillets on the baking sheet. Sprinkle the fish with fleur de sel and pepper. Place 1 sesame dough square atop each fish fillet. Press the dough gently to adhere to the fish. Remove the unused paper. Bake until the dough is golden around the edges and the fish is just cooked through, about 10 minutes.

(continued)

Vegetables

1½ tablespoons extra virgin olive oil

24 baby carrots, peeled and blanched

24 cherry tomatoes, halved

3 tablespoons finely chopped crystallized
ginger

1½ cups pepper cress or watercress (for garnish)

MEANWHILE, PREPARE THE VEGETABLES

Heat the oil in a heavy large sauté pan over medium heat. Add the carrots, tomatoes, and ginger. Sauté just until heated through, about 5 minutes. Season the vegetable mixture to taste with fleur de sel and pepper.

TO ASSEMBLE AND SERVE

Divide the vegetable mixture equally among 6 deep serving bowls.
Spoon the sauce over the vegetables. Place the fish fillets, crust side up,
atop the vegetables. Garnish with the cress and serve immediately.

ROSE PETAL VINEGAR

Believe it or not, rose petals were once a favorite seasoning in American cuisine. Vinegar infused with rose petals is good on any kind of salad, and also goes well with shellfish. The vinegar will keep for at least three months.

MAKES ABOUT 2 CUPS

1 cup dried pesticide-free rose petals
2 cups distilled white vinegar

Place the rose petals in a bottle. Bring the vinegar to a simmer in a heavy small saucepan. Using a funnel, carefully pour the hot vinegar into the bottle to cover the rose petals completely. Seal tightly. Store at room temperature for 2 weeks before using.

DO AHEAD: *The vinegar can be made 3 months ahead. Keep airtight at room temperature.*

FRUIT CHUTNEY WITH GINGER AND FENUGREEK SPICE

This is an excellent condiment for fish, pork, and chicken. Note: Though technically a fruit, chayote is usually referred to as a squash. You can find it in most Latin markets.

MAKES ABOUT 2 CUPS

3 tablespoons acacia or wildflower honey
1 cup diced cored peeled pineapple
1 cup diced pitted peeled mango
1 cup diced pitted peeled chayote
1 cup diced cored peeled Granny Smith apple (from 1 apple)
¾ cup ruby red grapefruit segments (from 1 grapefruit)
¾ cup diced seeded tomato (from 2 tomatoes)
½ cup minced peeled fresh ginger
4 teaspoons ground fenugreek seeds

Cook the honey in a heavy medium saucepan over medium heat until it becomes a dark amber color, about 3 minutes. Add all the remaining ingredients. Reduce the heat to low and cook until the juices evaporate and the mixture is thick, stirring occasionally, about 1 hour.

DO AHEAD: *The chutney can be made up to 1 week ahead. Cover and refrigerate. Rewarm before serving.*

WHOLE FOIE GRAS COOKED IN WHITE BEANS AND BACON

More often than not, sliced foie gras is seared and the pan drippings discarded. Here, the whole goose liver is placed in a pot to impart its juices and flavor to a trove of white beans. The outcome is a wonderfully hearty dish packed with earthy flavor.

2 MAIN-COURSE SERVINGS

1 cup (about 8 ounces) dried Great
    Northern white beans, rinsed
2 bouquets garnis (including fresh
    rosemary,
    thyme, bay leaf, flat-leaf parsley, and leek)
1 onion, halved
1 large carrot, peeled and quartered
1 garlic clove
2 1-pound whole foie gras
    Fleur de sel and freshly ground pepper
¼ cup finely diced bacon
¼ cup finely diced carrot, blanched
¼ cup finely diced onion, blanched
4 cups (about) Chicken Stock (page 239)

Place the beans in a large pot. Pour enough water over the beans to cover by 4 inches. Let soak overnight at room temperature. Drain the beans and return the beans to the pot. Pour enough water over the beans to cover by 4 inches. Add 1 bouquet garni, the halved onion, quartered carrot, and garlic. Bring the water to a boil over medium-high heat. Reduce the heat to medium-low and simmer, uncovered, until the beans are almost tender, about 30 minutes. Drain the cooking liquid. Discard the cooked onion, carrot, bouquet garni, and garlic. Cool the beans slightly.

Sprinkle the 2 whole foie gras with fleur de sel and pepper. Place the foie gras in the large pot. Cover the foie gras with the beans. Add the remaining bouquet garni, bacon, diced carrot, and diced onion. Pour the chicken stock over to cover completely. Poach over low heat until the foie gras is just warm in the center and the beans are tender, about 35 minutes. Season the mixture to taste with fleur de sel and pepper.

TO SERVE

Cut the foie gras into ½-inch-thick slices. Ladle the beans and broth mixture into 2 wide shallow soup plates. Top with the foie gras and serve.

ROASTED SQUAB WITH CHOCOLATE-PORT SAUCE AND BLACK CURRANT COULIS WITH MANGO, CORN, APPLE, AND CELERY ROOT CHUTNEY

For the most part, I like to cook light, but every now and then I want something rich and hearty, something worthy of a king. Chocolate on squab may sound like some nouveau affectation, but in fact it's an ancient sauce used to mute the strong flavor of game. Here, the sauce is lightened by fruit.

4 MAIN-COURSE SERVINGS

Chocolate-Port Sauce and Black Currant Coulis

- ½ cup good-quality dry red wine
- ½ cup ruby port
- 3 ounces good-quality bittersweet (not unsweetened) chocolate, chopped
  Fleur de sel and freshly ground pepper
- ½ cup fresh or frozen black currants
- 2 tablespoons sugar
- 1 tablespoon water

Squab

- 2 tablespoons extra virgin olive oil
- 4 12-ounce squab

Garnish

- 12 ⅛-inch-thick slices peeled celery root
- 2 tablespoons unsalted butter
- 1 cup fresh corn kernels
- 1 cup Mango, Corn, Apple, and Celery Root Chutney (recipe follows)

FOR THE CHOCOLATE-PORT SAUCE AND BLACK CURRANT COULIS

Boil the wine and port in a heavy small saucepan over high heat until reduced to ¼ cup, about 8 minutes. Remove from the heat. Add the chocolate and whisk until melted and smooth. Season the sauce to taste with fleur de sel and freshly ground pepper.

Combine the currants, sugar, and water in another heavy small saucepan. Simmer over low heat until the currants release their juices, about 2 minutes. Using a hand blender, blend the coulis until it is smooth. Season to taste with fleur de sel and freshly ground pepper.

DO AHEAD: *The sauce and coulis can be prepared up to 8 hours ahead. Cover separately and refrigerate. Rewarm before serving.*

FOR THE SQUAB

Preheat the oven to 450°F. Lightly oil a heavy rimmed baking sheet. Tie the squab legs together with kitchen string. Lightly coat the squab with oil, then sprinkle with fleur de sel and pepper. Place the squab, breast side up, on the baking sheet. Roast until the squab are golden brown and an instant-read meat thermometer registers 135°F when inserted into the thigh, about 18 minutes. Remove the squab from the oven. Let stand for 5 minutes.

TO FINISH AND SERVE

Cook the celery root slices in a large saucepan of boiling salted water until crisp-tender, about 2 minutes. Drain well.

Melt the butter in a heavy large sauté pan over medium heat. Add the celery root and corn kernels. Sauté until the corn is heated through, about 3 minutes. Season to taste with fleur de sel and pepper.

Remove the breast meat and leg and thigh pieces from each squab. Arrange the squab pieces decoratively on 4 large plates. Lightly coat the squab with the chocolate sauce. Spoon the mango, corn, apple, and celery root chutney alongside the squab. Drizzle the black currant coulis around the chutney. Arrange the celery root slices and corn atop the chutney and serve immediately.

MANGO, CORN, APPLE, AND CELERY ROOT CHUTNEY

MAKES ABOUT 2 CUPS

2 lemons

2 mangoes, peeled and pitted, one cut into
⅓-inch dice and one pureed

1 Granny Smith apple, peeled, cored, and
cut into ⅓-inch dice (about 1 cup)

1 celery root, peeled and cut into ¼-inch
dice (about 1 cup)

1 cup fresh corn kernels

½ cup white wine vinegar

⅓ cup sugar

Fleur de sel and freshly ground pepper

Using a vegetable peeler, remove the peel from the lemons. Using a small sharp knife, trim away all the pith from the peels. Cut the peels into ⅓-inch diamond-shaped pieces (makes about ¼ cup total). Place the peels in a small saucepan of water. Bring the water to a boil. Drain. Rinse the peels under cold water. Repeat this process once.

Combine the lemon peels with all the remaining ingredients in a heavy medium saucepan. Simmer over low heat, stirring frequently, until the mixture is thick and transparent in color, about 40 minutes. Season the chutney to taste with fleur de sel and pepper.

DO AHEAD: *The chutney can be made up to 1 day ahead. Cool. Cover and refrigerate. Rewarm before using.*

SWEET ONION TART WITH
CURRY AND PARSLEY SAUCE

Curry is all about flavor—intense and complex, yet subtle enough to be almost mystifying, as if you're walking through a forest where unseen strangers are whispering behind every tree. Combined with the softly cooked onions and parsley, it plays delicately on the tongue.

4 FIRST-COURSE SERVINGS

Sweet Onion Tarts

    Nonstick cooking spray

2 tablespoons unsalted butter

3 Maui, Vidalia, or other sweet onions
    (about 1½ pounds total), cut into
    ½-inch pieces
    Fleur de sel and freshly ground pepper

1 10-ounce piece of Puff Pastry Dough
    (page 242)

Parsley Sauce

2 bunches fresh flat-leaf parsley,
    stems removed

2 tablespoons unsalted butter

1 teaspoon Curry Powder (page 241)

FOR THE SWEET ONION TARTS

Spray four 4-inch nonstick cake pans with cooking spray. Melt the butter in a heavy large sauté pan over low heat. Add the onions and sauté until the juices evaporate and the onions are translucent but not brown, about 20 minutes. Season to taste with fleur de sel and pepper. Divide the onions among the prepared pans.

Roll out the puff pastry dough on a lightly floured work surface into a 20 x 5-inch rectangle that is about ¼ inch thick. Using a small sharp knife, cut out four 4½-inch rounds of puff pastry; discard the pastry trimmings. Transfer the pastry rounds to a small baking sheet. Cover and refrigerate until cold.

DO AHEAD: *The tartlets and pastry rounds can be prepared up to 8 hours ahead. Cover separately and refrigerate.*

FOR THE PARSLEY SAUCE

Cook the parsley in a large saucepan of boiling salted water until the leaves are very soft but still green, about 3 minutes. Drain the water. Transfer the parsley to a large bowl of ice water to cool. Drain again. Transfer the parsley to a food processor and purée with 3 ice cubes until smooth. Heat the parsley sauce in a small saucepan over medium-high heat until hot but not boiling. Whisk in the butter. Season to taste with fleur de sel and pepper.

TO FINISH AND SERVE

Preheat the oven to 400°F. Place 1 pastry round atop the onions in each pan; tuck in the edges of the pastry. Place the pans on a baking sheet. Bake the tartlets until the pastry rises, about 20 minutes. Reduce the oven heat to 350°F. Continue baking the tartlets until the onions on the bottom and sides of the pans are golden brown, about 15 minutes longer.

Run a small sharp knife around the edges of the tartlets to loosen. Set 1 plate, top side down, on each tartlet. Turn the tartlets and plates over together to invert the tartlets onto the plates. Remove the pans. Replace any onions that may have become dislodged. Drizzle the parsley sauce around the tartlets. Sprinkle with the curry powder, fleur de sel, and pepper. Serve immediately.

CINNAMON AND ROSEMARY-INFUSED CHICKEN BREAST WITH BABY VEGETABLES

I was just playing around one day when I stumbled into the beautiful combination of cinnamon and chicken. The cinnamon highlights the sweeter side of the poultry, while the rosemary anchors it in savory goodness.

4 MAIN-COURSE SERVINGS

2 cups Chicken Stock (page 239)
1 cup Veal Demi-Glace (page 238)
1 cup verjus
4 fresh rosemary sprigs
4 fresh lemon thyme sprigs
2 Ceylon cinnamon sticks
4 boneless chicken breasts
8 baby carrots, peeled
8 baby turnips, peeled
2 tablespoons unsalted butter
  Fleur de sel and freshly ground pepper

Preheat the oven to 200ºF. Combine the first 6 ingredients in a heavy 5-quart pot. Cook over medium heat until the liquid is 170ºF. Add the chicken, carrots, and turnips. Poach until the chicken is cooked through but still tender and the vegetables are crisp-tender, adjusting the heat as needed in order to maintain the temperature of the poaching liquid, about 30 minutes. Transfer the chicken, carrots, and turnips to a heavy large baking sheet. Place in the oven to keep warm.

Boil the poaching liquid over high heat until it is reduced to 1 cup, about 20 minutes. Strain the sauce into a small bowl. Whisk in the butter to form a smooth sauce. Season the sauce to taste with fleur de sel and pepper.

Arrange 1 chicken breast, 2 carrots, and 2 turnips on each of 4 large plates. Spoon the sauce over and serve immediately.

MEYER LEMON TART

Meyer lemons are truly special. They're especially sweet and contain all the essence of lemons without the mouth-puckering tartness. Needless to say, they make a delicious tart.

MAKES ONE 10-INCH TART

Sugar Crust

- 1 cup all-purpose flour
- ½ cup powdered sugar
  - Pinch of fleur de sel
- ¼ cup (2 ounces) chilled unsalted butter, cut into 1-inch pieces
- 1 large egg, stirred to blend

Lemon Curd Filling

- 1⅓ cups strained fresh Meyer lemon juice (from about 6 Meyer lemons)
- 2 cups granulated sugar
- 4 large eggs
- 1 cup (8 ounces) unsalted butter, cut into ½-inch pieces
- 2 tablespoons minced grated Meyer lemon peel (from about 6 Meyer lemons)

FOR THE SUGAR CRUST

Mix the flour, powdered sugar, and fleur de sel in a food processor to blend. Add the butter. Using on/off turns, blend until the mixture resembles a coarse meal. Drizzle 2 tablespoons of the beaten egg over the dough; discard the remaining egg. Using on/off turns, blend just until the dough begins to form. Gather the dough into a ball; flatten into a disk. Wrap the dough in plastic wrap; chill for at least 30 minutes and up to 1 day.

Preheat the oven to 350°F. Roll out the dough on a lightly floured surface to a 12½-inch round. Transfer to a 10-inch tart pan with a removable bottom. Gently press the dough in the pan to cover completely. Press any overhanging dough against the top edge of the pan to trim. Cover and refrigerate the crust until it is cold, about 10 minutes. Line the crust with aluminum foil and fill with pie weights. Bake the crust until the sides are set, about 15 minutes. Carefully remove the weights and foil. Bake the crust until it is golden on the bottom, about 15 minutes longer. Cool the crust in the pan on a rack.

FOR THE LEMON CURD FILLING

Bring the lemon juice to a boil in a heavy medium saucepan. Whisk the sugar and eggs in a medium bowl to blend. Gradually whisk in the hot lemon juice. Return the mixture to the saucepan. Stir over low heat until the mixture thickens, about 5 minutes (do not boil). Remove from the heat. Gradually whisk in the butter, then the lemon peel. Transfer the lemon curd to a medium bowl. Press plastic wrap directly onto the surface of the curd; refrigerate until cold.

TO ASSEMBLE AND SERVE

Spoon the cold lemon curd into the crust at least 1 hour before serving, or up to 8 hours ahead. Cut the tart into wedges and serve.

PAIN D'EPICES

I think you'll find that every bite of this spice bread is like walking through the door of a spice shop for the first time. The spices arise through your nostrils, so that your nose will taste the bread before your mouth does.

MAKES 1 LOAF

Nonstick cooking spray

1½ cups all-purpose flour

1 tablespoon grated orange peel, minced

2 teaspoons grated lemon peel, minced

2 teaspoons freshly ground
   Ceylon cinnamon

2 teaspoons freshly ground star anise

1 teaspoon freshly ground nutmeg

½ teaspoon freshly ground cloves

½ teaspoon fleur de sel

¼ teaspoon freshly ground cumin

⅔ cup sliced almonds, toasted and finely chopped

⅓ cup shelled pistachios, toasted and finely chopped

⅓ cup hazelnuts, toasted, husked, and finely chopped

⅓ cup candied fruit, finely chopped

⅓ cup raisins, finely chopped

1¼ cups water

¾ cup honey

½ cup sugar

2 tablespoons dark rum

1 tablespoon baking soda

Preheat the oven to 325ºF. Spray an 11½ x 4 x 3-inch loaf pan with nonstick spray. Whisk the flour and next 8 ingredients in a large bowl to blend. Set the flour mixture aside. Mix all the nuts, candied fruit, and raisins together in a small bowl. Set the nut mixture aside.

Stir the water, honey, sugar, and rum in a heavy medium saucepan over high heat until the sugar dissolves. Bring the syrup to a boil. Immediately whisk the boiling syrup into the flour mixture, stirring just until blended. Whisk in the nut mixture. Whisk in the baking soda.

DO AHEAD: *At this point, the batter can be prepared up to 1 day ahead. Cover and refrigerate. Stir to blend before continuing.*

Transfer the batter to the prepared pan. Smooth the top. Bake until a toothpick inserted into the center of the bread comes out clean, about 55 minutes. Cool the bread in the pan for 5 minutes. Invert the bread onto a rack, and cool completely.

MY MOM'S CHOCOLATE CAKE

This dessert is for people who really like chocolate. It's dense, like a brownie, but much softer.

8 SERVINGS

8 ounces good-quality bittersweet (not unsweetened) chocolate, chopped
8 ounces unsalted butter, cut into pieces
1 cup sugar
1 cup water
4 large eggs, room temperature
1 cup all-purpose flour
Vanilla Sauce (page 152)

Preheat the oven to 350°F. Lightly butter a 3-quart (8-inch) charlotte mold. Stir the chocolate and butter in a medium bowl set over a saucepan of simmering water until melted and smooth. Set aside; keep warm.

Stir the sugar and water in a heavy small saucepan over medium-high heat until the sugar dissolves. Bring to a boil. Remove the sugar syrup from the heat. Set aside; keep hot.

Whisk the eggs in a large bowl just to blend. Sift the flour over the eggs and whisk to form a smooth, thick batter. Gradually add the hot sugar syrup, whisking to ensure that no lumps remain. Whisk in the warm melted chocolate mixture to form a smooth batter. Pour the batter into the prepared charlotte mold.

Place the mold in a heavy roasting pan. Add enough hot water to the roasting pan to come halfway up the sides of the mold. Carefully transfer the pan to the oven. Bake until the outer 1-inch perimeter of the cake is set and the center 3 inches are still slightly loose (do not overbake; the cake will become firm once it has been chilled), about 1 hour. Remove the mold from the roasting pan. Transfer the cake in the mold to the refrigerator. Chill until the cake is cool, at least 2 hours. Cover and keep refrigerated until cold.

Bring a medium sauté pan of water to a simmer. Remove from the heat. Place the mold in the hot water for about 1 minute (this will help release the cake from the mold). Run a small sharp knife around the edges of the cake. Invert the mold onto a platter, shaking gently to release the cake from the mold. (If the cake does not release easily from the mold, return the mold to the hot water for 1 minute more.) Remove the mold. Cover the cake and refrigerate.

DO AHEAD: *The cake can be prepared up to 1 day ahead. Keep the cake covered and refrigerated.*

Heat the blade of a large sharp knife over a medium flame just until warm. Slice the cake with the warm blade into 8 wedges, rewarming the blade slightly in between slices. Transfer the wedges to plates. Spoon the vanilla sauce around the cake and serve cold.

QUINCE JAM WITH NOSTRADAMUS SPICE

I once read that Nostradamus's favorite spices were cinnamon, green cardamom, cloves, and star anise. I don't know if this spiced quince jam will help you predict the future, but I do predict you'll find it delicious on your morning toast, and with cheese.

MAKES ABOUT 2 CUPS

3 fresh quince (about 1¼ pounds total), peeled, cored, and coarsely chopped

1 cup sugar

2 cups water

1 teaspoon freshly ground green cardamom seeds

1 teaspoon freshly ground Ceylon cinnamon

½ teaspoon freshly ground star anise

¼ teaspoon freshly ground cloves

Combine the quince and sugar in a heavy medium saucepan. Add the water to cover the mixture completely. Cook over low heat until the quince are soft and the liquid is syrupy, stirring occasionally, about 1 hour. Transfer the mixture to a food processor. Add the spices. Using quick on/off pulses, process just until the spices are blended into the quince mixture (the mixture should not be smooth). Serve warm, room temperature, or cold. Store the jam in the refrigerator for up to 2 weeks.

ALMOND RICE PUDDING WITH CITRUS JELLY

There's something about the way rice pudding fills you up that makes for a happy tummy. But most traditional versions are too sweet for my taste. Here, the bitter citrus jelly gets into a playful tug-of-war with the sweet pudding, and the result is delicious. Almond milk can be found in Indian and Middle Eastern groceries and on the Internet (see Resource Guide on page 246).

4 SERVINGS

Rice Pudding

  3 cups whole milk
 ½ cup Arborio rice
 ⅔ cup sugar
 ¼ teaspoon fleur de sel
  1 vanilla bean, split lengthwise
 ¼ cup almond milk
 ½ cup heavy whipping cream
  3 large eggs
  3 large egg yolks

Citrus Jelly

 ½ cup strained fresh ruby red
      grapefruit juice
 ¼ cup strained fresh orange juice
  1 teaspoon sugar
 ¼ teaspoon unflavored gelatin
  2 oranges, segmented

  1 ruby red grapefruit, segmented
      Citrus Zest Confit (page 244)

FOR THE RICE PUDDING

Combine the whole milk, rice, sugar, and fleur de sel in a heavy medium saucepan. Scrape the seeds from the vanilla bean into the milk mixture; add the bean. Bring to a simmer over medium heat. Reduce the heat to medium-low and cook until the pudding is thick and the rice is very tender, stirring often and scraping the bottom of the saucepan so that the milk does not scorch, about 45 minutes. Remove from the heat. Cool slightly. Stir in the almond milk. Remove the vanilla bean.

Whisk the cream, eggs, and egg yolks in a large bowl to blend. Gradually stir the rice mixture into the cream mixture. Return the rice mixture to the saucepan. Stir constantly over very low heat until the pudding thickens slightly and an instant-read thermometer registers 160°F (do not boil), about 8 minutes. Divide the rice pudding equally among 4 wide soup plates or pasta bowls. Refrigerate until cold. Cover and keep refrigerated.

DO AHEAD: *The rice pudding can be prepared up to 8 hours ahead. Keep refrigerated.*

FOR THE CITRUS JELLY

Combine the grapefruit juice, orange juice, and sugar in a heavy small saucepan. Sprinkle the gelatin over and let stand until the gelatin softens, about 5 minutes. Stir the juice mixture over medium-high heat until it begins to simmer. Remove from the heat and whisk until the gelatin dissolves. Transfer the citrus jelly to a small bowl. Cover and refrigerate until the mixture resembles a loose jelly but is not firm, at least 8 hours or overnight. Stir to loosen before using.

TO ASSEMBLE AND SERVE

Arrange the fruit segments atop the pudding. Spoon the citrus jelly over, garnish with the citrus zest confit, and serve.

LEMON SORBET WITH SAFFRON

What could be more refreshing in the heat of summer than a lemon sorbet? The addition of saffron softens the citrus taste while adding an almost mystical dimension. The saffron lends the sorbet a beautiful orange hue, like the color of sunset. The sorbet is best when made no more than eight hours before serving. If you must freeze it longer, let it melt back to a liquid in a bain-marie and return it to the ice cream maker until soft-solid.

MAKES ABOUT 1 QUART

1³/₄ cups purified water (such as Evian)

1¹/₂ cups sugar

 ¹/₈ teaspoon coarsely crumbled saffron
      threads

1¹/₄ cups strained fresh lemon juice

 5 tablespoons light corn syrup

Combine the purified water and sugar in a medium saucepan. Bring to a boil over high heat. Add the saffron. Cover and steep for 5 minutes. Whisk in the lemon juice and corn syrup. Cover and refrigerate until cold.

Process the lemon mixture in an ice cream maker according to the manufacturer's instructions. Transfer the sorbet to a container. Stir to distribute the saffron evenly. Freeze until soft-solid, stirring occasionally, about 6 hours.

BASIC RECIPES

PART *IV*

A FEW WORDS ABOUT STOCKS.

ALL SERIOUS COOKS (OR EVEN SEMISERIOUS COOKS) OUGHT TO HAVE A VARI-ETY OF STOCKS STORED IN THEIR FREEZERS, READY TO GO FOR LAST-MINUTE APPLICATIONS. FREEZE THEM IN ONE-CUP PORTIONS AND BAG THEM IN PLASTIC. THAT WAY, YOU'LL REDUCE THE LABOR INVOLVED FOR PREPARING ANY NUMBER OF DISHES, AND YOU'LL BE ABLE TO IMPROVISE IF THE MOOD STRIKES YOU. NEVER ADD SALT TO STOCKS WHEN COOKING BECAUSE, AS YOU REDUCE THEM, THEY BECOME TOO SALTY. CLARIFY STOCKS BY STRAINING THEM THROUGH CHEESECLOTH, AND YOU GET A CONSOMMÉ, THE PERFECT FOUNDATION FOR ANY SOUP. REDUCE A STOCK BY HALF AND YOU'VE GOT A DEMI-GLACE, WHICH IS HALFWAY TO A SAUCE (JUST ADD A LITTLE COGNAC, SHERRY, OR VEGETABLE STOCK FOR FLAVOR). REDUCE A STOCK BY THREE-FOURTHS AND YOU HAVE A THICK GLAZE TO SPREAD OVER MEAT OR FISH; A GLAZE ADDS COLOR AND INTENSIFIES FLAVOR. I LIKE TO TAKE ADVANTAGE OF A GLAZE'S STICKY CONSISTENCY BY SPRINKLING HERBS OR SPICES ON TOP. STOCKS SHOULD BE COOKED SLOWLY; AVOID BOILING THEM OR THEY'LL BECOME CLOUDY, AND SKIM STOCKS EVERY THIRTY MINUTES OR SO. IF THE FLAVOR IS TOO PALLID AT THE END, YOU CAN STILL ADD MORE GARLIC, ONIONS, OR OTHER APPROPRIATE INGREDIENTS, AND REDUCE FURTHER TO FORTIFY THE TASTE.

BEEF STOCK

What to do with all that leftover beef after the stock is finished? In France we make hachi à la Parmentier—the French version of shepherd's pie. Grind the cooked meat, place it in a shallow pan, cover it with mashed potatoes, and top with Parmesan cheese. Place it in a 300-degree oven until just warm.

MAKES ABOUT 8 CUPS

4 pounds beef chuck, cut into 1-inch pieces

¼ cup canola oil

1 carrot, chopped

1 onion, chopped

1 leek, chopped

3 whole shallots, chopped

3 quarts cold water

½ lemon

5 fresh thyme sprigs

3 fresh bay leaves

Toss the beef with the oil in a large bowl to coat. Heat a heavy large wide pot over high heat until it is very hot. Working in batches, add the beef and cook until it is a rich dark brown color all over, about 10 minutes. Using tongs, transfer the beef to a large bowl.

Drain any excess oil from the pot. Add the carrot, onion, leek, and shallots. Sauté until brown, about 10 minutes. Add the water, scraping up any browned bits from the bottom of the pot. Add the lemon, thyme sprigs, and bay leaves. Return the beef to the pot. Bring to a simmer over high heat. Reduce the heat to medium and simmer for 2½ to 3 hours, skimming the stock every 15 minutes to remove the fat and foam that accumulate at the top.

Strain the stock through a fine-mesh strainer. Cool in the refrigerator. Remove the fat from atop the stock. Cover and refrigerate for 2 days before using.

DO AHEAD: *The stock can be made and refrigerated up to 3 days, or frozen up to 3 months.*

LAMB STOCK

¼ cup plus 2 tablespoons canola oil

4 pounds lamb bones

2 ripe tomatoes, chopped

1 leek, chopped

1 carrot, chopped

1 onion, chopped

3 shallots, chopped

1 whole garlic bulb, halved crosswise

2 tablespoons tomato paste

1 whole onion, halved

5 quarts cold water

3 fresh thyme sprigs

2 fresh bay leaves

2 large fresh flat-leaf parsley sprigs

Preheat the oven to 450°F. Pour ¼ cup oil into a heavy large roasting pan; place the pan in the oven until the oil and pan are very hot, about 3 minutes. Add the lamb bones to the pan, turning to coat with the oil. Return the pan to the oven and roast until the bones are a rich dark brown color, turning the bones occasionally, about 45 minutes. Add the tomatoes, leek, carrot, chopped onion, shallots, garlic, and tomato paste. Stir to mix well. Return the pan to the oven and roast until the vegetables are a rich brown color, about 30 minutes.

Meanwhile, line a heavy medium sauté pan with aluminum foil. Heat the remaining 2 tablespoons oil in the pan over high heat. Place the onion halves, cut side down, in the pan. Cook until the onions are black on the bottom, about 8 minutes. Set aside. (This will lend a depth of color and flavor to the finished stock.)

Transfer the roasting pan to atop the stove. Add the cold water, scraping up any browned bits from the bottom of the pan. Add the thyme, bay leaves, and parsley. Bring to a simmer over two burners on medium-high heat. Add the blackened onions. Reduce the heat to medium-low and simmer for 3 to 4 hours, skimming the stock every 15 minutes to remove the fat and foam that accumulate at the top.

Strain the stock through a fine-mesh strainer. Cool in the refrigerator. Remove the fat from atop the stock. Cover and refrigerate for 2 days before using.

DO AHEAD: *The stock can be made and refrigerated up to 3 days, or frozen up to 3 months.*

VEAL STOCK

MAKES ABOUT 8 CUPS

¼ cup plus 2 tablespoons canola oil

6 pounds veal bones

¼ cup tomato paste

2 carrots, chopped

1 leek, chopped

1 onion, chopped

2 whole garlic bulbs, halved crosswise

1 whole onion, halved

6 quarts cold water

3 ripe tomatoes

5 fresh thyme sprigs

5 fresh bay leaves

3 large fresh flat-leaf parsley sprigs

Preheat the oven to 450ºF. Pour ¼ cup oil into a heavy large roasting pan; place the pan in the oven until the oil and pan are very hot, about 3 minutes. Add the veal bones to the pan; turn to coat with the oil. Return the pan to the oven and roast until the bones are a rich dark brown color, turning the bones occasionally, about 1 hour. Stir in the tomato paste to coat the bones. Add the carrots, leek, chopped onion, and garlic. Stir to mix well. Return the pan to the oven and roast until the vegetables are a rich brown color, about 30 minutes.

Meanwhile, line a heavy medium sauté pan with aluminum foil. Heat the remaining 2 tablespoons oil in the pan over high heat. Place the onion halves, cut side down, in the pan. Cook until the onions are black on the bottom, about 8 minutes. Set aside. (This will lend a depth of color and flavor to the finished stock.)

Transfer the roasting pan to atop the stove. Add the cold water, scraping up any browned bits from the bottom of the pan. Add the tomatoes, thyme, bay leaves, and parsley. Bring to a simmer over two burners on medium-high heat. Add the blackened onions. Reduce the heat to medium-low and simmer for 3 to 4 hours, skimming the stock every 15 minutes to remove the fat and foam that accumulate at the top.

Strain the stock through a fine-mesh strainer. Cool in the refrigerator. Remove the fat from atop the stock. Cover and refrigerate for 2 days before using.

DO AHEAD: *The stock can be made and refrigerated up to 3 days, or frozen up to 3 months.*

NOTE: *To make a veal demi-glace, simmer 4 cups of the finished veal stock in a heavy medium saucepan until reduced to 2 cups, about 25 minutes.*

CHICKEN STOCK

4 pounds chicken bones, necks, and feet
1 carrot, chopped
1 onion, chopped
1 leek, chopped
5 fresh bay leaves
2 large fresh flat-leaf parsley sprigs
3 quarts cold water

Rinse the chicken bones, necks, and feet in cold water. Place the chicken pieces in a heavy large stockpot. Add the carrot, onion, leek, bay leaves, and parsley. Add the cold water. Bring to a boil over medium-high heat. Reduce the heat to medium-low and simmer gently for 3 to 4 hours, skimming the stock every 15 minutes to remove the fat and foam that accumulate at the top.

Strain the stock through a fine-mesh strainer. Refrigerate the stock until cold. Remove the fat from atop the stock. Cover and keep refrigerated for 2 days before using.

DO AHEAD: *The stock can be made and refrigerated up to 3 days, or frozen up to 3 months.*

DUCK STOCK

3 tablespoons canola oil
3 pounds duck bones (from about 2 ducks)
3 ripe tomatoes, chopped
1 carrot, chopped
1 leek, chopped
1 small onion, chopped
1 tablespoon tomato paste
3 quarts cold water
2 large fresh flat-leaf parsley sprigs

Preheat the oven to 450°F. Pour the oil into a heavy large roasting pan; place the pan in the oven until the oil and pan are very hot, about 3 minutes. Add the duck bones to the pan; turn to coat with the oil. Return the pan to the oven and roast the bones until they are a rich dark brown color, turning the bones occasionally, about 1 hour. Add the tomatoes, carrot, leek, onion, and tomato paste. Stir to mix well. Return the pan to the oven and roast until the vegetables are a rich brown color, about 30 minutes.

Transfer the pan to atop the stove. Add the cold water, scraping up any browned bits from the bottom of the pan. Add the parsley. Bring to a boil over two burners on medium-high heat. Reduce the heat to medium-low and simmer gently for 2 to 2½ hours, skimming the stock every 15 minutes to remove the fat and foam that accumulate at the top.

Strain the stock through a fine-mesh strainer. Cool in the refrigerator. Remove the fat from atop the stock. Cover and refrigerate for 2 days before using.

DO AHEAD: *The stock can be made and refrigerated up to 3 days, or frozen up to 3 months.*

LOBSTER STOCK

MAKES ABOUT 5 CUPS

3	pounds lobster heads and shells
¾	cup canola oil
1½	cups Cognac
3	ripe tomatoes, chopped
1	onion, chopped
1	carrot, chopped
1	leek, chopped
¼	cup tomato paste
1	whole garlic head, halved crosswise
5	fresh thyme sprigs
2	quarts cold water

Working in batches, blend the lobster heads and shells in a food processor until the shells are finely chopped and the juices become creamy. (Note: Chopping the lobster pieces lends much more flavor to the finished broth than if the shells are used whole.) Heat the oil in a heavy large wide pot over medium-high heat until the oil is very hot and almost smoking, about 2 minutes. Add the lobster mixture and sauté until the juices evaporate and the mixture becomes a rich dark brown color, about 30 minutes. Add the Cognac. Simmer for 2 minutes. Add the tomatoes, onion, carrot, leek, tomato paste, garlic, and thyme. Add the cold water. Bring to a simmer over medium-high heat. Reduce the heat to medium-low and simmer gently for about 1½ to 2 hours, skimming the stock every 15 minutes to remove the fat and foam that accumulate at the top.

Strain the stock through a fine-mesh strainer. Cool in the refrigerator. Remove the fat from atop the stock. Cover and refrigerate for 2 days before using.

DO AHEAD: *The stock can be made and refrigerated up to 3 days, or frozen up to 3 months.*

FISH STOCK

MAKES ABOUT 5 CUPS

¼	cup olive oil
1	onion, very finely chopped
1	leek, very finely chopped
1	fennel bulb, very finely chopped
3	shallots, chopped
2	pounds fish bones, chopped (do not wash the bones in order to preserve all their flavor)
½	cup good-quality dry white wine
5	cups cold water
3	fresh bay leaves
2	fresh thyme sprigs

Heat the oil in a heavy 5½-quart stockpot over medium-low heat. Add the onion, leek, fennel, and shallots. Sauté until the vegetables begin to release their juices (do not allow them to brown), about 10 minutes. Add the fish bones. Cook until the bones are opaque (do not allow the mixture to brown), stirring often, about 10 minutes longer. Add the wine. Bring to a simmer over medium-high heat. Add the cold water, bay leaves, and thyme. Bring to a simmer. Reduce the heat to medium-low and simmer gently for about 30 to 40 minutes, skimming the stock every 15 minutes to remove the fat and foam that accumulate at the top.

Strain the stock through a fine-mesh strainer. Refrigerate until cold. Remove the fat from atop the stock. Cover and keep refrigerated for 2 days before using.

DO AHEAD: *The stock can be made and refrigerated up to 3 days, or frozen up to 3 months.*

CURRY POWDER

This is a versatile curry powder that complements any kind of fish. A dash or two added to soups and vegetables will brighten them considerably. Make the powder two weeks in advance and store in a tightly sealed container to let the flavors mingle. The curry powder will retain its pungency for about a month.

MAKES ½ CUP

20 green cardamom pods

16 whole cloves

4 whole star anise

2 tablespoons coriander seeds

2 teaspoons cumin seeds

1½ teaspoons coarsely grated dried ginger

1 teaspoon crumbled shredded mace

¾ teaspoon fennel seed

½ teaspoon white peppercorns

½ teaspoon fenugreek seeds

1½ tablespoons turmeric

1¼ teaspoons cayenne pepper

Combine the first 10 spices in a heavy medium sauté pan. Stir over low heat until fragrant, about 5 minutes. Transfer the spices to a spice grinder. Add the turmeric and cayenne pepper to the same pan and stir over low heat until fragrant, about 3 minutes. Transfer the turmeric mixture to the whole spices in the spice grinder. Finely grind the toasted spices.

Transfer the curry powder to a jar and seal tightly. Store airtight at room temperature for 2 weeks to allow the spices to blend.

FOUR SPICES POWDER

In France, four spices powder (quatre épices) is widely used for just about everything, especially fish. Instead of cinnamon, which is usually the fourth spice, I prefer to use cloves, which gives the mixture a softer character. The spice powder is best when used within two weeks, after which it loses its pungency.

MAKES ABOUT ⅓ CUP

4 whole nutmegs

¼ cup dried coarsely grated ginger

1½ teaspoons whole white peppercorns

1 teaspoon whole cloves

Combine all the ingredients in a spice grinder. Grind into a fine powder. Transfer the spice powder to a jar and seal tightly.

DO AHEAD: *The spice powder can be prepared up to 2 weeks ahead. Keep airtight at room temperature.*

PUFF PASTRY DOUGH

This is a very flexible recipe, equally suited to desserts and more savory dishes, such as vegetable tarts.

MAKES 2½ POUNDS

3¼ cups all-purpose flour

  2 teaspoons fleur de sel

  4 ounces chilled unsalted butter, cut
      into 1-inch pieces

1¼ cups (about) cold water

14 ounces unsalted butter, room
      temperature

Mix the flour and fleur de sel in a food processor. Blend in the chilled butter. With the machine running, gradually add 1 cup of the water through the feed tube, blending just until a soft dough forms and adding the remaining ¼ cup water if needed. Transfer the dough to a lightly floured work surface; knead until smooth. Roll out the dough into a 15 x 12-inch rectangle. Brush away any excess flour. Spread the room temperature butter over two-thirds of the dough. Fold the unbuttered third over the center third, then fold the remaining buttered third over the folded two-thirds as is done for a letter. Refrigerate for 45 minutes.

Return the dough to the lightly floured work surface and turn the dough so that the long edges of the dough are parallel to the edge of the work surface. Roll out the dough into a 15 x 12-inch rectangle. Brush away any excess flour. Fold the narrow ends of the dough in to meet at the center, again brushing away any excess flour. Fold the dough in half again as is done when closing a book. Cover the dough and refrigerate for 30 minutes. Repeat turning, rolling, and folding the dough 3 more times, refrigerating the dough for 30 minutes in between each turn.

Cut the dough crosswise into 4 equal pieces (each weighing about 10 ounces). Wrap each piece separately in plastic wrap.

DO AHEAD: *The puff pastry dough can be made and refrigerated up to 1 day or frozen up to 1 week. If frozen, defrost the dough in the refrigerator before using.*

SPICED WHITE BREAD

Spiced with sultry nigella seed (sometimes confused with black cumin) and sumac, this bread tastes like a walk in the forest on a hot summer day. Look for these spices at your local spice shop, or see the Resource Guide on page 246. Spiced White Bread makes excellent croutons.

MAKES 1 LOAF

⅓   cup warm water (105° to 110°F)

2   tablespoons active dry yeast

3½   cups all-purpose flour

1   tablespoon sugar

2½   teaspoons Four Spices Powder
       (page 241)

2   teaspoons fleur de sel

1¼   cups whole milk

3   tablespoons unsalted butter, melted
       and warm

1   large egg, beaten to blend

1   teaspoon ground sumac

1   teaspoon whole nigella

Stir the water and yeast in a small bowl. Let stand until the yeast dissolves, about 10 minutes. Using an electric stand mixer with a hook attachment, stir the flour, sugar, four spices powder, and fleur de sel in a large bowl to blend. Mix in the milk and yeast mixture. Knead to form a soft dough. Gradually mix in the melted butter. Knead until the dough is smooth and elastic, about 2 minutes. Transfer the dough to a lightly floured work surface; form the dough into a ball. Lightly oil the bowl; return the dough to the bowl. Cover and refrigerate until the dough doubles in volume, about 1 hour.

Oil a 12 x 4 x 3-inch loaf pan. Punch down the dough; shape into a 10-inch rectangular loaf. Place the loaf into the prepared pan. Cover and let rise in a warm draft-free area until almost doubled in volume, about 20 minutes.

Preheat the oven to 375°F. Lightly brush the top of the bread with some of the egg. Dust the loaf generously with the sumac, then sprinkle the nigella over. Bake until the loaf is brown on top and an instant-read thermometer registers 200°F when inserted into the center of the loaf, about 50 minutes. Cool the bread in the pan for 5 minutes. Transfer the loaf to a cooling rack. Cool completely.

CLARIFIED BUTTER

Clarifying butter removes milk solids and evaporates the water from the butter, leaving it clear and golden. It has a much higher smoke point than regular butter, and therefore has a number of uses. Fish poached in clarified butter, for example, comes out remarkably soft. I also like to use it for frying potatoes.

MAKES ABOUT ¾ CUP

1   cup (8 ounces) unsalted butter

Cook the butter in a heavy small saucepan over medium heat until melted and beginning to simmer (do not stir). Remove from the heat. Spoon off the foam from atop the butter. Carefully pour the clarified butter into a small bowl, leaving the liquid whey and milk solids behind. Cool the clarified butter. Cover tightly and refrigerate.

DO AHEAD: *The clarified butter can be prepared up to 1 week ahead. Keep tightly covered and refrigerated.*

LEMON CONFIT

This thin, diaphanous syrup retains all the essence of lemon without the acid. In fact, I used to love to drink it poured over ice! Drizzle a little on fish or pork, after cooking, or over ice cream.

MAKES ABOUT ½ CUP

4 lemons
3 tablespoons sugar

Preheat the oven to 400ºF. Line a baking sheet with foil. Wrap each lemon individually in aluminum foil. Place the lemons on the foil-lined baking sheet and bake until they are very soft, turning occasionally, about 40 minutes. Cool the lemons in the foil.

Remove the foil and cut the lemons in half. Spoon the lemon pulp and juice into a fine-mesh strainer set over a heavy small saucepan. Press on the lemon solids with the back of a rubber spatula to release as much liquid as possible. Discard the solids. Add the sugar to the lemon mixture. Bring the lemon mixture to a boil. Remove from the heat.

DO AHEAD: *The lemon confit can be prepared at least 1 day ahead, but will lose its essence after a few days or so. Cover and refrigerate. Return to room temperature before using.*

CITRUS ZEST CONFIT

Like lemon confit, this recipe is good with fish and meat. I also use it to make Citrus Marmalade (page 245) and as a garnish for desserts. The tartness of grapefruit and the slight bitterness of the citrus peel are softened and rounded out nicely by the sugar.

MAKES ABOUT 1 CUP

1 ruby red grapefruit
1 orange
1 lemon
2 limes
½ cup sugar

Using a vegetable peeler, remove the peel from the fruit. Using a small sharp knife, trim away any pith from the peels. Cut the peels into ⅓-inch diamond-shaped pieces (makes about ¾ cup total). Place the peels in a small saucepan of water. Bring the water to a boil. Drain. Rinse the peels under cold water. Repeat this process once.

Meanwhile, juice all the fruit to extract about 1¾ cups total. Strain the juices through a fine-mesh strainer; discard the solids.

Combine the peels and juices in a heavy small saucepan. Simmer gently over medium-low heat until the peels are tender, about 25 minutes. Add the sugar and cook until the juices become syrupy, about 15 minutes.

DO AHEAD: *The zest confit is best when prepared no more than 2 days ahead. Cover and refrigerate.*

CITRUS MARMALADE

A tangy, refreshing condiment for your morning toast, this marmalade also goes well with veal and pork.

MAKES ABOUT 2 CUPS

2 oranges

1 ruby red grapefruit

1 Meyer lemon

Citrus Zest Confit (page 244)

1 tablespoon extra virgin olive oil

Fleur de sel and freshly ground pepper

Using a small sharp knife, remove the peel and white pith from the fruit. Cut out the fruit segments from between the membranes. Cut the fruit segments into ½-inch pieces. Transfer the fruit pieces to a colander and let stand to drain excess juices, about 15 minutes.

Just before using, combine the fruit segments, citrus zest confit, and oil in a medium saucepan. Cook over medium-low heat just until warm. Season to taste with fleur de sel and pepper.

VANILLA ICE CREAM

What really needs to be said about vanilla ice cream? Well, maybe one thing. The key is in the quality of the vanilla, so it's important to get the best you can find.

A note about ice creams and sorbets: Although you can freeze them indefinitely, they're far better served fresh, preferably the same day they're made. They're also best served soft. If you make ice cream or sorbet a day in advance, place it in a bain-marie until it softens, then return it briefly to the ice cream maker.

MAKES 1 QUART

2 cups whole milk

⅔ cup sugar

½ cup heavy whipping cream

1 vanilla bean, preferably Tahitian, split lengthwise

8 large egg yolks

Combine the milk, sugar, and cream in a heavy medium saucepan. Scrape in the seeds from the vanilla bean; add the bean. Bring to a simmer over medium-high heat. Remove from the heat. Remove the vanilla bean.

Meanwhile, whisk the egg yolks in a large bowl to blend. Gradually whisk in the hot milk mixture. Return the mixture to the saucepan. Using a heat-resistant rubber spatula, stir over low heat just until the custard thickens and leaves a path on the back of the spatula when a finger is drawn across, about 8 minutes (do not allow the custard to boil). Strain the custard through a fine-mesh strainer and into a large bowl. Stir the custard over another large bowl of ice water until cold. Cover and refrigerate for at least 2 hours.

Transfer the custard to an ice cream maker. Process according to the manufacturer's instructions. Spoon the ice cream into a container. Cover and freeze until the ice cream is semi-firm, at least 4 hours.

DO AHEAD: *The ice cream can be prepared up to 8 hours ahead. Keep frozen.*

RESOURCE GUIDE

Browne Trading Company

Merrill's Wharf
260 Commercial Street
Portland, ME 04101
207-766-2402
207-766-2404 Facsimile

All fish

Danko Foods Inc.

Dan Ketelaars
P.O. Box 7013
Laguna Niguel, CA 92607
www.dankofoods.com

Importer of fine foods, including seafood and wild game

D'Artagnan

280 Wilson Avenue
Newark, NJ 07105
800-327-8246
www.dartagnan.com

Foie gras, squab, game, and truffles

Dean and DeLuca

www.deandeluca.com

Spices, plus Banyuls vinegar and acacia honey

Derrick S. Foy Corporation

Derrick Foy
825 16th Street
Santa Monica, CA 90403
310-828-3154
310-829-3075 Facsimile

European kitchen supplies and equipment, silver, china, and crystal, including Priority cookware featured in the photographs in this book

Dorothy McNett's Place

800 San Benito Street
Hollister, CA 95023
831-637-6444
www.happycookers.com

Verjus from Perigord, France

Earthly Delights

www.earthly.com
800-367-4709

Hard-to-find ingredients, including argan oil, fleur de sel, and juniper berries

Energy Bee Farm

Jeff Erb
California
310-671-9054

Honey and pollination

Energy Muse Jewelry, LLC

1145 Artesia Blvd.
Suite 204
Manhattan Beach, CA 90266
1-866-674-4367
www.energymuse.com

Handmade crystal and gemstone jewelry designed to activate your intentions, including a necklace inspired by Ludo Lefebvre

Fish Warehouse

Philippe Levy
1020 East 7th Street
Los Angeles, CA 90021
213-627-5039
213-627-6588 Facsimile

Specialty fish by mail order, including loup de mer, John Dory, and red mullet

Fitzgerald's

J. Fitzgerald Kelly
10483 S. MacDonough
Reedley, CA 93654
559-638-3136
559-638-4146 Facsimile

Premium ripe tree fruit

Four Story Hill Farm

Stephen & Sylvia Pryzant
HC 62, Box 38
Honesdale, PA 18431
570-224-4137

Milk-fed veal, capons, and poultry

Jeo Shin Int'l Co.

Alex Chuang
2038 Mountain View Road
S. El Monte, CA 91733
626-582-8002
626-582-8091 Facsimile

Seafood

Kosmo Ranch

2025 Ravoli Drive
Oxnard, CA 93035
805-985-2054

Apples

Le Sanctuaire

Jing Tio
2710 Main Street
Santa Monica, CA 90405
310-581-8999
310-581-8991 Facsimile
www.le-sanctuaire.com

Precious vinegars and oils, exotic seasonings, spices, produce, and prime-source seafood

Liaison West

18322 Ward Street
Fountain Valley, CA 92708
714-593-9277

714-593-9288 Facsimile

Olive oil, mushrooms, truffles, truffle oil

Maggie's Farms

Dennis Peitso
13953 Panay Way #2
Marina Del Rey, CA 90292
310-578-1865

Fresh herbs

Montana Gourmet Garlic

The River Bottom Ranch
15999 East Mullan Road
Clinton, MT 59825
406-825-3007
406-825-3008 Facsimile
www.montanagourmetgarlic.com

Garlic farm

Newport Meat Company

16691 Hale Avenue
Irvine, CA 92606
949-474-4040
949-474-8383 Facsimile

Premium meats

Navarro Vineyards

5601 Highway 128
Philo, CA 95466
800-537-WINE
www.navarrowine.com

Verjus

Oakville Grocery

800-973-6324
www.oakvillegrocery.com

Verjus

Penzey's Spices

P.O. Box 924
Brookfield, WI 53150
www.penzeys.com

Spices, including green cardamom pods, lemongrass, and ground blade mace

Petrossian Distribution, Inc.

321 North Robertson Boulevard
West Hollywood, CA 90048
310-271-6300

310-271-8256 Facsimile
www.petrossian.com

Caviar

Petrovich Caviar, Inc.

Pierre Beylier
6762 South Centinela Avenue
Suite B
Culver City, CA 90230
310-572-4454
310-572-4452 Facsimile

Caviar

Polito Family Farms

Bob and Mary Polito
11920 Betsworth Road
Valley Center, CA 92082
760-749-1636
760-749-3674 Facsimile

Specialty citrus

Scarborough Farms

P.O. Box 1267
Oxnard, CA 93032
805-483-9113
805-247-1803 Facsimile

Fresh herbs and salads

Surfas

8825 National Boulevard
Culver City, CA 90232
310-559-4770
www.surfasonline.com

Escargots

True Foods Market

877-274-5914
www.truefoodsmarket.com

Almond milk and almond flour

www.wine-searcher.com

Vin jaune (yellow wine)

World Cuisine

Christian Jarry
3960 Landmark Street
Culver City, CA 90232
877-778-2711
www.world-cuisine.com

Culinary equipment, including Priority cookware featured in the photographs in this book

INDEX